Your Complete 2020 Horoscope

Your Complete Forecast 2020 Horoscope

BEJAN DARUWALLA
with
NASTUR DARUWALLA

Ranvir Books

HarperCollins *Publishers* India

First published in India by
HarperCollins *Publishers* in 2019
A-75, Sector 57, Noida, Uttar Pradesh 201301, India
www.harpercollins.co.in

2 4 6 8 10 9 7 5 3 1

Copyright © Bejan Daruwalla 2019

P-ISBN: 978-93-5357-289-1
E-ISBN: 978-93-5357-290-7

The views and opinions expressed in this book are the author's own
and the facts are as reported by him, and the publishers are not in any
way liable for the same.

Bejan Daruwalla asserts the moral right
to be identified as the author of this work.

All rights reserved. No part of this publication may be reproduced,
stored in a retrieval system, or transmitted, in any form or by any means,
electronic, mechanical, photocopying, recording or otherwise,
without the prior permission of the publishers.

Typeset in 10.5/13.7 Sabon at
Manipal Digital Systems, Manipal

Printed and bound at
MicroPrints India, New Delhi

Contents

Aries (21 March–19 April) 1

Taurus (20 April–20 May) 28

Gemini (21 May–20 June) 58

Cancer (21 June–22 July) 88

Leo (23 July–22 August) 117

Virgo (23 August–22 September) 144

Libra (23 September–22 October) 171

Scorpio (23 October–22 November) 200

Sagittarius (23 November–22 December) 224

Capricorn (23 December–22 January) 252

Aquarius (23 January–22 February) 281

Pisces (23 February–20 March) 307

Ready Reckoner for All Twelve Signs	335
The Signs and Their Elements	337
World Horoscope	338
Our Future	342
Achievements	345
Personalities	348
Modi and India	350
In Memorium	354
Astro-analysis of Terrorists and Suicide Bombers	355
ESP and Astrology	357
Cartoons and Comedy (Effect of Mercury)	359
Ramana Maharshi's Truth	360
Your Bonus for 2020	361
Bejan Opens Out	368
Mantras	370
About the Authors	371

ARIES

21 March–19 April

Symbol: The Ram
Ruling Planet: Mars
Fire-Cardinal-Positive
The Sign of the Pioneer, the Explorer
Ganesha summarizes you in the three As: Ambition, Aggression, Achievement

In the name of Ganesha, I have used a new method specially for you. It is the philosopher's stone that represents the planet Mars. It means control of anger and unruly emotions – direct your energy towards positive action, bravely take risks, act courageously and vigorously. The planet Mars is an active force in our lives, strengthening our energy, creativity and sex drive. Mars is the god of war, whose sword indicates direct action as he stands poised above the vessel – the philosophic egg. The strike of his sword symbolizes the purifying fire that heats the vessel.

Your colour is red, your number is nine and your direction is south.

My book is mainly by Western astrology. But the mantra I give for you is from the Vedas. The mantra is '*Om Kram Kreem Krom Sa Bhowmaya Namah*'. You may recite it nine times every Tuesday. But I always say the choice is yours and I do not force people into anything.

This picture shows you all about your own planet Mars. A picture is worth a thousand words.

JUPITER

Jupiter will be in your tenth angle from 2 December 2019 to 18 December 2020 which means, in simple language, that you will be at the height of your powers. It means prestige, power, position, perks – the four Ps – will be yours. Responsibility in irreversible, monumental proportions will be thrust upon you, but that will give you the authority and ability to handle pressure – and that's ultimately important. Prestige does a huge pole vault; parents figure in your scheme of things, inheritance and possession will show up on the Internet of your individual life. You learn to play splendidly with all kinds of gizmos and new-fangled gadgets, and the various media of communication. The health of parents, elders and in-laws could, however, cause concern; and the same goes for your boss and superiors. Your proficiency and performance will be at an all-time high and this should give the necessary confidence to achieve your targets / goals. In practical terms, this is what astrology is all about – giving confidence. Honours, awards and rewards sum it all up nicely.

My experience of sixty-five years in astrology has convinced me that Jupiter stands for prosperity, progress, pious deeds, achievements and divine blessings.

SATURN

In simple language, Saturn means duty, responsibility, karma and right action. Saturn is the controller who sometimes whips you for your own good. Yes, I agree, Saturn is many times the chief cause of suffering, pain and misery but to me, that is life. You may or may not agree with me. I keep an open mind.

Saturn will be also be in your tenth angle from 1 January 2018 to most of 2020. In simple language, whether you like it or not, duty, responsibility and looking after others will be thrust upon you. I repeat word for word what I said about Saturn in 2019.

Saturn in your tenth angle means power and push. But if you cross the limits, it certainly means a downfall, a big crash from a great height. I do not want you to do that. Luckily for you, in 2019, Saturn is helped by Neptune, the planet of imagination and vision. Therefore, do think of yourself. But also think of others. Let me make it very clear: In any matter that has to do with organization, industry, handling large groups of people, social work, heavy complexes and plants, new projects and ventures, you will have the ability, skill and confidence to push ahead bravely and powerfully. This could be used as a tool or a wedge to gain your ends. In short, be venturesome, be brave but also respect the desires and wishes of others. Let me put it all in a different way. Be a great commander. But also, be a fine listener. That is the secret. Rise is certain but fall remains in your own hands. Your ambition is great, your drive is tremendous. I agree to it. But try to control your ego and all will be well.

But there is one important difference. Jupiter will also be in your tenth angle along with Saturn. Therefore, it means that what you did not achieve last year, you will do it now, your suffering will be less, your power and prestige much more. Let me put it in a different way. Your opportunities and chances of happiness and joy will be much more. Most Ariens have the capacity to take the rough with the smooth. But now the smooth part will be more evident.

As Uranus has changed signs from March 2019, it will be excellent for you in 2020.

BLUEPRINT FOR THE ENTIRE YEAR

January: Up and about, hard-working, you will be ready to be on the go, be it home or office.

February: Fun and games, friendship and fraternity, gains and gaiety.

March: Too many things happening all together; see that you conserve your energy/vitality.

April: Month of progress, prosperity, pelf and getting things done.

May: Loans, funds, deals, transactions, buying and selling.

June: Assignments, communication, transport, ties, trips, relatives.

July: Home, house, family, shopping, renovation, decoration, alteration.

August: Trips, ceremonies, rites, fame and name, future plans.

September: Work, health, rewards, service, pets, projects, colleagues, promotion.

October: Love, marriage, law cases, relationships, travel, contracts, communication, enemies.

November: Joint finance, loans, funds, immigration, moving, shifting, capital formation, passion, sex.

December: Joy, publicity, travel, ceremony, functions, parties, invitations, import and export, collaboration, contacts and happiness because of abundance.

Listen carefully, mighty Ariens, your main planet is forceful, egoistical Mars. In other words, Mars is the warrior of the entire zodiac. I am not encouraging you to go to war. But when you want to achieve your desires and complete your plans and deliver the goods as we say, I have given the time for it below, because your own planet will guide and help you. From 19 November 2019 to 2 January 2020, Mars will help you in terms of finance and romance. From 3 January to 15 February 2020 is wonderful for travel, research, freedom and opening the vistas of your mind. From 31 March to 12 May, friends, socializing and group activities give you health, wealth and happiness. This may be a cliché but it will come true. From 28 June to 6 January 2021 is possibly your period of name, fame, opportunities, recognition, awards and rewards. In other words, June onwards, you will be at your very best. Ganesha blesses you.

In one word, Aries is the ignition key to life itself.

Your happiness quota will be 79 per cent.

WEEKLY REVIEW BY PHASES OF THE MOON

10 January: Full Moon in Cancer

The overlying theme of this week is finance and you will be busy with loans, funds, buying and selling of personal assets, even trying your luck in the stock market. It is time for new beginnings and you are keen to make your work more profitable. You will be motivated to maintain a regular fitness regime including relaxation exercises which will help you enjoy good health. There will also be harmony at home and good times with your spouse/partner and other family members. The year starts well and you can look forward to great times.

17 January: Moon's Last Quarter in Libra

The moon in your own sign helps you consolidate the gains of the recent past. You will be daring and enterprising, and even a pioneer of sorts. Money trends are positive as you ponder your goals and aims for the current year. Setting goals, making plans and implementing them will occupy you and keep your energy levels high. You push ahead with all guns blazing and see most of your plans being realized. There will be adventure and daring in all your interactions and you may be drawn into several affairs of the heart. Ganesha advises you not to neglect work and to be discreet in romance lest it spill over into work and the home, and lead to problems/worries.

24 January: New Moon in Capricorn

You have a creative streak and find ingenious solutions to your money and relationship problems. Despite it, you are plagued by a sense of insecurity deep down. It is possible that you feel restless and dissatisfied with your life and this could spill over into your intimate relationships. Children and pets could be a source of worry. Travel for work/pleasure will be beneficial; you attend meetings, seminars and conventions and win applause for your prowess in work. This is also a good time to start laying the foundation for a spiritual quest through meditation, relaxation techniques and chanting.

2 February: Moon's First Quarter in Taurus

This is a time to slow down but it won't be easy as your sights are firmly fixed on making more money. Children/siblings/extended family will crave and need your attention and your time. Health may need attention too and alternative therapies will prove effective. Visits to places of worship will calm your agitated mind. You look for truth and the meaning of life, and may seek out a guru for guidance. But you have nothing to worry on the material plane as your bank balance is quite strong. Your life is fairly well balanced but there could be stagnation in relationships. A change in perspective combined with an open-minded and flexible attitude will help bring about harmony here too.

9 February: Full Moon in Leo

Your interest in money matters continues and you think of ways and means to increase your assets. You love making money and spending it too. You can also be flamboyant and make it a point to display your material worth. Meetings with financial planners and dealing with loans, funds, assets will keep you occupied. There will be fun times too with social outings with loved ones. This is a good period in life and you taste success in whatever you do.

19 February: Moon's Last Quarter in Scorpio

This financially hectic period of the past few weeks slows down and there is a sense of a quiet and calm now. This low-key period could propel you to seek out adventures and shake things up a bit. Nothing ventured, nothing gained

– so true in your case, and you are ready to try your luck, gamble away your money, and also seek out adventures of the heart. You might even find the courage to propose to your sweetheart, and then there may be an engagement or marriage on the cards, Ganesha urges you to be bold and brave and to keep your wits about you to extract the most out of this phase.

23 February: New Moon in Aquarius

Keep your bags packed as you may have many trips this coming week. Yes, says Ganesha, be prepared to take overnight trips or short getaways for both work and pleasure. Meeting new people and even those you have lost touch with – personally or through email, phone or snail mail – is not ruled out. Check out new technology to raise your communication levels. There will be some obstacles at work but the family and close friends are behind you like a rock to motivate and support you. So don't lose heart. You manage to make progress despite the odds. Your determination and enterprise will ensure that you pull through difficult situations.

2 March: Moon's First Quarter in Gemini

It is definitely 'relationship time' now as the new moon phase draws your attention to those who have added value to your life. You also have the cooperation and support of your boss and co-workers. People find you pleasant and agreeable as you go out of your way to help others in need. There may be a windfall now and you could gain a lot from an inheritance which you didn't expect. Loans/interest/bonuses and even payments stuck for a long time will now be accessible to you. Don't go overboard and spend it all. Exercise control and be moderate, says Ganesha, and success is yours.

9 March: Full Moon in Virgo

A really busy week, even a hectic one, as everyday chores take your time. Despite leaving you totally engrossed and sometimes exhausted, it is still an enjoyable week. You also manage to find time for your spiritual aspirations. Apart from work, there are social interactions and quality time spent with friends, family and loved ones. You love entertaining and being entertained, and there will be a plethora of outings, picnics and get-togethers. You will be the soul of the party. Your emotions are more intense now and you may have to keep a tab on mood swings. There will be opposing energies at play and you will have to keep the balance. Take care of your health in this phase.

16 March: Moon's Last Quarter in Sagittarius

Your fine interactions with people, especially with family members/work associates have been enjoyable and even empowering. The introspective phase gives way to more pressing, earthly concerns. The welfare and security of your loved ones is of paramount importance now and you need to take care of their needs and wants. There could be unexpected expenses as you overreach yourself to help others. Your efforts are now diverted towards building up the family assets and also your personal wealth.

24 March: New Moon in Aries

Your sustained hard work now bears fruit. It is payback time now and Ganesha showers you with rewards. Salary raises, promotions and perks are part of this well-deserved package, and you will have to take care that it doesn't bloat your ego further. Other money-related matters such as funds, loans, deposits, taxes, trade, agencies, legal matters could give you gains, both expected and unexpected, and could become a cause of great jubilation at home. There could be overseas travel and some medical issues to attend to. The health of an older family member may be a cause for concern.

1 April: Moon's First Quarter in Cancer

You love to make money and you make a lot of it quite effortlessly, as the new moon in your own sign initiates a trend of gains. Money continues to flow into your coffers through rents, leases, loans and promissory notes. A good bank balance makes you feel secure. You may have to spend a lot of time on negotiations and deals, buying/selling of assets and making acquisitions. Your life is on an upswing in this monthly trend and you work at a new image for yourself. You may go in for a makeover and change your wardrobe, hairstyle and even body image. You may take on a club membership which will help expand your social circle. You spend on yourself but isn't that also a type of investment?

8 April: Full Moon in Libra

It is definitely money that is in focus this week. A strong financial foundation is what you hanker after, as it gives you a feeling of security. You do this through prudent and long-term investment in land, property, assets and stock holdings. This will give you the necessary push to achieve success and, in the process, develop your identity too. Everything falls smoothly into place like the pieces of a jigsaw puzzle, almost preordained and without any great effort on your part. Ganesha seems determined to ensure that you are in the right time and so it is no surprise to see how swiftly your efforts bear fruit. But it is possible that over-involvement with work could cause you to neglect your spouse/home/kids and even your health. Fortunately, in the end, all your efforts will be rewarded.

14 April: Moon's Last Quarter in Capricorn

You have been working very hard these past few weeks and could have neglected your emotional relationships in the bargain. Romantic matters now come into sharp focus and you bond with your partner in a powerful way. You feel good about it and this, fortunately, infuses a feel-good factor which also colours your ties with your colleagues, co-workers, siblings and even extended family. The mood is contagious and everyone is happy. Those who are unattached can expect to find love too. A sense of joyousness permeates your being and you feel physically fit too.

23 April: New Moon in Taurus

Carpe diem! (Seize the day!) This is the motto that truly defines this exciting time in your life. Drink to life and savour each mouthful to the fullest, says Ganesha. You can have it all, if you want. Love, romantic relations, fun and games, partying, socializing, get-togethers – yes, all these appeal to you and fill your plate till it is overflowing. Relationships, both personal and professional, give you great pleasure and benefit you in manifold ways. You look towards the future with hope and optimism in your heart. Nothing dims your happiness and you are eager to help those less privileged than you. You find a strange satisfaction at work and this joyful spirit adds colour to your life. You couldn't have asked Ganesha for more, could you?

30 April: Moon's First Quarter in Leo

A whole new trend begins this week and Ganesha predicts that it will definitely be the main theme in August too. It involves the evolution of your fast-moving, impulsive nature into a calmer, more sober one in which you develop a love for humanitarian activities. No half measures here, as you go all out to share your resources with the underprivileged. You are at the forefront, making things happen at home, work and in the community. You go about getting things done, whether it is helping new people adjust to the workplace or introducing new methods of functioning. You are socially and environmentally aware and also very humane, helping orphans or even stray animals find new homes or developing new initiatives for senior citizens in your locality. You also set about developing deeper bonds with your partner. The time could be just right for you to start a family if you wish to, says Ganesha.

7 May: Full Moon in Scorpio

The theme of relationships is taken further this week and you focus strongly on communicating with your loved one. You do not generally enjoy going too deep into any issue but at this stage in your life, you do just that. They do say God is in the details, don't they? This is also the time to make yourself more visible, perhaps even the right time to update that résumé, says Ganesha. Networking opportunities/the tools of modern communication are aplenty and it is easy to meet new people and old friends, and even have interactions for professional gains and career growth. There could be travel, new collaborations and much professional success.

14 May: Moon's Last Quarter in Aquarius

Developing and maintaining relationships is the definite trend for this month, and you may have already seen strong indications of this since last week. You will continue to strengthen your professional relationships through good communication and a thoughtful attitude. Thanks to the changed perspective and your efforts, you will also see immediate rewards. You are ready to involve other people in new projects and the money starts flowing in. You are also happy to share the profits with your partners and co-workers. This certainly helps boost their morale and leads to a pleasant working environment. If you are in business, you will be eagerly looking at the many lucrative opportunities open to you. The domestic environment will also be harmonious and will reflect your success. It is a happy period by any account.

22 May: New Moon in Gemini

Two themes run parallel this week. On the one hand, you add to your resources through loans, funds, rent, leases, legacies and inheritances. On the other hand, as you seek an intense connection with your partner or beloved, the possibility of a strengthened emotional bond charges you with adrenaline. You are filled with passion. Last month's romantic adventures and interludes are still playing on your mind and you are eager to take them to the next level. Honey and money, love and finances, amour and pelf – yes Ariens, this phase gives you the two best reasons to be happy! But, underlying all this, quite paradoxically, will be a streak of spirituality and mysticism which draws you into esoteric practices/tantra and mantra. There are many colours on your palette to dip into.

30 May: Moon's First Quarter in Virgo

Fun, frolic, friendships, finances – these four Fs have demanded your fair share of attention in the past week and you have gone all out to do them justice. Now, you want to take things easy and rest a bit. There is the danger of going to the other extreme – from intense activity to absolute indolence. Other-worldly matters bubble up, urging you to search within and get the answers to esoteric questions. Visits to holy places, short trips and pilgrimages, meditation centres, religious gatherings attract you as Ganesha offers you a chance to build up your spiritual base. You could also meet a spiritual guru/mentor to guide you in your search for the meaning of life.

5 June: Full Moon in Sagittarius

You can't be kept down for too long and you think your goals and targets afresh for the month to come. Life beckons and you push ahead with your characteristics forthrightness. Hard work, creativity, innovation and optimism colour your actions as you make brilliant progress. Communications, contacts, correspondence – these three Cs – are the main trend for this month, not just in your work but even in all your personal and intimate relationships. Romantic gestures/leisure activities/outings/movies/family gatherings keep you excited and happy. Your home is your haven and you spend special moments with your spouse/partner/children/extended family. This energizes you, gives you renewed zest for living. Great times are in store for you.

13 June: Moon's Last Quarter in Pisces

You realize the need to organize your time and work routine as you push ahead with the goals set last week. You introduce systems, streamline procedures and increase your efficiency at the workplace. This endears you to your colleagues and subordinates. Yes, it's action time and you may find yourself tackling many projects at one go and multitasking furiously and successfully. There will be travel, expansion and growth.

You will be mentally rejuvenated, will perform wonderfully at work and will have a loving relationship with spouse, children and family elders. Finances are on the upswing and you reach the pinnacles of success.

21 June: New Moon in Cancer

The attention you have given to relationships over the past few weeks has opened your eyes to the great value they have in your life. It is no longer enough for you to think only about yourself, your personal goals and ambitions. You have to include others in your dreams. There are high expectations from spouse/partner/older relatives/children/colleagues and workmates, and this could stretch your time and resources. Their needs are important too and you may not have the time, energy or the money to fulfil their desires. This bothers you no end. Meditation, going for quiet walks or indulging in some other relaxing activity will be necessary to sort this situation out. Don't allow yourself to get ensnared in emotional dramas. You have to guard against such emotionally volcanic situations.

28 June: Moon's First Quarter in Libra

The moon in your sign makes you want to shine in the world. You aim to be the best you can in your work and in your relationships and also want to be the centre of attraction. A strong self-image and a successful persona is what you want to project, especially to those who look up to you. Money makes both personal relationships and family interactions sweeter and you enjoy domestic bliss. You are filled with contentment as you go about your work and domestic affairs.

5 July: Full Moon in Capricorn

You feel a strong pull to explore new facets of your personality. Till now you have focused on your work and home and have seen glimpses of complex emotional issues emerge. You have tackled the professional front efficiently (your energy and drive are legendary, no doubt about that) but now you are eager to explore the creative side of your personality. Hobbies, children, pets and intimate relations are highlighted and you feel the urge to create something new. Innovation and ingenuity are the keywords here. Art, theatre, cinema, films, writing, designing or any creative pursuit could interest and inspire you. You have developed good people-skills which will hold you in good stead in your personal as well as your professional life.

12 July: Moon's Last Quarter in Gemini

Ganesha rewards you with closer bonds, genuine love and romance. This fills you with a sense of peace and well-being which no amount of money or material success can buy. These relationships are your bedrock, inspiring you to take giant strides in your chosen field. At work, a new outlook – one that is caring and tolerant – will get you the cooperation and support of your workmates and this will increase the kudos coming your way. Family members provide moments of true companionship but there could be health-related issues of older relatives that would need to be tackled. Children will be a source of joy.

20 July: New Moon in Cancer

You switch from the relationship-rich period of the last few weeks to professional concerns. Personal associations have been supportive on the road to material success, but you now realize that renewed efforts are required to push ahead. Spouse/lover/children/parents/servants/helpers look to you for direction and you provide it. You need a balance for life to be more harmonious and must make time for family obligations too. You have a tendency to take off on a tangent which you must curb.

27 July: Moon's First Quarter in Virgo

This is a pleasant phase. You have delivered virtuoso performances in both the important sectors of your life – home and work. You are the toast of everyone, the blue-eyed boy/girl and also the centre of envy. Your confidence and chutzpah, combined waters and emerge victorious. But this is not all, says Ganesha. Another trend overlaps: finances engage your attention too. Funds, loans rentals and leases, or MoUs demand your attention. You may see an overlap as professional relationships turn more personal and there is a mixing of business and pleasure. You are the key person in these dealings/negotiations and Ganesha helps you to take the right action at the right time. Relations improve as you spend quality time, not just with your beloved, but also with your children/parents/siblings/in-laws. There are happy times to be had by all.

2 August: Full Moon in Aquarius

The successful pursuit of your goals requires out-of-the-box thinking and you wholeheartedly accept the challenges that confront you. Ganesha motivates you to seek greener pastures. You could be busy with funds/loans negotiations and deals, a job change or even a surge in responsibilities (should be accompanied by promotions and in privileges). You could be also looking out for collaborations, partnerships and even dealerships. As a carryover from last week, you may still find yourself restless and so you will be drawn to a quest for peace and spiritual solace. This is a week in which you can expect the unexpected. The focus will shift, as the week unfolds, to spiritual practices, meditation and other relaxation techniques which will help you tide over the bumps of this period gracefully and safely.

11 August: Moon's Last Quarter in Taurus

Your spiritual practices have given you fortitude and the courage of your convictions. You feel much more calm and peaceful and ready to face life's challenges with equanimity. This doesn't mean that you are lethargic and laid-back; quite the contrary really. Ganesha says that you will be full of energy and vigour, a joie de vivre, an unalloyed enthusiasm, which helps you fulfil your responsibilities at home and at work. You will do remarkably well at work and will be suitably rewarded. Meeting deadlines with superlative ease in child's pay for you.

19 August: New Moon in Leo

There is a repetition of last month's theme (to a lesser degree, though) as the moon is once again in Taurus. The spotlight continues to shine on you at work, thanks to your awesome performance. Relationships are on the upswing with interpersonal tensions sorted out. Your home is your haven and you enjoy warm and caring interactions with your near and dear ones. Socializing, partying and entertaining your friends and family helps you unwind. Your popularity soars and you are the darling of your friends, family, kith and kin. Curb unhealthy ego drives or you will be the target of envy.

25 August: Moon's First Quarter in Sagittarius

This phase kick-starts a trend of hardwork and fervent play. Dedicated efforts and large doses of luck give you success on the domestic and professional fronts. You are more organized at work and read the fine print. You are also enthusiastic, confident and filled with a new energy which ensues success. You use your resources in a prudent manner, introducing innovative and effective measures at work, revive old contacts and friendships and clear the air with those you may have had a run-in with earlier. There is also room for interesting tie-ups and romantic liaisons. You will also hit the gym or take up some form of health improvement scheme.

2 September: Full Moon in Pisces

The work formats put into place last week take your productivity levels to dizzy heights. There is a lot of work but the systems are in place and so while the productivity increases, the effort doesn't. This not only makes your work easier but also gives you more time to devote to domestic affairs. You will have tender moments with your loved one as you multitask and juggle several projects effortlessly. You may have to attend out-of-town meetings, conferences, conventions for collaborations/negotiations/tie-ups. Certain unforeseen legal matters could crop up; though not serious, they could be time-consuming. It is a week of many facets and immense possibilities.

10 September: Moon's Last Quarter in Gemini

You need a break from the hectic activities and events of the past weeks. Stress levels are high and you need to recuperate.

You look at social work and may spend time at old people's homes and other charities. You look at ways to give back to society. Those in the healthcare professions – such as nursing, psychiatry, psychotherapy, counselling, etc. – could scale new heights, perhaps even win international acclaim for their work. Almost all of you will have unusual intuition which is actually quite different from your normal leanings, but this phase makes it happen. You have made enough money and are now hankering after spiritual gains.

17 September: New Moon in Virgo

You internalize and intellectualize your emotions this week, which is a natural progression of the trend that started at the full moon of last month. Astrology is a logical science, says your Ganesha devotee, and you can definitely see the proof. You indulge in genuine self-evaluation and self-awareness, and life inspires you to make changes that may be against your basic nature but which help you reach your higher self. You are usually very impatient and hasty to get your work done (even guilty very often of cutting corners, isn't it?) but this phase demands accountability. Self-mastery is the key to gains in this phase. The three Cs – contacts, contracts and correspondence – are of paramount importance too, says Ganesha. You will make rapid progress on all fronts and become a much more whole and rounded personality.

24 September: Moon's First Quarter in Capricorn

With your restored and enhanced perception of life, you will take it easy, be relaxed, a bit laid-back too. You are happy and optimistic and take time away from work with your lover or for social outings with friends, children and parents. You find joy in building and maintaining valuable partnerships and have a gentle, loving attitude which helps foster intimate bonds. It is not all as rosy as it sounds and you could face hurdles, setbacks and delays coupled with sluggish funds and unexpected expenses. But you will continue to socialize. There will be fun and frolic in your life, which energizes you. Somehow, you don't allow trifles to bother you.

2 October: Full Moon in Aries

There has been a steadily increasing awareness of the importance of relationships in your life for the past few weeks. So, a further strengthening and bonding, both at work and at home, can be achieved through mutual care and respect. Strife and friction, when they occur, should be tactfully and diplomatically handled. As we all know, peaceful solutions will lead to greater growth and progress. Control your ego and allow wiser counsel to prevail. This will be particularly relevant on the home front in your dealings with your spouse/partner. At work too, supportive colleagues and co-workers will help you perform better. Planning, delegating and working as a team player could reduce work pressures and improve output. Overall, it is a fantastic week for putting down the roots for stupendous long-term success.

10 October: Moon's Last Quarter in Cancer

You are determined to sustain the growth you have achieved and even build further on it. This is an action-packed week as you find your hands full at work, much more than you can handle. This moon phase in your sign reinforces the focus on your priorities and values as you push forward to take advantage of the myriad possibilities that have presented themselves to you. The rewards are immediate and, buoyed, you push ahead frenetically. This could lead to a burnout, causing more harm than good. So use available resources judiciously to avoid such an eventually. Spending time in the company of small children/pets and on hobbies/leisure pursuits could energize you.

16 October: New Moon in Libra

The hectic work situation slows down to some extent in this phase. You are satisfied with the way your projects have turned out and now you feel relaxed enough to spend time with your loved ones. Home matters occupy your mind and you may even delve deep into the history of your family. Family trees, older relatives, extended family, visits to the ancestral home, even taking stock of ancestral property are some of the ways the current trend may manifest in your life. Some of you, says Ganesha, may be overburdened by mundane domestic chores and so an outlet in terms of a hobby, creative pursuits, shopping, learning new skills will serve as a great release.

23 October: Moon's First Quarter in Aquarius

You now allow yourself to become more relaxed and enjoy a 'chilled out' time, as they say, with your loved ones. Unattached Ariens could find many opportunities to spend happy, even ecstatic, moments with someone special. The married may want to renew their marriage vows or go on a second honeymoon. This intensely passionate time also affects your money angle. You do have to pay for all your indulgences and so a tab on expenses will be prudent. It may be a good idea to avoid any new undertakings at this time.

31 October: Full Moon in Taurus

You have worked hard to consolidate your position and now feel confident that your finances are stable. You have taken a lot of risks earlier which could have led to some degree of loss at work. You are now cautious and read the fine print carefully. There is better rapport too between you, your co-workers and boss. You could be involved in developing new contracts or more business for your company, and will be travelling on work. This receives the full support and approval of your boss/superiors. Those in the media strike a purple patch, do remarkably well, and are applauded for their efforts.

8 November: Moon's Last Quarter in Leo

Having all aspects of your life running smoothly like the well-oiled wheels of an engine, you feel content as acknowledgement and appreciation pour in for your brilliant performances at work. You now enjoy an enhanced stature in society, and this is very gratifying, especially if you look back at the hard work and sacrifices you have made to get there. But now there is a complete contrast, a veritable volte-face, as you move away from the absolute grind of the past weeks to the present mood of pure elation. The frenzy of achievements has dimmed and you now want to take it easy, revelling in glorious passions with your spouse/lover, partaking of luxuries and sweet moments. Romantic energies pervade all your interactions and could lead to tricky situations vis-à-vis love affairs and secret liaisons. Children and/or hobbies provide fun and frolic. Ganesha advises you to develop healthy habits to be able to ride this exciting phase safely. Try to rein in indiscretions.

15 November: New Moon in Scorpio

Your confidence as well as the caring side of your nature will be at an all-time high as you give and get love and affection in equal measure from your family and loved ones. The past week has given you some exceptionally special moments, heart-warming and thoroughly enjoyable, with your spouse/lover and children/parents. The temptation of going overboard and showering them with the most precious gift of all – your time – will fill you with pure joy and happiness. The intense sharing and caring are there but, at the same time, there will be a need to consider the ground realities of your financial situation. A restricted cash flow could cause dissatisfaction and unhappiness and could need extraordinary efforts to get them back on track. Neglecting domestic duties and responsibilities could be an offshoot of your extreme involvement at work but you needn't be unduly worried as your lover or spouse/partner and even family elders provide you with the necessary support and backing (both financial and emotional). The feel-good energies of this phase will give you the strength and stamina required to achieve your business/professional goals, which could have been, at a standstill due to varied reasons. This is a period in which you make enormous progress.

22 November: Moon's First Quarter in Pisces

Happiness and contentment come into your personal life through the blessings of Ganesha. There is closeness and warmth in all your relationships leading to greater pleasure and cheer. Your spouse/lover showers you with love and you reciprocate. It is a lucky week in which unexpected profits flow in and allow you to enjoy the fruits of your labour. There is exultation and exuberance in your life as material successes pale in front of the ecstasy of soul-stirring relationships. The euphoria that you now experience translates into radiant health.

30 November: Full Moon in Gemini

Professional pursuits hold your interest. You set gargantuan goals and expect to achieve them. Each and every aspect of your life is at its peak and fills you with a heightened sense of self-worth. There are monetary gains too. Your accomplishments fill with you with pride and you are on a roll, but the tendency to neglect intimate relationships, children and health issues could again cause roadblocks in your progress. You attract trust, belief and faith and are filled with the confidence that you can realize the awe-inspiring dreams within your heart.

8 December: Moon's Last Quarter in Virgo

You will experience true inner peace and contentment this week. You have worked hard, conscientiously and consistently, and the results have been superlative; you were absolutely deserving of the awards and rewards that came your way. Your performances at the workplace has been stellar, to say the least, but now you look at issues far removed from the workplace. You are less fiery and ambitious and are more complacent and calm in your interactions. You mentor, guide and motivate youngsters and this gives you a sense of fulfilment. As an extension of your renewed outlook, public welfare schemes concerning the underprivileged, the needy and the destitute, make you reach out and provide solace physically, emotionally and monetarily. You feel blessed, light-hearted and spiritually satisfied.

14 December: New Moon in Sagittarius

You will be closer to people now, enjoying the new bonds you have forged in the past few weeks. You look forward eagerly to widen your personal horizons and the scope of your interactions and relationships. All kinds of gains have come to you but now a completely different dimension of connections, communications and collaborations open up. Geographical/physical boundaries and limitations are no longer a hindrance as a fresh universe virtually opens up before you as you make full use of the latest networking tools. With your feet placed firmly on the ground, you work hard. Finances could be tight as you dream big and need huge amounts to invest. You tap loans and the market and push ahead confidently. You are filled with optimism and energy and feel you can move mountains. Nothing seems impossible in this phase.

21 December: Moon's First Quarter in Aries

Ganesha gives you just about everything that you wish for. But your focus will continue to remain on your work. A strong network of friends/relatives, in-laws is your lifeline as you immerse yourself completely into professional commitments. Your efforts are scintillating, sparkling and truly divine. You plumb the depths of your inner being to bring forth creations of supreme innovation, novelty and originality. This is an excellent time for those in artistic professions. You are also assailed by intensely passionate energies, concerned with the physical expressions, and enjoyments of love, and even manifesting themselves in illicit, secret affairs/romantic liaisons/behind-the-scenes deals and activities. There could be health issues which need attention and wild mood swings too. Travel, especially short trips, could be beneficial.

30 December: Full Moon in Cancer

Once again, as at the beginning of this year, you come face to face with one of the most important aspects of your life. Becoming financially stable has been the cornerstone of almost all your efforts. You have persisted and persevered in planning and executing financial matters with good results. You have managed to leverage not only your profile but also your organization's kitty. Awards, rewards, funds and income from varied sources have made you and your loved ones happy. You have tasted success far beyond your wildest imagination and are now not keen to rest on your laurels. You are infused with new hope and confidence and want to push ahead without stops. Bonds with children/young people/parents/siblings provide immense joy. You look forward to 2021, especially in the areas of money/love/spirituality. Ganesha's blessings are with you.

Taurus

20 April–20 May

Symbol: The Bull
Ruling Planet: Venus
Earth-Fixed-Negative
The Sign of the Builder, the Producer

The mystic John Donne says, 'Contradictories meet in May.' Therefore, in digital terms, the sign Taurus signifies the builder, the producer, the artistic, the practical, the stubborn, the generous and the lawyer.

JUPITER

Please count yourself lucky. Why? Jupiter, the planet of plenty and prosperity, moves into your ninth angle of good fortune from 2 December 2019 to 18 December 2020. What will be the benefits? It means education, law, religion, foreign affairs, intellectual pursuits, plans for the future, a long journey and working on long-range aims.

TAURUS

- Faith and devotion in religion, spiritualism, cult, sect, God Almighty, lower deities, Congregationalism, Unitarianism and cosmopolitanism. Sometimes faith, but no attendance at religious place and no activity at home or at any religious place or gathering or at place of worship or prayers.

- Ideals, principles, known as hidden activities or any religious or spiritual formation, organization, *panth*, *marg/math*, sect/cult or religious group.

- Creation/establishment of a religious/spiritual order/panth/marg/organization/formation/group, etc.; its ideals and principles; other legal or illegal, social or unsocial activities under the cover of that organization or formation, etc; its impact on society and on the individuals and their families; on the general neighbourhood.

- Creation of an educational/social welfare/medical welfare formation/organization/group/order/ association for the given ideals and principles; or for some other hidden activities under the cover of that formation or organization.

- Renouncement of worldly life (*grihastha life*) and staying at one place/ashram/own premises/secluded permanent cottage; or leading a constant nomadic life except the four months of the rainy season, or nomadic life even during the rainy season (referral houses first, fourth, fifth and seventh, sometimes twelfth house also).

- Individual's last wishes/wills/sermons and guidance for others for the post-renouncement period or the post-death period, including brief, etc., also donation of eyes or kidney, last religious rites/gifts/charities/contributions/*daan*, etc.

- Respect or disrespect, obedience or disobedience towards one's gurus, teachers, priests, preachers, other elders in general.

- Partnership in business/professional/self-employment/industrial venture or any other income-generating activity (referral houses fourth, tenth and eleventh).

- Partnership with colleagues/co-workers, friends (such partnerships normally for side or part-time business/activity); financial implications and results; success or failure with impact on relationship.

- Tendency and intentions to help and serve others without any motive, selfishness, without reservation/restriction of any kind, neither of caste/colour/community/religion/status (referral houses first and fifth).

- Touring/repeated travels, inland/foreign for education/official/social welfare/religious/spiritual/charitable/pilgrimage or any other purposes of self or related to source of income or duties and responsibilities (referral houses fourth, fifth, tenth, eleventh and twelfth).

- Help and assistance or refusal to give it by progeny of self in any kind of good or bad activity of self (referral houses fifth and seventh).

- Marriage/physical relationship with brother/sister or cousin of the dead spouse (referral houses third, seventh, and also fifth in case of any child or children from the first marriage).

SATURN

Saturn continues to be in your ninth angle this year also of *bhagya* or good fortune from 21 December 2017 to most of 2020. Therefore, I am repeating from my last year's book. It will help you in:

- Higher learning and evolution.
- Journey and ceremony.
- Publicity, communication, contacts, computer knowledge and skills.
- Inspiration and intuition.
- The right time to plan well ahead, and believe me, this is the master key to success.
- Like it or lump it, you will be dealing with your in-laws and relatives, so why not put in a little of the charm for which you are so justly famous, and get on with it?
- Try to be a creative listener too, though I know this is difficult for you!
- It would be fatal to neglect contacts and correspondence or get into needless arguments about trifles, just to prove that you are right. Leave well alone should be your motto.
- As I had warned you, be firm but not inflexible and rigid to a fault.

Lastly, religion, research, spirituality, pilgrimage, pious deeds, tours and travels and ties, journeys and all matters to do with your higher self and your consciousness will be mighty important. In other words, it is time for a complete renovation and evolution of your own self. This is truly a mighty powerful and necessary asset for your own personality and development.

URANUS

Uranus, the planet of change and technology, moves into your fifth angle from 5 March 2019 to 6 July 2025. Specially in 2020 to 2024 birth of children, powerful creativity, great entertainment, profound sorrow and misery, and the complete use of your organizational and managerial faculties will be in great evidence. Therefore, this is the time to go all out and be at your brilliant best. It is the time to do or die.

Food, family and finance go naturally with you Taureans.

VENUS

Your main planet or the captain of your ship is Venus. Venus means charm, money, luxury and all the things which make life worth living. Venus is also beauty and design. Therefore, Venus is like the breeze which brings many good things and lays it on your table specially for you.

Venus turns very favourable for you between 14 January and 17 February 2020 and will give you a variety of goods between 5 March and 3 April. Therefore, you should be ready to grab it and take full advantage of it. Again, from 3 to 27 October and specially 22 November to 15 December, Venus helps you in marriage, contacts and partnerships. It is possible that you may realize your heart's desire. Ambition will be fulfilled, and money will jingle in your pockets. What more do you want?

BLUEPRINT FOR THE ENTIRE YEAR

January: Three Cs – contacts, communication, computers.

February: Home, house, parents, in-laws, property, retirement for the elderly, foundations for new projects.

March: Entertainment, love, engagement, hobbies, sports, games of chance; in a word, creativity.

April: Health, employment, pets, subordinates, colleagues, debts and funds.

May: Marriage, legal issues, friends and enemies, trips and ties, collaborations, competition; it is a mixed bag.

June: Money, passion, joint finance, buying, selling, shopping, taxes, real estate, insurance, focusing on health and strain and drain (on the purse and perhaps on you physically).

July: Leapfrog to fame, publicity, spirituality, fulfilment, journey, education, future plans, relations.

August: Tough decisions, health of elders, parents, in-laws are possible.

September: Friendship, the social whirl, romance, material gains, hopes, desires, ambition; happy days are here again.

October: Expenses, losses, contacts, love, secret deals, journeys, spirituality – a paradox, a big contradiction.

November: Confidence, power, gains, happiness, right timing, the realization of wishes.

December: Finances, food, family, taxes, buying, selling, shopping, property, functions and meets. You will be a crowd-puller! That's great.

It is my observation that gardening and the culinary arts (cooking) are often the speciality of you Taureans. The numbers three, six and nine are often lucky but my parting shot is that your lucky colour is blue, and blue is the colour of the millennium.

You Taureans love food and are generally on the fat side. Do not drain yourself too much. New research shows that a kind of bacterium called *Firmicutes* favours obesity and is found in higher number in the gut flora of obese persons. Conversely, another type of bacterium called *Bacteroidetes* is found to be present in higher amounts in the gut of lean persons. Therefore, all the fat people of the world can find consolation and relief in their gut.

Your happiness quota is 84 per cent.

WEEKLY REVIEW BY PHASES OF THE MOON

10 January: Full Moon in Cancer

The year starts with an excellent period for sustained hard work. You will be intensely ambitious and will reach for the moon and the stars. Money and honey – Ganesha blesses you within these twin themes at the beginning of the new year. Taureans are tenacious and resolute and crave financial security. They love all the comforts that money can buy and do not mind putting in a lot of extra hours at work to earn the 'moolah' to pay for comforts and luxuries. They are highly ambitious and self-motivated. As the year unfolds, you go about setting goals. You are keen to increase your bank balance and you will gladly welcome new opportunities for doing so. Fund, loans, deposits, dividends, stocks, shares, realty and other instruments of financial investments will interest you. The beginning of the new year finds you on a high as romantic relations and family ties occupy your time and attention. There will be some intensely pleasurable moments too. Those in banking or the media, in particular, will do remarkably well. There could be awards and kudos from the highest quarters. But Ganesha warns against ill health. You are firing on all cylinders and will have to take care of your diet and exercise to prevent illness or even hospitalism. You attract stress and so frequent breaks will be a good idea.

17 January: Moon's Last Quarter in Libra

The hard work continues this week as you pursue your goals with great zest and enthusiasm. Money matters continue to hold centre stage as you delve into ways and means of expanding your current business/work. The toils and cares of the world will engulf you this week and you could be stressed out. This could result in ill health and so Ganesha advises you to keep a cool head. Relationships, both personal and professional, require work and patience. You are dedicated in your approach to work and Ganesha tells you that awards and rewards are not far behind.

24 January: New Moon in Capricorn

Ganesha is pleased with your toil and labour but also reminds you that life is not only about money. Relationships are at the forefront of the new trend that begins with the current phase of the moon. You will now spend even more time in spiritual pursuits and at the same time you will understand the value of harmonious relationships. Romantic liaisons, intimate relations with your beloved/spouse, love affairs, engagements, weddings, strengthening bonds with your loved ones – be it your lover, your children, or even your extended family, some or all these – will occupy your time. Your domestic situation is harmonious and this fills you with a sense of well-being. Money-wise too, this is a good week as gains from your past investments fill your pockets.

2 February: Moon's First Quarter in Taurus

The esoteric energies of last week dissipate (though not completely) as you enter the beginning of a hectic work phase. This trend will continue for a few weeks at least. But Ganesha reassures you that though you will be quite busy, it will not be with just work. Expect to put on your party shoes even before you are out of your office. Work hard but play harder – this seems to be your motto this week as socializing, meeting friends, partying, entertaining at home and fun and frolic take up much of your time. Your money situation could turn a bit tricky with so much socializing and partying, and so juggling and balancing your accounts gains top priority. Relationships also require a lot of attention and you will need to guard against resentments and flare-ups too.

9 February: Full Moon in Leo

This phase in your own sign gives you rock-solid determination to progress in your career. After the intensive and hectic activities of last week you now seek to improve your living conditions. You love your home as it is your sanctuary and Ganesha says that your attention will now be vested in renovating and beautifying it. Home-improvement projects occupy you this week. Money-wise you are in a

TAURUS

positive phase and this is a good time for investments – the stock market, mutual funds, fixed deposits, whatever. Choose what is most suitable for your situation as you take determined steps towards financial security which is an issue that is very close to your heart. Taureans love to make money and lead a comfortable life.

19 February: Moon's Last Quarter in Scorpio

You have built up a system of work that is both self-driven and self-sustaining. The hectic period of work in the recent past could have taken its toll and you now look for a much-needed change in your routine. Hobbies or spending quality time with children (your own, if you have them) could be the breath of fresh air in your humdrum life. Nature walks, visits to art exhibitions and artistic places and music concerts help rejuvenate your spirit. You might have to travel for work as gains filter in through prudent use of your charms and your highly developed communication skills. Ganesha asks you to be very vigilant with your money this week as you could have a tendency to be careless with it. You could lose money in the share market or even through impulse shopping.

23 February: New Moon in Aquarius

Ganesha is pleased with your dedication to work and personal relationships and rewards pour in. There are monetary gains and stronger bonds of love with those who matter to you. You could find yourself delving deeper into the issues of the higher self/dharma/karma/tantra and mantra in search of spiritual power and strength. Your search could lead you to unusual religious groups or cults or sects. Exploration of all kinds will be beneficial and it could give you mental peace and happiness. You do gain in many other ways too as your mental well-being will lead to physical well-being.

2 March: Moon's First Quarter in Gemini

Your journey within will see you divert your attention towards spending pleasurable moments and fun times with friends and close family members. You are on a high. Leisure activities, indulging in your favourite hobbies or even spending time with your loved ones will help you pass your time happily. There is little material progress now but it is a good time to set action plans for the attainment of goals which are close to your heart. Your energy levels may be low which could make you irritable and easily offended. Ganesha advises you to remain calm. Like a jeweller who burnishes his gold with constant heating, Ganesha strengthens you mentally, physically and emotionally so that you can come out with flying colours in the game of life.

9 March: Full Moon in Virgo

You begin this new phase with a load of responsibilities and duties. The fun-filled days of last week now morph into days and even nights of labour and hard, unrelenting work as you catch up with unfinished projects and other official paper work. There is no respite. A strained cash flow and interpersonal tensions could be the result of the overwhelming energies at play in this phase. Communications could go haywire leading to hurt feelings and even resentment.

16 March: Moon's Last Quarter in Sagittarius

The full bag of responsibilities of the previous week continues to weigh you down but Ganesha now gives you the gift of accepting your situation gracefully and partaking of life to the fullest by being in the moment. You play as hard as you work and your conservative nature takes a back seat as you indulge yourself. Some Taureans could even explore a new way of life – a life of austerity and going back to the basics. You could be a person of extremes here – a life of either utmost decadence or piety.

24 March: New Moon in Aries

Water seeks its own level. Thanks to all your experiments you have learnt many new things about yourself which may have surprised, even shocked you. A little tightening of belt may be demanded of you this week, not just in your personal expenditure but also at work. You are a whiz at money matters as you plan out strategies to help tide over this slack period. You comb your financial outgoings to see if you can make any savings through bargains and discounts. Sudden changes in your workplace could make you jittery and could even lead to fights with your spouse. But having made you walk the spiritual path for the last few weeks, Ganesha ensures that you are carried to safety.

1 April: Moon's First Quarter in Cancer

The new month begins with the events of last week, still fresh in your mind. Everything has turned out much better than you expected and you heave a sigh to relief as you ponder over your financial matters. Contracts, commissions and collaborations are some of the Cs that you will deal with this week but it will have to be done with the big C – yes, I am referring to 'commitment'. Your favourite astrologer also reminds you that your loved one could be feeling neglected with your over-involvement in work. Romantic dinners, overnight trips and shopping for self or home are some of the ways you could bring cheer. There is a possibility of overspending but indulge if it makes you feel good. You are quite capable of augmenting your finances when the need arises.

8 April: Full Moon in Libra

Matters of the heart and hearth occupy you this week as your domestic responsibilities finally catch up with you. You now have to schedule in all neglected home matters and so are busy with repairs, renovations, constructions, additions to property, buying of assets, debts, rentals, leases, property loans, house/office/godown/warehouse/shops and such. Spouse, children, elders and even dependents and pets could require your soothing and calm presence. The ill health of your loved ones or even extended family could cause panic but Ganesha guides you to happily overcome these obstacles.

14 April: Moon's Last Quarter in Capricorn

The full moon in Libra reminds you of the importance of strong and solid relationships in your life. Small and big victories at work give you satisfaction and the home environment is also harmonious. Your partner displays understanding and care and this motivates you to reciprocate. You are innovative and ingenious at work and win applause. You will gain professionally and personally. Some of you may have to deal with legal matters which could require you to travel. Ganesha counsels you, Taureans, to take a balanced approach to all issues if you want to derive the maximum benefits from them.

23 April: New Moon in Taurus

The feel-good factor in your life comes through the positive and loving vibes you share with your loved ones. Even your co-workers and the people you associate with feel enveloped in these warm feelings as they interact with you. You are able to put yourself in the other person's shoes and this helps you to take humanitarian decisions at work. This also endears you to all, at home and at the office, even the upper management. At the same time, your gentle approach to situations at home makes it a safe haven, where you can relax in the company of your loved ones, far away from the hustle and bustle of everyday life. Even though you may not have surplus money at this time, there is fun and laughter at home and beautiful moments with loved ones.

30 April: Moon's First Quarter in Leo

You initiate the search for true happiness and it is possible that the trend will carry on over the next month too. You are flamboyant in your expressions of love. Your efforts to find bliss and strengthen your love life meets with success as your partner is intensely attracted to you. You may get depressed too sometime during this new moon phase and feel like pondering esoteric issues, the purpose of life/karma/dharma/the inner self. Religion and spirituality are the fields that you want to explore at this time. Meditation/relaxation techniques/chanting could help you to become more positive. This is also a good time to set financial goals and even make plans for the successful completion of your various projects. It will also serve as a good diversion from troubling thoughts.

7 May: Full Moon in Scorpio

The new moon in your own sign in your birth month is the time to get back in touch with your sensual and earthly desires. It is okay to indulge in the three sinful Cs – chocolates, caviar and champagne – without any feelings of guilt. It is your birth month after all and you do deserve a treat. Other feel-good pursuits could include oil massages, visits to the spa and even to hot water springs and therapeutic resorts. This could be a good time for some of you to undergo a makeover. A new look, including a new hairstyle and even a new wardrobe, could give you dual gains – add a spring to your step – and at the same time enhance your prospects at work. If you are unattached, you could attract renewed attention which could develop into a relationship with excellent prospects for the long term. This is also a good time to take stock of your assets and monetary worth. Ganesha says that making efficient and productive financial plans at this time will give you greater gains in the days ahead. There could be gains from inheritances too.

14 May: Moon's Last Quarter in Aquarius

Your financial plans of last week are giving you expected gains. At the same time, you continue to explore other options that could make your finances even stronger. A new trend this week overlaps the money-focused one of last week. Artistic and aesthetic activities interest you as do spending time in the company of your beloved. Art and artworks may appeal to you as lucrative forms of investment. Your relief at having successfully overcome challenging aspects of the previous weeks could cause you to overindulge, leading to health and other problems. Ganesha suggests that you slow down and take stock of the situation.

22 May: New Moon in Gemini

Your untiring efforts, steadfastness of purpose and precise planning deserve a reward and Ganesha gives you your dues. Hard work, combined with a helpful and generous attitude, puts the spotlight on you at work, enhancing your image. You have the luck of the draw and plans fall into place even as you think about them. So can the three Ps – power, pelf and privileges – definitely the outcome of your labours – be far behind, asks Ganesha, and quite rightly so! Watch out because fame could make you swollen-headed and arrogant resulting in abrasive behaviour, both with your workmates and even with your family. The relationships that may be ruptured might never be healed, so nip this tendency in the bud and use all your negotiating skills to ensure win-win situations. It is also advisable to keep your legendary temper in check.

30 May: Moon's First Quarter in Virgo

Your ceaseless efforts at work or in your business have possibly given you tremendous gains. But the last week of this month sees this emergence of a new trend. The latest technology and better procedures to make your work more efficient could provide you with enough free time to pursue your favourite leisure activities. You enjoy spending time and money on entertaining friends and generally having a good time. Ganesha says that the admiration and adulation of your colleagues could make you complacent and even lethargic. This could be harmful in the longer term as you could end up losing the advantage you may have gained over your competitors. Spiritual pursuits and facing life-changing questions of death and salvation could be the key that fulfils your metaphysical yearnings. You develop a loving relationship with yourself even as Ganesha blesses you with harmonious and deeply loving relations with your near and dear ones. You make substantial spiritual gains in this period.

5 June: Full Moon in Sagittarius

The slowdown of last week is transformed into a hectic period in which the most obvious trend relates to people, people and people. Yes, buildings bridges – not literally – and creating connections with people, renewing contacts/contracts, travel – both long-distance journeys with stopovers and short/overnight trips included – can provide monetary gains. People-related professions, especially those in public relations/event management/tour organizers/wedding planners/hotel management will do well. Setting goals to expand your business or work beyond the boundaries of your city/state/country could excite you but watch out for enemies and critics at work. Do not retaliate and decide to repay them in their own coin. Ganesha feels that the best way is to 'go with the flow' and 'surrender to the higher energies'. Relaxing at home with leisure pursuits – watching plays and movies, attending seminars and workshops with your children/siblings/spouse/partner could help steady your nerves and also add to domestic harmony.

13 June: Moon's Last Quarter in Pisces

A lucky phase begins. You are like a magician – whatever you desire appears in front of you, just like magic. Luck favours you and this could be a good time to buy the lottery ticket too. You feel cheerful and satisfied with the way your life has shaped up midway into the new year. You will now pay attention to the finer details of your business and fine-tune the procedures that help you to carry out your work more effectively. Wealth generation and regeneration are areas that concern you this week as you overcome a few organizational glitches and tensions at work.

21 June: New Moon in Cancer

Your basic nature is conservative and serious and you rarely let your hair down. But this full moon in Sagittarius will completely change this perception that people have about you. You are quite the party animal now. 'Where's the party tonight?' will be your motto as you dance away evenings in the company of friends and family. Relationships with parents/in-laws give special joy, and children (especially your own) spread cheer in your life. The money angle is also good at this time and so you are able to enjoy life without worries. People will still look up to you for advice and guidance in familial and fiscal matters. Take care of your health as all the overindulgence could get to you. This is a fantastic week and you express your deep gratitude to Ganesha for the wonderful and priceless gifts he has bestowed upon you.

28 June: Moon's First Quarter in Libra

You will continue to feel lucky and speculative activities could give you huge gains. But Ganesha cautions you not to go overboard. You continue to develop your material assets/insurance policies/term deposits to assure the financial security of your loved ones. You put in sustained efforts in all aspects of life and are rewarded for it. There is romance and you may wear your heart on your sleeve. The object of your attraction will not be able to escape your attention. If married, there will be intense bonding. If single, a serious romance which begins now could take you to the altar.

5 July: Full Moon in Capricorn

The new moon in Cancer brings with it the luck of the draw and you find your coffers filling up with returns from your investments. You are flush with funds and will be intent on making purchases. You realize that luck is favouring you now and will continue with your speculative activities. Peers, colleagues and friends seem to love your company and this gives you a warm feeling of satisfaction. People connections are truly electric and they are a source of much joy in your life. You will shower gifts on your beloved and pamper him/her thoroughly. Luck, both in love and in work, is very rare indeed! But very true for you this week, says Ganesha.

12 July: Moon's Last Quarter in Gemini

Last week, you concentrated your efforts on work and on your most intimate relationships and this gave you multifold returns. This week you get an opportunity to expand the sphere of your interactions with people from different aspects of life. Your reputation also grows at your workplace and at home, your family (which could include your spouse, children, siblings and even parents and in-laws), not only find you delightful company but are also visibly impressed with your tremendous skills, extensive knowledge and common sense. Neighbours, community representatives, friends and acquaintances approach you with their problems as they realize that you genuinely care about them and are ready to go out of your way to help them. As you leave no stone unturned in your efforts you realize that the leadership role thrust on you gives you great pleasure and makes you appreciate the significance of life. You love feeling wanted and being the centre of attraction.

20 July: New Moon in Cancer

Recent events have turned you into a new person. Earlier, your behaviour was often boorish and aggressive, often bordering on selfishness. The new you is still assertive in pushing ahead in business – and you are keen to expand into unexplored/virgin/foreign territories and fields – but now you welcome out-of-the-box thinking and encourage fresh, innovative ideas from your subordinates. Awards and rewards pour in due to your sustained efforts. You are careful not to hog the limelight and are willing to share the credit with your teammates. You go out of your way to help and guide your co-workers and subordinates. You have a great sense of style and impeccable manners and you present a picture of true success. Money matters are on the right track and there is harmony in domestic affairs. Incomplete and pending issues from previous weeks continue to put irritating obstacles in your path and you get down to tackling them. If you don't tackle them firmly and soon, they could blow out of proportion.

27 July: Moon's First Quarter in Virgo

There is peace of mind and also money from several sources. Dividends from games of chance could make your pocket heavy and your heart light. With Ganesha's blessings you are doing well in your job and in your relationships. This is even more satisfying as it happens without extra cost. You have redefined the values and principles which govern your life and this has helped reduce the stress and tension. The week is coloured by a celebratory mood and so dinners, parties, get-togethers et al., get the thumbs up. There is a lot of entertaining and relationships continue to hold an important position in your life. You are loved and appreciated by all, and isn't this a great way to be, asks Ganesha.

2 August: Full Moon in Aquarius

A lot depends on your perspective this week. You will question whether your life is fulfilling. What would give you true happiness and peace? You have to deal with both non-materialistic and material issues and this is a time to make tough choices. A toss-up between family and work could cause fights and unpleasant situations at home. You may have to remain absent from a family function because of work issues and this could cause fissures in your domestic set-up and relationships if not handled with maturity. You may also explore new investment opportunities. Ganesha advises you to keep your mind alert and calm to prevent unnecessary losses. There could be a conflict between the higher self and your shadow self. This could be a period of great learning if you take the right approach.

11 August: Moon's Last Quarter in Taurus

You have been wavering between material and spiritual pursuits for the last couple of weeks but this ends now, as circumstances compel you to give your full attention to more earthly issues. Your down-to-earth, pragmatic nature comes in handy in your dealings with realty, rentals, leases, insurance and taxation matters. Spending time with an elderly parent/relative, their health issues or visits to hospitals could put a drain on your resources. You don't begrudge it but you now put in renewed efforts into your work (maybe you will even have to moonlight) or business to make up for the unexpected expenses. One way you could generate additional income is through monetizing your hobbies.

TAURUS

You could find yourself giving interviews, travelling for this purpose, communicating with influential people, and even being headhunted. This is a period for hard, sustained work and you don't shy away from it.

19 August: New Moon in Leo

This week it is all about you, and only you. Funds, friends, family, food, fashion – yes, the total mix of things that give you utmost pleasure – will become more important. You have a deep organic relationship with food; savouring exquisite delicacies and even cooking gives you considerable pleasure. Wining and dining with loved ones/family/friends takes your time. There will be makeovers too which could include your home/garden/neighbourhood; the permutations and combinations are unlimited and you do all this very stylishly and gracefully. All this would require a lot of expenditure but you have made the necessary arrangements. You radiate an aura of success this week and nothing can block your progress, says Ganesha.

25 August: Moon's First Quarter in Sagittarius

This week sees the birth of a trend that could carry on at least till the beginning of October. A stable family life is very important for Taureans and any kind of upheaval stresses you. The love and devotion of your spouse and children (the unattached may want to propose at this time so this phase could see a lot of engagements and weddings) motivate you to devote your stupendous energies to wealth generation. Yes, Taureans are capable of building huge, even gargantuan financial empires with extremely durable roots. You put in the requisite efforts, cheerfully and unhesitatingly, to build a strong and secure future for your loved ones. Work will be hectic and will require you to be super-efficient and organized. Success is yours for the asking, assures Ganesha.

2 September: Full Moon in Pisces

In continuation of last week, you will have to be on your toes at work. Your hands could be full with a large number of projects with looming deadlines and all of them requiring your detailed personal participation. But this period is not only about hard slogging; you can expect to be busy attending official receptions, business lunches and dinners, conferences, conventions, trade fairs, networking meets, etc. Your interpersonal skills, combined with your proficiency in your profession, could make you the key person in negotiations, deals and collaborations. Your boss and upper management respect you and even help you at work. Despite such a hectic schedule, you might be compelled to study further, gain knowledge and scholarship as an additional academic qualification. But your love life and domestic interaction could both suffer as you will be slogging away. It will be a good idea to steal some time away from your work for those you love. You will be busy but not bored, chortles Ganesha, as you achieve success in whatever you undertake.

10 September: Moon's Last Quarter in Gemini

This week's full moon gives rise to introspection. The hectic professional manoeuvrings of the last weeks are finally over, and may have led to a burnout. Prayers, piety and philosophy – these three Ps aptly sum up the pursuits of this week. You might find yourself delving deeper into the metaphysical aspects of life. You are very sensual but now your spiritual cravings need to be satisfied. There could be conflicts between work and your other-worldly pursuits and you may seriously seek out solitude to search inwards and think things over. Social service/providing medicine/healthcare/food/clothes/education to the underprivileged will help you in your inner healing. The support of your family, especially your spouse/beloved/partner in this mission, strengthens your spirit and faith and this is what makes this phase really worthwhile.

17 September: New Moon in Virgo

You have had a streak of good fortune in the past. You yearn to give back to society and this process may already have begun since the last moon phase. It intensifies this week as you involve yourself in charitable activities. But be chary of too much involvement as it could lead to false allegations of self-interest and at the same time lead to frayed tempers and relationships. Children, with their charming freshness and innocence, will add a sparkle of purity and freshness in your life. Domestic affairs will be harmonious and there will be monetary benefits through communications; those in the media will do very well both monetarily and performance wise.

24 September: Moon's First Quarter in Capricorn

This is a perfect time to set goals for your relationships and finances. Shower your loved one with constant attention if you want to retain the charm and excitement of the courtship years. Relationships ranging from intimate ones to even those at the workplace come to the fore. There are interrelational issues, resentments and past grievances to deal with. It will not be all smooth sailing, but this is the right time to find answers to troublesome issues, with your tactful and generous nature. Your mate and you will bring back the much-required element of romance in your relationship. You wish to spend more time in the company of your children, parents and elders but you also need to provide for the family. You are a practical sign and understand the value of money in your life. Therefore, you will try to balance both in this Libran quarter.

2 October: Full Moon in Aries

Ganesha says that this week you will need to concentrate on your career/business if you are seriously looking at progress and upward mobility. Upgraded and efficient machinery and processes make you more productive and you are a veritable dynamo at work. Your energy levels are high and you need to find ways to let off steam. Your achievements are rewarded and your stock rises in your workplace. Money makes the world go round and the joy of making money and spending it is contagious. The family is happy and there is domestic bliss.

10 October: Moon's Last Quarter in Cancer

You could have some hidden or secret information revealed to you which, at first, may be shocking. Your working style has become much more professional and you are reaping the rewards. You could be the brand ambassador of your organization, and pursuing new projects and gaining new business for your company could be at the top of your agenda for the next quarter. There may be some hindrances to your rapid progress due to family matters, like the ill health of a spouse or accidents/death of a relative. There is a possibility, but it may not happen. Ganesha advises you to remain patient. Everything in life has its own time frame and it won't help to rush things. Be calm and look at innovative strategies to get around old problems.

16 October: New Moon in Libra

Your home is truly your castle and you are now keen to upgrade it to reflect your status and financial worth. Renovations, redecorating, repairing – these three Rs are uppermost in your mind as you make the relevant changes in your residential property. You might even want to relocate to a better locality. There are indications of seeking out an overseas posting if the prospects are good. You desire a happy home life and loving and respectful relations with people as well. There may be several romantic liaisons and this could lead to complications. Travel, either for work or pleasure, could give unexpected gains. Take care of your health too.

23 October: Moon's First Quarter in Aquarius

Money, or 'moneta' as the Italians call it, is the key focus of this week. A strong financial position is what you crave, and you go all out to fulfil this desire. You love money, not for itself, but for the security it can provide you and your family. Power, privileges, pleasure, pride – these four Ps are the offshoots of a strong monetary position and this is what you aim for in this week. Your financial skills and prowess ensure that money multiplies easily and you laugh all the way to the bank. There is a dark side of the week too, though. There could be the misuse of power, jealousy, possessiveness, secret deals, extramarital affairs and so on. Ganesha advises prayers and meditation. You are charged with energy and it is important that your direct it well.

31 October: Full Moon in Taurus

The deeper the well, the sweeter the water, says Ganesha as he advises you to go deep within yourself to find the answers that you are looking for. This is the time for introspection. But it will not be enough to restrict your research to metaphysics. There is a great demand for your services/products and you make huge profits. You feel good about yourself and it also makes you more loving in your relationships. But, relationships with extended family and in-laws may not be smooth; even colleagues and peers could blow hot and cold this week. Maintaining a balanced and open outlook will help you to navigate this phase successfully.

8 November: Moon's Last Quarter in Leo

Ganesha brings you a fun-loving week at the beginning of the month and you are ready to enjoy the fruits of last month's labour. At work, besides your regular dedicated efforts, you feel the need for a change and will try to introduce new strategies at work. You also bring in new elements to spice up your love life. Your body and mind need a recharge and you work towards it. Despite all the distractions, you manage to make steady progress at work, and give a good account of yourself.

15 November: New Moon in Scorpio

Your inner and outer self are one and you are at peace with yourself and the world. The tremendous efforts at work have drained you of your vital energies and so it is time to recoup. Mini vacations, celebrations and visits to relatives and friends energize and refresh you. The moon in your own sign enhances your positive points and really energizes you. Ganesha warns you against lethargy, sloth, procrastination and overindulgence in food and sleep. Handle inflammable situations with calmness and patience to prevent flare-ups and keep your cool at all times.

22 November: Moon's First Quarter in Pisces

You are back with your nose to the grindstone but this time there is a kind of flamboyance in your attitude. Large/mega projects interest you and you go all out to attract big business. Relationships require new and fresh inputs. If cracks have developed recently, they need to be mended at the earliest to prevent further tears in them. Your spouse and your children are the proud recipients of the fruits of your hard work. Your love is reciprocated and you could find yourself taking trips with your loved ones and bonding deeper with them. There could be some health scare in the family but Ganesha's blessings are with you and it won't be a major source of worry.

30 November: Full Moon in Gemini

Your creative energies are making you restless and you are like a bubbling volcano waiting to burst forth with new ideas. This is a good time to identify the most workable ones and then set down action plans to achieve them. You may have to go beyond your comfort zone to make substantial progress but you are not one who shies away from hard work. You have now learned to temper your self-confidence with patience and goodwill and are less brash and cocky. So people don't really resent your spectacular successes. The same dedication may be required to handle events at home but Ganesha guides you out to tight situations.

8 December: Moon's Last Quarter in Virgo

If you have been solitary for long or not communicating too much with others, this is the time to come out of your shell and face the real world head-on. This is the only way to resolve matters that seemed insurmountable. Working together with close associates will provide exponential growth. Whether it is co-workers, bosses or subordinates, your spouse/partner, children or even extended family, you will have to work out a win-win agenda. There is a danger of accidents due to carelessness or absent-mindedness at home/work/while travelling. So be alert at all times.

14 December: New Moon in Sagittarius

Ganesha continues to send you his blessings for both personal and professional success. Events that began in September could now find fruition. Health, wealth and work form the trinity for you, and with the grace of Ganesha, you can see definite enhancements in these areas. The three big Cs – computers, correspondence and contacts – could benefit you tremendously if you can overcome your in-built resistance to the unusual and the unexpected. Don't be too conservative, and open your mind to the prowess of technology. There could be long journeys related to work. The more you commute/communicate/contact, the more you benefit, says Ganesha. This applies to the home front too, Ganesha adds.

21 December: Moon's First Quarter in Aries

You have made enough money and now it is time to seek answers within. It has been a hectic period and you long for some peace and solitude. You are fatigued by the continuous interactions with people. You look to the scriptures for answers and ponder questions about life, death and destiny. It is the end of the year and there are deadlines to be met, the mood is celebratory and there are several responsibilities for you to deal with. So you are hard-pressed to find time for spiritual pursuits. This moon phase can give splendid benefits to those involved in working behind the scenes like researchers, detectives, archaeologists, writers, software engineers, talent scouts, HR executives. It is an action-packed period and you are truly stretched, and have much to do, even though the year is ending.

30 December: Full Moon in Cancer

It has been an exceptional year even by your high standards. You have slogged away and won accolades and built up a reputation as well as a bank balance. You are grateful to Ganesha for his blessings. You end the year on a high note feeling very satisfied with yourself. There have been tough moments but you have managed to sail through. You take stock of the year and plan ahead. You are ambitious and money means a lot to you. You also have the stamina to build your career literally from scratch. A lot of highly successful people are Taureans, born with the gifts of determination and unstinting hard work. You are the plodders of the zodiac. Having attained most of your material goals, you will now be keen to continue your search for inner peace and true happiness and could meet a guide who could hasten this process. Awards and rewards were aplenty this year and Ganesha whispers into my ear to convey to you that many more are in the offing in 2021. Inculcate a little tact, strategy and patience in your life and rein in your legendary temper and there will be no stopping you Taureans, the mighty bulls of the zodiac.

GEMINI

21 May–20 June

Symbol: The Twins
Ruling Planet: Mercury
Air-Mutable-Positive
The Sign of the Inventor, the Artist.

Former US president Barack Obama used to say, 'We are all interconnected.' Interconnection is possible through communication and dialogue. All of it comes under the orbit of the planet Mercury. In short Mercury means contacts and communication. You are the great communicator the zodiac.

JUPITER

Jupiter the great benefactor and the glue of the zodiac comes in your eighth angle from 2 December 2019 to 18 December 2020. The focus will be on finances. In finances we include legacies, inheritance, money of all the partners, real estate, taxes, revenues, rents, private transactions, wills and codicils, funds for the welfare of others, trusts, sudden gains by gambling, hidden treasures and money gained from unknown means and ends. Money gained from other sources like horse racing, smuggling, games of chance, prayers for the dead and the living. Hidden treasures come to light resulting in great gains.

Concealment and storage of contraband goods, normal merchandise goods of high value on behalf of others without involvement in sale or purchase of the goods; consequences with regard to responsibility or legal implications for the custodian (referral houses fourth and twelfth)

Ancestral money, pious deeds and ceremonies for the living as well as the dead. This is truly remarkable, and I have seen it happen.

It is a great time for tantra and mantra and using words of power and hymns to gain what you desire.

Joint finances should be given special attention.

Religious or social or spiritual rallies, demonstrations, processions or meetings; peaceful functioning disturbed by rival groups; antisocial gangs; by hoodlums with ulterior motive of looting, molesting or terrorizing or giving communal colour to the disturbances/riots (referral houses fourth, ninth and twelfth).

Different kinds of phobias, including that of water, river, sea, darkness, height as that of mountains/hills/high-rise buildings, valleys, road journeys by automobiles, train journey (specially that across water or on mountainous regions), riding a horse, camel, elephant; phobia of rallies and dog bite or jackal bite; phobia of weapons including firearms; phobia of poisonous snakes, reptiles and scorpions, lizards etc.; phobia of schoolteachers; phobia of police personnel or any person attired in police-type uniforms (referral houses sixth and twelfth).

MERCURY

Here is a fine observation about Mercury from *The Philosopher's Stones*. Mercury means quicksilver. Volatile new ideas can yield great results. Be prepared to go to rapid and dramatic change. Communicate wisely with those who can help you. Like the metal quicksilver Mercury is represented by the god of travel. Mercury is the messenger of the gods, whose sacred sites were marked by stones along the road. Thus, the god rules the initiate's journey to find primal matter and to decode the many curious symbols and phrases found in alchemical manuscripts. The planet then exerts its influence over the initial operations of the work. This is a gaseous stage when the matter starts to darken and sinks to the bottom of the vessel in preparation for the dramatic stages to come.

I have purposely reserved the different meaning of Jupiter in your eighth angle. It means life, death and regeneration. In simple terms it means you will be able to pass through all the difficulties and trials of life. In other words, you will succeed in the end. This should be of great and mighty satisfaction to you, dear Geminis, who often change their life and their course.

SATURN

Saturn, the planet of duty, responsibility, limitations and balancing the scales of life itself will be in your eighth angle from 21 December 2017 to most of 2020. The spin-off will be the total finance scene comprising earned income, funds, loans, investments, legacy, joint finance and capital formation. The works, in fact, are favoured. It will, in many ways, make the trends and tendencies of last year run into this one. However, it's not only money but the entertainment and communication world that keeps you occupied – food, fads and fashions, family life – all the Fs, counting finance. Food could even extend to include dietary and nutritional concerns vis-à-vis the household and domestic matters, which cannot really be relegated to second place, even though business is your major thrust. You'll just have to push that little bit extra

Talking about food, let me give you an illustration of the largest fondue (dish of melted cheese), in the world. As you know, America is symbolized by the largest, and largest fondue was prepared on the 28 February 2007, under the supervision of chef Terrance Brennan, owner of the Artisanal Cheese Centre in New York. The fondue weighed 2,100 lbs. Its major ingredients were 1,190 lbs of Gruyere cheese from Wisconsin, 120 lbs of white wine and some spices. It was prepared in a 220-year-old 2-ton cast iron kettle brought from Louisiana.

The greatest lesson Saturn teaches you Geminis is health is wealth. You need to do exercise, build up your muscles and have an extra dose of strength and stamina. This is mighty important. Also taxes, joint finances and property, improving your self-confidence, trying to save wherever it is truly possible but not to be miserly. In short, a fine balance between lending and borrowing. Trusts, wills, dealing in property matters and insurance and, if you are old, preparing for a graceful retirement are a must for you Geminis because of the simple reason that you live on your nerves and sometimes rash decisions and actions which might prove unfavourable. I would say in short that care and caution will be better than enterprise and taking new challenges. But I have always maintained that astrology is not perfect and the final decision is always yours. I can only suggest and comment to the best of my limited abilities.

As Saturn continues throughout the year in your eighth angle the same results will apply. But there is also a change for the better. Why? Because Jupiter, the planet of plenty and prosperity, also stays in your eighth angle along with Saturn. Let me put it all in simple, easy-to-understand words. This year will be a great improvement than the last year in every possible way. Delays and disappointments and hurdles will not stop you from gaining your goals and wanting what you desire. Congrats.

BLUEPRINT FOR THE ENTIRE YEAR

January: Money, honey, riches, beautification, augmentation of income, good food, jewellery.

February: Research, contacts, communication, correspondence, brothers, sisters, relatives.

March: Home, house, property, renovation, decoration, alteration.

April: Love, romance, children, relationships, hobbies, sports.

May: Health, pets, servants, job, hygiene, colleagues.

June: Love, marriage, divorce, journeys, reaching out to people, also separations and law cases.

July: Joint finances, funds, loans, legacy, family issues and problems.

August: Sweet-and-sour relationships, publicity, conferences and meets, inspirational and intuitive moves and manoeuvres.

September: Prestige, status, power struggle, perks, new ventures and means of communication.

October: Socializing, group activities, marriage, love affair, happiness, laughter, the goodies of life.

November: Secret activities, health expenses, visits to hospitals, welfare centres, medical check-ups.

December: Fulfilment, happiness, money, marriage, confidence.

Summary: Pressures and opposition bring out the best in you. Also, Jupiter helps you in money, journeys, publicity, ceremony, discoveries.

Your happiness quota is 79 per cent.

WEEKLY REVIEW BY PHASES OF THE MOON

10 January: Full Moon in Cancer

As the new year dawns, your attention will be drawn towards laying strong foundations for your finances. Though you are in a stable financial position, you realize that you need to make more money and make your family more secure. Dig the well before you need the water – this proverb could aptly describe your mindset as you explore investment options that will give you lucrative returns. International connections/projects/people could bring you unexpected gains but Ganesha advises you to keep the details of your deals a secret. Be ready for great changes/transformations in your domestic situation which could be positive or negative, depending on your perspective. Life is never a bed of roses all the way and Ganesha warns you about the ill health of your spouse or the loss of your job. But you manage to cope well with flexitime at your workplace and even starting a side business. Freelancing/consulting/collaborations will fulfil both your creative and material needs. Some of you, depending on your personal horoscope, will profit through lotteries/lucky draws/sports. There will also be happy times with the family throughout the year.

17 January: Moon's Last Quarter in Libra

You continue to make determined efforts towards strengthening your financial position, and explore every investment opportunity. Geminis are generally restless and are always on the lookout for action of some kind. Travelling for work/higher studies/business is a possibility this week. You are always open to learning new strategies that could help you in your career and yet also indulge in play in equal measure. Your industrious, result-oriented nature finds approval from your boss. You show the same mindset towards stocks/shares/mutual funds/property or anything else that you invest in. You display a more caring and nurturing attitude towards your loved ones and children. You have always been a dutiful son/daughter and shall continue to be so – that being one of your strengths.

24 January: New Moon in Capricorn

You have been involved, till now, in seriously and conservatively building your family's nest egg. You have been a responsible child/parent/spouse/friend/employee and have won kudos for your cool, caring and calm nature. Now, at this phase, you could feel an upsurge of emotional energy which could cause restlessness and loneliness. You may indulge in disruptive and decadent behaviour and shock your loved ones. Illicit affairs, infidelity (both physical and emotional), underhand deals and indulging in games of chance are possible under these energies; you may not have any qualms or feelings of guilt either. Ganesha advises you to understand the repercussions of your actions on your family and suggests using safer ways to dissipate these for thrill urges. Cash-flow problems could arise if you spend indiscriminately. Spending time with your beloved and your children (if you have them) will provide pleasurable moments and divert your mind from any action which you may repent later.

2 February: Moon's First Quarter in Taurus

You have been devoting too much of your energies to work and this has been causing difficulties in your relationships. The new moon gives you an opportunity to make amends with your loved ones. Socializing/partying with close family members and friends takes your time and you showcase your fun-loving /outgoing/generous/caring nature. You are benefited too as improved ties and bonds give you great joy and harmony. Besides your close family, you show interest in the activities of your local community and even volunteer to help out. There could be collaborations with international partners (franchising/import–export)/job opportunities in a multinational company, and your reputation at work could receive a huge boost. You earn applause and are the toast of all.

9 February: Full Moon in Leo

Your natural inclination is towards spirituality and you involve yourself in studying the scriptures/visiting holy and sacred shrines/meditation/chanting. Finances continues to occupy your attention but Ganesha advises you to stay alert in all money matters. This is the right time for parking your money in safe and stable investments and not risking or squandering it away in get-rich-quick schemes. You will enrich your life on an esoteric level and find great joy in simple domestic pleasures. You will also find solace and material rewards in creative and artistic pursuits.

19 February: Moon's Last Quarter in Scorpio

You are on a high as you involve the three Cs – communications, contacts and correspondence – to take your career/business up the next rung of success. Your stupendous interpersonal skills attract attention and just dividends. You could be tempted to venture into risky territory; the indications are all there and you will have to control yourself. Ganesha advises caution in money matters, love affairs and in overindulgence. Bold declarations and dynamic gestures of love are possible, leading to indiscreet romantic liaisons. There could be niggling health issues and Ganesha strongly advocates prudence in all your actions.

23 February: New Moon in Aquarius

Money matters continue to demand attention. But along with that friends/loved ones/extended family demand your attention and you do not hold back as you respond. You overextend yourself to bring peace and harmony in all your relationships, both professional and personal, and the results are spectacular. Ganesha blesses you with happy bonding. You have pleasurable moments with your lover and, if a parent, great times with your kids. There will also be happy occasions with siblings/parents/in-laws and extended family.

GEMINI

This is a great week as you win accolades at work too. You could begin to gain clarity about your goals and this helps you achieve success with both money and love. Ganesha's blessings are with you.

2 March: Moon's First Quarter in Gemini

You have an inherent edge in communicating with people and so any relationship issue with children/family elders/siblings can be sorted out by talking. Friends are the source of fun and frolic and you will enjoy partying virtually all week long. You manage to give equal and quality time to both your career and your children. Spirituality and religious matters also interest you. The money position is strong and Ganesha is pleased to inform you that at least on this score you have little to worry – for the coming months at least.

9 March: Full Moon in Virgo

The moon in your own sign gives you significant gains, especially in relationships. The trend of the past few weeks continues and you put in dedicated efforts in all your projects and initiatives. The focus has shifted from work to home and this requires detailed planning. All issues related to the home are highlighted – from restorations/renovations/additions to investments in property, land, leases and loans. There will be very intense bonding and you spend memorable moments in the company of loved ones. Along with peace of mind and contentment, this period also brings closure to delayed or unattended topics, including blocked payments and projects. Tact and diplomacy are required to tackle awkward issues and to resolve them to everyone's satisfaction.

16 March: Moon's Last Quarter in Sagittarius

The three Cs – contacts, communications and correspondences – are this week's theme and so there will be a flurry of letters, emails, SMS as well as travel and trips. You will be in touch with the world and there will be many new work projects. A personal situation/work issue could put you in a dilemma but you manage to come through unstuck with some deft manoeuvring. There is a good chance to meet up with extended family and friends in religious functions/family get-togethers/celebrations. There are chances of fruitful journeys too. Expenses on frivolous and risky ventures could put your family budget under strain resulting in domestic problems. It will be important to plan ahead. This is also a good time to start a fitness routine.

24 March: New Moon in Aries

You have continued to work hard and diligently even in the midst of all the interpersonal drama in your private life, winning approval with your superiors. Your reputation will soar. Prestige, promotions and pelf are the results of your own hard work and dedication, and you deserve it. As your self-esteem and self-confidence – along with your social standing – soar, you manage to, thankfully, retain your helpful and gracious attitude with all and sundry irrespective of their status in life. You are called upon to attend to matters connected to loved ones and even extended family/relatives. You are loved and admired for your generous/caring/hard-working nature. You are destined to go places.

1 April: Moon's First Quarter in Cancer

You are now determined to put in your all towards building your dreams which includes both your career path and the lifestyle you aspire to. You have received rewards for your efforts, but now breaking the status quo and pushing ahead calls for some risky moves. There may have been hindrances before but now you want it all. So you equip yourself physically and mentally through determined and disciplined efforts/research/studies, 'out-of-the-box' thinking and a 'can-do' attitude. You are filled with confidence and energy and will put your ideas at work into motion. There is good bonding at home and the support and goodwill of people/friends/relatives/bosses is available to you in plenty. Ganesha advises you to use contacts well.

8 April: Full Moon in Libra

The trend that began in the full-moon phase continues and you put in superhuman efforts at work. You are a rock star and your achievements are in the spotlight but you don't allow it to distract you from the larger vision. There are obstacles and potholes ahead but you have the stamina and strength to move ahead. You may step on a few toes in the process but you also manage to quell any untoward incident and defuse a difficult situation before it blows up. Rewards, returns and revenues – these three Rs – are the result of relentless efforts and rigorous hard work. You are motivated and determined to bring prosperity and cheer to your family. You also manage to party hard and enjoy dinners/get-togethers/sleepovers. Children/pets/hobbies help you to relax and even maintain good health in spite of your back-breaking agenda at work.

14 April: Moon's Last Quarter in Capricorn

You learn to let go a bit at work this week but continue to get amazing results from your associations and connections.

Supportive and cooperative ties with your colleagues and workmates will energize you. The domestic situation will also require your intense dedication and focus and so you are occupied on all fronts. Children/pets/dependents/older relatives could also take your time once again this week too, but you are generous with yourself and they love it. You gain love and affection and are filled with goodwill. You also make substantial career progress; your accomplishments are many and will happen easily as the luck of the draw is clearly with you. You could be attracted, at this time, to projects or activities that could give you a supplementary income. The additional workload may lead to undue stress. You should take proper care of your health – it will be imperative.

23 April: New Moon in Taurus

Having set the ball rolling in your workplace, with Ganesha's blessings and your dedicated efforts, you will now be receptive to the myriad opportunities that have fallen into your lap. You have energy and a positive mindset and success is ensured. You will complete all your tasks and keep your deadlines. Proper management of resources and time allows you to indulge in your favourite pastimes without compromising tight work schedules. You win kudos for your efforts and an elevated sense of self-assurance and confidence will double your pleasure both at home and work. There will be many new associations and several happy moments.

30 April: Moon's First Quarter in Leo

You somehow, magically, revolutionize your relationships, thanks to a makeover and a spanking new persona. There is a sea change in the way you conduct your affairs, both personal and professional, and a feeling of exultation runs through all your interactions. Having made these changes, you will find you have gained immensely. Work will occupy you as you set your plan into motion. There will also be outings/get-togethers/dinners/shopping with your loved ones including your partner/children/friend/extended family. Your days will be happy and filled with joy. With a comfortable cash flow, you drink deeply of the splendours of life.

7 May: Full Moon in Scorpio

This week will see a turnaround in your priorities as the work-driven focus of last week will diminish to some extent and shift to your personal ties and association. On display will be the new you, more mature, loving, caring and demonstrative. Friends – both old and recent – and relationships just forged or revived from the distant past will fill you with a sense of warmth and happiness. Tender and memorable moments shared with your spouse/partner and children/dependents, while ignoring pressing demands on your resources (physical/monetary), will strengthen mutual love and bonding. Travel will enhance your engagement with life. This is certainly an interesting period of any account. Overwhelming spiritual urges, involvement with charitable/relief organizations and matters of global concern will all be felt. You will be in a very introspective frame of mind.

14 May: Moon's Last Quarter in Aquarius

You are on a high this week, as you allow nothing to hold you back in your pursuit of pleasure and profit. You will be eager to partake of fun and you also have a backup plan to ensure that funds keep coming in. It is your time to shine and you will go much beyond the call of duty in your fulfilment of domestic obligations. Health of elders/dependents/boss and even in-laws could require your prolonged involvement. But you help out without qualms. 'Being in the moment' in each aspect of life will enhance your happiness. Ganesha's blessings are with you and you will be able to tackle any obstacles/hindrances in your career path.

22 May: New Moon in Gemini

The professional arena will now demand intense commitment. You are a high achiever, nobody can deny that, and you will continue to work on your projects without letting up, and are not ready to brook any interference. You will set very high standards, not just for your subordinates, but also for yourself. This uncompromising attitude could alienate your co-workers and supporters leaving you to complete the bulk of the work alone. But this doesn't deter you and you ensure that every project is completed in time. Ganesha is pleased with your passion for work but reminds you to employ tact and diplomacy in your dealings. Being tolerant of peoples' foibles and shortcomings and patiently encouraging them to become a part of your team will help a great deal. Co-operation, collaborations and work are the key themes of this week and shall continue to be so for the remaining days of the month.

30 May: Moon's First Quarter in Virgo

Once again, relationship issues will distract you from your work, making you lose focus, and this could have harmful long-term repercussions. Details at your work will be important at this time and reading the fine print could help you avoid heartaches in the future. You could have the

GEMINI

tendency to be laid-back and even casual about things, and carrying this attitude into your workspace could cause grief. You might have to take swift and wise decisions in certain matters and may face animosity and negativity, and undergo a lot of stress leading to health issues. Gaining mastery over your subject/job/work or even additional knowledge or an added qualification could occupy your time, leaving you very little time for family and loved ones. But it is their love and support that help you tide over this stressful period. You are filled with gratitude, leading to deeper bonding.

5 June: Full Moon in Sagittarius

For the better part of May, you have been involved in tackling varied issues on the home front. This will result in the strengthening of family ties which you now realize is important for your mental peace and harmony. Health-related concern for children (your own, if you have them) could create panic and stress. This week could put a strain on your budget too and you will have to attend to money matters urgently. Prudent steps taken now to build a strong financial foundation, through conservative and reliable investments, will provide exponential returns in the future. You will also continue to devote a large part of your energies to higher studies, research and new learning. Ganesha helps you ascend a higher plane to lead a more meaningful life.

13 June: Moon's Last Quarter in Pisces

All the trends of the preceding week continue to require your intense involvement. Spiritual leanings and insights of the last week will grab your attention. Even now and you look hard for rest, relaxation and inner peace. Family funds and assets are relevant at this time as there could be unexpected demands on your time and money. Although you experience relief at the favourable conclusion of a court case or legal matter, there is a chance of getting into big trouble if you overcommit your limited resources in solving problems that don't really concern you or your loved ones. The dual nature of Gemini will come into play as you are inventive, hardworking, and yet imaginative and frivolous. You will find the time to relax and meditate and also discharge your duties and responsibilities. You could also be impatient, arrogant, and squander away your gains, and alienate kinfolk through hurtful words and actions. Ganesha advises you to exercise control and not lose your head. Words spoken in anger can cause a lot of damage and can never be withdrawn. So exercise prudence and caution.

21 June: New Moon in Cancer

Your main focus and thrust now – in your birth month phase – and continuing almost till the middle of July will be on relationships, especially with your spouse/lover and family which could include your children, dependents, parents, siblings and in-laws, and even colleagues and co-workers. You will be motivated to extend yourself, not just physically but even emotionally, to consolidate all your ties and associations. Communications, contracts and collaborations will be very relevant professionally and also in your personal life. It is not all smooth sailing, though, as unexpected events, accidents and losses could have an adverse impact on your partnerships. Remaining alert and flexible will help minimize the damage. Additionally, long-drawn-out legal procedures and processes could find this difficult as you may be drawn to be engrossed with other-worldly matters. There is not much clarity in your life now but you will endeavour to do your best.

28 June: Moon's First Quarter in Libra

This is a period of intense activity. Connections, friendships, links and associations formed now will not only be just career-related but even personal, and this is largely due to your helpful nature. Tightening your belt and investing in sure-shot winners – be it stocks, shares, mutual funds or government bonds – will give you a healthy balance sheet which will be a big blessing in these times of increasing expenses. Ganesha also ensures that you have perks, pelf and privileges, maybe even an inheritance or two. Romantic relationship, domestic interactions and celebrations will be the icing on the cake.

5 July: Full Moon in Capricorn

You may have left doubly blessed as you enjoyed a profoundly stimulating union with your mate last week. But now Ganesha showers his grace on you further. You are extremely happy as even health and wealth are in top-notch condition. You will glow with an inner sense of harmony and well-being as you experience and live joyfully each and every aspect of your life. You will be on a high as you experience amorous relationship with your lover/sex partner. Minor financial and health worries/delayed and running-behind-schedule projects could cut short your joy, but you will be able to take it in your stride because your intensely loving connection with your significant other more than makes up for it.

12 July: Moon's Last Quarter in Gemini

There is a lot of activity this week requiring you to juggle both money and relationship issues. Though you will feel intensely passionate and gloriously romantic in your personal life, it will not be wise to neglect matters pertaining to your work/profession. Cash transactions, overdrafts, loans, credit ventures will occupy you, but Ganesha advises you to keep all such deals under wraps if you want to derive maximum benefit this week. You give of your best to both areas of your life and reap the whirlwind. Ganesha blesses you.

20 July: New Moon in Cancer

Expanding your knowledge through intensive spiritual practices will occupy you this week. You are charged and highly motivated. Wisdom and confidence will be yours. You will have no respite this week both from work and family commitments. Though you continue to invest your time and effort in these areas, you will also set a game plan for the future. Rising expenses on the home front could cause worry and the stress could lead to health problems. Look for creative solutions to these pressing problems. Ganesha's blessings are with you.

27 July: Moon's First Quarter in Virgo

From money concerns, you now turn your attention to the state of your relationships. A compromised financial condition, or strained personal ties, could have caused you to become impatient and abrupt with your associates and loved ones. This attitude has helped no one, last of all you, and in fact may have even caused you undue stress and unhappiness. Having realized this, you will now make a genuine effort to become more tolerant and available with all your contacts and connections. This change in approach will reap immediate dividends and will be greatly appreciated. There could be salary hikes, awards and recognition at the workplace. Ganesha chips in with another big blessing – a recurring legal matter is resolved, bringing you both relief and revenue. You seek guidance and solace and search for it within, through mantra/tantra/meditations, and even penance.

2 August: Full Moon in Aquarius

Further accomplishments are now yours. You shine brilliantly as you make it clear that there is no goal you cannot achieve and no peak you cannot scale. If you decide to do something, you will do it. Growth and advancements is on the cards and you will be highly energized and enthused to undertake specialized courses and higher studies or even take up a new position of responsibility. Your passionate energies spill over into all aspects of your life and you socialize/party and have a ball! Ganesha has bestowed an enchanting week on you.

11 August: Moon's Last Quarter in Taurus

You may have a tendency to go overboard in your relationships. Your physical and emotional intimacy with your lover/partners is at an all-time high. Family ties with children, sibling or parents could go through a transformation. But, as your associations widen, you may have to reach out to your extended family on several issues. There are chances of strife and conflicts leading to face-offs, arguments and quarrels. You will need large dollops of tact and diplomacy to prevent a conflagration. You will also need to pay attention to money, communication and relationships. Take special care of your health now.

19 August: New Moon in Leo

You are handling personal and professional issues in a deft manner much to the satisfaction of everybody. There is harmony both at home and in the office. You go out of your way to strengthen the ties of affection. You, luckily, manage to hold on to your ego and handle the situation well. You also manage to make more money and enjoy the luxuries of life. You pamper loved ones and spend time and money home renovation. But a new inclination crops ups this week and you delve deep into your psyche in search of answers. You explore metaphysics, tantra, mantra, astrology and even undertake studies of religious scriptures. Ganesha blesses you and guides you on the spiritual quest.

25 August: Moon's First Quarter in Sagittarius

Many new experiences will strengthen your faith. You are now capable of assimilating differing and contrasting viewpoints and attitude. This adds to the existing harmony all around and you are happy. You are well loved and deserve the spotlight. Your self-belief and identity get a leg-up and you become even more secure about your talent and skills. But beware of overconfidence. This could lead you to develop a casual and careless approach with repercussions on both your career and home life. You could put mental and financial stability of your loved ones into jeopardy with an I-don't-care approach. Apart from this, it is a wonderful week for setting up efficient system at work and home.

2 September: Full Moon in Pisces

This is another grand week, full of joys and achievements, and not just restricted to your professional milestones. After a fantastic week devoted to your partner and other personal issues, you are now all charged up and ready to tackle pending projects. You work hard and execute all your plans and meet your deadlines. Schedules will be hectic. You may get involved in grand projects not just at the locality/community level but at the national and international level too. You will be involved with issues of global concern where your enthusiastic participation will be appreciated. You will feel greatly blessed with the love and affection showered on you, the monetary rewards and the rise in status. Your family is proud of you and this is more valuable than any material success.

10 September: Moon's Last Quarter in Gemini

A marvellous time begins which brings you everything that your heart desires. This has not come without effort because there are no free lunches in life. You have put your nose to the grindstone and now it is time for payback. There is heightened reputation at work, plus several other monetary perks. Your career graph soars. This is a brilliant time to explore new and exciting avenues, even thoughts and ideas, and to bring a high level of creativity, innovativeness and ingenuity to all that you do. You can look forward to a bigger bank balance and a prominent leadership role. Your colleagues and peer groups are in awe of you. You experience the true happiness that can only come with a balanced, successful life, and this is what Ganesha blesses you with.

17 September: New Moon in Virgo

The fine trend and good interactions of last week reach a crescendo as awards, rewards, gifts and prizes and acknowledgements start rolling in. Having taken stock of your status in life, you will feel pleased to see that your aims and ambitions – both for yourself and for your loved ones – are now in your grasp. The best part is that all your achievements have been ethical and above board. This works beautifully for you, especially in your interactions with your boss and senior colleagues. Income from varied sources finds its way on to your kitty and further enhances your life. But life will not be all work and no play. You will enjoy a hectic social life in which interesting interactions/unusual leisure pursuits will add a new dimension to your life. You will also be happy and peaceful. As the week draws to a close, both health and wealth show an upward trend. You thank Ganesha for his generosity.

24 September: Moon's First Quarter in Capricorn

With your restored and enhanced perception of life, you give yourself leeway to take life easy now. You will be relaxed and laid-back. Your positivity and optimism are the basis of your enjoyment of life's pleasures. There is intimate bonding with your partner and many happy moments with friends. You also have a gentle and loving attitude which helps. On the other hand, there could also be unexpected expenses. But you manage to tide over it all and continue to socialize happily.

2 October: Full Moon in Aries

Life is a state of constant flux and this will be amply proved this week. You will now enjoy opening up to new people, experiences and expectations with gusto and fervour. You are in furious communication mode and reach out to all and sundry. You also make the most of new technology and explore new areas of work and play. Solitary activities no longer hold any charm and you revel in group interactions. It is not all smooth sailing or egos, miscommunication and even unexpected delays could tell on your health. Don't worry too much, advises Ganesha. You are quite capable of handling everything smoothly and well. In the end, it will all work out in your favour.

10 October: Moon's Last Quarter in Cancer

Ganesha likes to reward genuine effort and you are well rewarded for your hardwork this week. You have overextended yourself and have persevered with your goals without hurting people's feelings or stepping on anyone's toes, winning approval from your superiors. You also bond well with the family as they are, and will always remain, a major priority in your life. A soothing, feel-good atmosphere at home is largely responsible for your cheerful and energetic ways. You leave no stone unturned to convert your high energy levels into gains for yourself and your loved ones.

16 October: New Moon in Libra

Your determination to succeed has been mind-boggling and it has yielded results. Despite it all, there could be some insecurity about yourself/your skills and you could be unsure and many even question the integrity of your relationship and associations. But you could begin to feel uneasy and restless. Substance abuse/destructive habits and even addiction are possible at this time, resulting in strained ties and impaired health. Try to be positive and have cheerful thoughts. This is also a good time to take recourse to spiritual practices, may be even to find a guru or master who could help and guide you. Your moral strength will be tested and this might be the best time to set down new and effective parameters to relate to other. There will be financial and monetary gains and, more importantly, a calm and content mind. Ganesha is watching over you.

23 October: Moon's First Quarter in Aquarius

Your obsession with mundane material pursuits now comes to an end. What once attracted you is no longer important for you, and you have a great need now to explore your inner consciousness. Selfishness and self-promotion, especially at work, is now a thing of the past as you are overcome by a great desire to give back to society. Your generosity and open-heartedness make the needy/destitute/underprivileged your beneficiaries. You are also equally generous with your loved ones and there is greater harmony at home. You enjoy enhanced vigour, prestige, pelf and power. You will be attracted to tantra/mantra/telepathy, alternative healing techniques such as reiki, acupressure, acupuncture, Tibetan meditation and chanting and the like. New vistas open up and you develop a more rounded and open personality.

31 October: Full Moon in Taurus

Your reckless behaviour is under control as you knuckle down to the sedate job of making a living and creating wealth. You are interested right now in fulfilling your professional and personal obligations. You determinedly slog away at your routine chores and commitments. There could be some problems at work which you will have to resolve, and accusations from the home front of being a workaholic could cause added stress. It will be a good idea to find a balance and spend more time with your family/loved ones. Anger and its expression could cause health and other problems. Ganesha advises walking the spiritual path. There is solace in spirituality and alternative healing.

8 November: Moon's Last Quarter in Leo

Ganesha blesses you with loads of financial luck in this phase. Fresh concept and your unceasing efforts result in promotions, perk and salary rises. You could be flush with funds, and not just from your regular income. Money finds its way to you in various ways and even from unexpected sources. All aspects of your life feel marvellous as you taste success, both at home and at work. You are buoyant and jubilant and this gives you an inner glow that succeeds in attracting love, creativity, more money and soul-warming encounters. Any hindrances and roadblocks in your projects and initiatives are quickly taken care of. Outings/get-together/parties with friends and family fill you with joy. There are expenses too but you manage well. Life is fulfilling. You bring a lot to the table and this is appreciated by all.

15 November: New Moon in Scorpio

In this phase, you will not only strive to keep focused at work but also ensure that you lead a multidimensional life. You have put in great effort and time in your business/jobs and the gains have been significant. But you also realize that carrying on in this manner can only lead to ennui and burnout. Taking time out for family, meditating, long walks, proper care of diet and sleep are necessary now. You continue to enjoy special moments with family and friends and, at the same time, your performance at work is superlative. Greater intuition will help you find the best solution to an important issue that has been bothering you for long. This will help to further your confidence and this spills over, with excellent results, into all your personal and one-on-one bond and ties.

22 November: Moon's First Quarter in Pisces

You have given a good account of yourself at workplace and the result have been stupendous. But you know that you cannot afford to rest on your laurels and so you continue to slog away. You are very clear in objectives: you desire material success as you can see it providing long-term financial security for your family. This goads you on to work harder. A hidden facet of your nature comes to the fore as you reach out to seek new bonds and forge new links. Reviving old relationships and friendships fills you with a deep-seated sense of contentment. In this last quarter of the year, your focus and clarity is at its peak as you work to put all your affairs (especially those relating to your partner/children/parents) on a firm footing.

30 November: Full Moon in Gemini

A lucky period begins for you now. All aspects of your life are under a favourable spell. Health, wealth and happiness are yours for the asking. There are monetary rewards, increased status and greater bonding with loved ones. Your immediate environment is a reflection of your inner feeling and you spend a lot of time and money to upgrade it. You will get amazingly lucrative opportunities and you will make the most of them. The money angle is in sharp focus; whether it is a business deal or a lottery ticket you can expect profitable returns. There could be panic in family as an elder member may need hospitalization, but with dedicated efforts and loads of luck you will definitely come out of crisis. Ganesha blesses you.

8 December: Moon's Last Quarter in Virgo

With your confidence, status and cash on the upswing, you are not tempted to let go and become complacent. You are determined to fine-tune the process to ensure that gains keep accruing from existing projects. Exploring, expanding and developing new vistas, markets and methods are all parts of your efforts to build upon what you have already achieved. You are the toast of everybody at the workplace: subordinates, colleagues, peers and superiors. There is increased bonding at home and you share your lovely moments with your partner. There is evidently a great time for you, Geminis. The family is proud of your achievements and you reciprocate their affection with tangible and intangible gifts. You are also seeking answers to deep spiritual, philosophical and existential issues. Way to go, says Ganesha!

14 December: New Moon in Sagittarius

You have understood the true value of mutually loving/ respectful relationship both in your workplace and at your home and this takes you further up the ladder of success. Your triumphs at work have been noteworthy, and you use tolerance and patience to navigate emotionally stressful situations. Communication and interaction with people will be wonderful, making this a truly auspicious time for the footloose and fancy-free. You could also meet up with old friends and lovers and there will be many moments of happy bonding. Donations and charitable work, even voluntary community service, give you the true joy of living. And this is really the most beautiful way to live, says Ganesha.

21 December: Moon's First Quarter in Aries

As the year draws to a close, the spiritual yearning of last week intensifies and you find yourself involved in esoteric practices, the reading of spiritual and even in the conducting of penances and rituals. Visits to holy places and holy people could be undertaken in your search for truth as you seek a deeper meaning to life. Things are looking up in your professional life and a strong cash position inspires you to indulge in altruistic and humanitarian work. All your varied relationships are blooming, supportive and harmonious. You seem well set to pursue future success. This new mindset is positive and result-oriented, and sets you off as a loving and achievement-oriented individual.

30 December: Full Moon in Cancer

As the year ends, your total persona undergoes a change for the better. You have had a wonderful year. A sensible and proactive approach to money has given you a strong asset base which greatly contributes to (a) your peace of mind (b) the quality of life you can lead. You shine in your career with your experience, attitude, innovativeness and ingenuity. The time and energy invested in your intimate relationship have also been fruitful and you now enjoy a new closeness with your loved once. You have redefined the focus of your professional commitments and have every aspect of your personal life. A strengthened family bonding, excellent prospects at your workplace and highly developed spirituality are Ganesha's gifts for you as you march confidently into 2021.

CANCER

21 June–22 July

Symbol: The Crab
Ruling Planet: The Moon
Water-Cardinal-Negative
The Sign of the Teacher, the Prophet

'Marriage is the silver link, the silken tie that heart to heart and mind to mind in body and in soul can bind.'

JUPITER

Why have I launched your ship with the above words? The reason is very simple. Jupiter in your seventh angle from 2 December 2019 to 18 December 2020 emphasizes partnerships, links, ties and collaborations of every sort. Most of us know that the biggest partnership is marriage. What happens after you marry is a different matter!

This is the time to be friendly, charming, responsive and outgoing. If you are into publicity, advertisement, Internet, TV or cinema, you should be able to slay the opposition completely.

CANCER

Let me put it all in a different way. You Cancerians are moody, sensitive and imaginative. But now there will be mood elevation, publicity, ceremony and evolution of the spirit. Research and higher learning and real wisdom, long-distance journeys and connections will accompany them. More importantly, future plans and blueprints and even successful campaigns can be planned as well as implemented. I know very well that you are responsible, understanding and generous. If you really want to be deeply appreciated and highly respected, this is the real way.

I may add to it journeys with a stopover, foreign connections, import and export, travel for leisure and pleasure and profit. In other words, be the first to extend your hand in friendship to others. Be sure that there will be a mighty response.

Yes, I fully understand that Saturn is also in your seventh angle. What I have said about Saturn the last year applies this year also.

SATURN

Saturn will be in your seventh angle from 21 December 2017 to most of 2020. The results will be bitter-sweet. Why? Saturn will be in direct opposition to your Sun. In simple words it means there will be a tussle between Sun (power) and Saturn (responsibility). Therefore, the only way out for you is to balance these two. The only way to do it is through compromise, diplomacy and conciliation. In other words, Saturn will blow hot and cold over you. This could disturb you enormously if you do not keep your cool, your poise, your equilibrium and your balance. If you believe in mantras, my special mantra for you is:

'*Hum Hanumantaye Rama Dutaye Namah*'. The other mantra is: '*Rama Charana Sukha Payo*'. The meaning of the first mantra is Ram controls Hanuman. The second meaning is you will find peace and relief by worshipping the footsteps of Ram. Modern people might find this stupid and superstitious. They are welcome to their belief. But I am a devotee of Hanuman, Ram and Amba Mata. My faith is my strength and my armour. Therefore, I believe in it. Belief becomes a certainty and a guarantee if you believe sincerely, and this belief should be in your blood, bones and even marrow. This is my opinion. At the same time, I admit that your opinion can be different.

To each his own, Saturn could lead to legal battles, sorrows, separations and sometimes the possibility of death, which is the final separation. I admit I do not have all the answers. But this I know, Saturn is duty. Duty is to me beauty. Therefore, to me the answer is to do your duty and leave the rest to your own maker.

Saturn in your seventh angle could sometimes lead to retirement or taking up a different set of values, a change of environment, competition. Be cooperative, try to understand the other person's point of view and please do not think that only you are clever, intelligent and wise. Please understand, my dear Cancerians, that in this world many people know all the tricks of manipulation and mischief and how to get work done from others. Therefore, you might face a tricky situation. Dalai Lama, the Cancerian, is my hero. Yes, I have met him.

What is my final answer to all this? It was the great storyteller, doctor, spy, Somerset Maugham who said: 'Goodness is its own reward.' This might be difficult for you to swallow. It could be a bitter pill but that, my dear readers, is my final answer. I am now eighty-eight. The world is a grand mix of goodness, technicalities, spiritualities, wickedness and sorrow as well as misery and evil. We human beings are complicated and complex. We have it in us to be gods or devils. The choice is yours.

SATURN

Saturn means delays, differences and disappointments. I know it very well but now Jupiter, the planet of friendliness and publicity, has joined hands with Saturn and therefore the evil effects and impact of Saturn will be much less. I am a Cancerian. But I have learnt to be optimistic, caring and helpful to one and all. The result is if you are consistent, others will also respond in a wonderfully nice way and therefore the interaction between you and others will not only lead to respect but also affection and love. In life, very few have both, namely love and respect. Here is your chance to have both. This chance does not come often. So take it up with both your hands.

URANUS

You have another planet going all the way for you. It is Uranus. Uranus is right now in your eleventh angle of friendship, gains, social work, helping others and being convivial. Convivial means friendly, lively and enjoyable. Uranus means surprise in every possible way. But this year, for you, Uranus will be a surprise in a splendid, rewarding manner for the simple reason that Uranus is in fine formation with both Saturn and Jupiter. So my advice is: Take a chance, move with courage and confidence, do not be timid and nervous and do remember the words of the mighty Sai Nath, 'Have faith in God and he will never let you down.'

I may add here that yours is the sign of the teacher and the prophet. You have tenacity, loyalty and intelligence. I admit that you are moody and could suffer from an inferiority complex. Therefore, have faith in yourself, those of you who could have been disappointed in your past, and others also. The flowers white lily, water lily and rose, and all trees which are rich in sap are immensely lucky for you. I have also found out that rowing in a boat rather than going in a steamer will be auspicious and lucky.

I must point out to you that I do not want you to be superstitious and believe in what I believe. What I have said may apply to many Cancerians but certainly not all. Therefore, I say it would be best to keep an open mind and be tolerant of others. This, I know, is the master key to life, love and living.

I am sure you Cancerians know very well that you love *Om* and are domesticated. But even if you are not, it is perfectly okay. Nothing in life is final and binding.

Finally, I am sure you know that the Moon is your main planet. But the Moon changes signs every two-and-a-half days. Therefore, writing about the Moon will take a book by itself. Instead of that I take Mars as an important planet for you. Mars will be lucky for you between 19 November 2018 and 2 January 2020. Also, 13 May to 27 August 2020 and again 28 August 2020 to 8 January 2021. In other words, you have much to look forward to. Try to implement and deliver the goods this year. That is my final suggestion. Action time!

CANCER

BLUEPRINT FOR THE ENTIRE YEAR

January: Power, pelf, perks, promotion, prosperity.

February: Finances and family.

March: Contacts and joy.

April: Property, parents, renovation/decoration, parents, in-law.

May: Joy, creativity, children, hobbies, you make news and win others over.

June: Work, funds, employment, health and medical check-up, servants, subordinates.

July: Marriage, ties, love, collaborations, romance, meeting and reaching out to people and places.

August: Health, funds, vitality, tantra and mantra, change of locale, moving.

September: Journeys, publicity, ceremonies, collaborations, functions, rites and religion.

October: Stepping up on efficiency, work, status, prestige, taking care of parents, elders.

November: Help, socializing, friendship, fraternity, camaraderie.

December: Expenses, losses, spirituality, helping others, charming, long-distance connections.

Summary: Romance and finance fuse happily for you. Health safeguards will be essential. Plenty of movement—physically, mentally, emotionally, spiritually—points out Ganesha, and his is the last word.

Your happiness quota will be 81 per cent.

WEEKLY REVIEW BY PHASES OF THE MOON

10 January: Full Moon in Cancer

The year gets off to quite a start. You feel grounded and secure, aware there are many things that you have to do – to undertake many changes and revamp your attitudes and thinking to streamline your advancement. Personal complexes and anxieties have held you back and it is time to get free of them. You have had a lot of false notions of yourself, causing ego hassles and clashes with people for no apparent reason. All this will now change. 'Home is where the heart is' for you; isn't it always, my dear Cancerians? So, quite naturally, you will be streamlining the house and home and making it all the more. Personal issues, property, real estate, family holding and soon grab your attention. Your family life is also important – of all the zodiac signs you are probably the most home oriented. You lavish love and affection on all your dear ones. You also look at your funds and career seriously. There is a lot to be done and several changes to be made on the work and personal front in order that you can achieve the desired success.

17 January: Moon's Last Quarter in Libra

This is heady time in more ways than one. Matters of finance are in sharp focus as also the family. Business and career will be put on the back burner. The finance angle, though, will come in as the family need it, and the two Fs – finance and family – go hand in hand. So you will work for the family and will be very busy. Indeed joint accounts, your bank balance, tax or estate problems need to be sorted out. They keep you busy and will require careful handling. It may be a good idea to keep your own counsel. It is good to be discreet and even secretive about money matters, to avoid problems or interference of any kind. Don't let anybody into your other affairs; also people around you may want to know more about your dealings. You will have to keep tight-lipped. The good times will roll later, promises Ganesha. This is also a very emotional phase and can be turbulent, so keep your emotions in check. You are not the fiery sort normally, but during this period you could often fly off the handle. Learn to keep cool and handle all the turbulence around you with a calm mind.

24 January: New Moon in Capricorn

As you run through January, life gets more and more intense. The Moon is now in your birth sign and there is a lot to do. You need all the tact you can muster to handle people both at the workplace and at home. There is still no getting away from finance and family. You need to step up your own efficiency and tolerance levels. It is not always about you; remember life is not always about 'I, me, myself'. You need to look at colleagues, superiors and subordinates with impartiality as you will need them for help and cooperation. Remember, it is teamwork that is important now. There is also buying and selling, speculation and plying the stock market, if so inclined. Last year, in 2019, this was the theme that was played too. You are not particularly money-minded, but the family is top priority and you will do anything for them, including making the greatest sacrifices. There is also love and warmth and generosity. You feel happy.

2 February: Moon's First Quarter in Taurus

The trends of January change now. There are different pressures and pulls at work. We don't have to revert to Charles Darwin, Carl Jung or other thinkers to know that nothing is permanent. You will be much more sociable and fun-loving and have a great time at parties, get-togethers and social gatherings, and indulge in good life. There is the powerful influence of Venus in your life right now and you could even end up putting on weight, with all the goodies being tucked into. Your mind is no longer in a whirl and you are more relaxed. Life is almost luxurious and you spend happily as you want to be surrounded by class and comfort. You love beauty and your home is your stronghold or heaven, away from the maddening world outside. There is love in the air too. If you are unattached there could be that special someone. And if you are already in love, the bond will only get deeper. Ganesha is blessing you in so many ways. But I must add that in the midst of all this, your mind is playing games with you, you are not centred and, sometimes, for no fault of yours, you feel you are moving in the opposite direction.

9 February: Full Moon in Leo

The crab is often very calculating and devious but now you get expansive and large-hearted as well. You get brilliant ideas and open up like the rainbow. You think along creative lines, and may even find fresh new lines of employment. You want to live life king-size and chase information and knowledge. It is the age of super consciousness and higher knowledge and what Sri Aurobindo called the making of the 'super mental man'. You understand all that perfectly.

More down to earth, you make valuable contacts and steady progress in whatever you embark on. Your moves are well directed. Money, home, comforts, love and expansion at all levels are foreseen. You have a sense of daring and are ready to take on all corners. Cancerians normally retreat into a shell when hurt, but in this phase, you are charged with inexhaustible and dynamic energy.

19 February: Moon's Last Quarter in Scorpio

The trends of last week will continue. You make several contacts and spread your wings really wide. There is creative expression and inspiration followed by some really hard, constructive work. It is not just theories, plans and hollow dreams. You will roll up your sleeves and get to work. You will be making great progress at all levels and will be reaching out to fresh horizons. There is the pursuit of pleasure too and you can also get indiscreet here, which you have to watch out for, warns Ganesha. But what is life without some fun; you can't be in expansion mode all the time and working your butt away, can you? Ganesha is with you, thankfully.

23 February: New Moon in Aquarius

You may start daydreaming now and live in a world of romantic fantasy. You will focus on your emotions and look at relationships. In this phase you may meet someone with a similar bent of mind and hit it off like a house on fire. In love too, there are happy tidings. You are floating on gossamer clouds. There is romantic love, appreciation. You are also extra-emotional and sensitive and that is saying a lot as Cancerians are anyway highly strung, emotionally. You live with an intensity of emotions and it makes its presence felt in every aspect of your life. Now, your emotions are in fifth gear, watch out!

2 March: Moon's First Quarter in Gemini

The trend shifts, and you will be looking ahead in several different directions. You are open to new ideas and progress. There will be many things for you to deal with and it will be difficult to decide the direction to take or what to prioritize. Money matters take a back seat. You are looking at so many avenues and are a bit confused too. This is a period of hectic mental, emotional and physical activity. Expenses may mount and health may need attention too. But you will ride out the storm and come up trumps. You may also get particularly emotional and sensitive now and can therefore be prone to making errors in judgement. Let the period pass before undertaking any serious decision making. This is valuable advice from Ganesha.

9 March: Full Moon in Virgo

You get rooted again and are thankfully, in a manner of speaking, taken away from all your illusions. There are domestic and family concerns to look into. Work and money also need attention. You may make plans to start a new project to achieve greater financial security. But, as usual, you will not neglect your familial responsibilities – that is not your way. Money is also in sharp focus in the form of property, family holding, shares and trust funds. Money is always at the back of your mind because it feeds the family; as we all know – money also buys freedom and respect. Left to yourself, you can make many compromises and live on very little. But you're concerned with your family welfare and progress. Again, your mind is in some sort of disarray as it may run in several directions like a headless chicken. The trend is bound to change and so, just hold tight.

16 March: Moon's Last Quarter in Sagittarius

You get even more focused and determined in this quarter. You are positive and ambitious and look at laying the foundations of a new project. Of course, you won't neglect the relationships and domestic angles, as well. But as of now, you will look seriously at making more money and tap several areas of work. You are not a cold, calculating type but now you survey several possibilities with a sharp and shrewd eye. You don't let others push you around. All this bluster and aggression could also affect your health, and you may need to relax in quite, harmonious surroundings. If it all gets too heavy, you may seek out fresh vistas and a radical change in your immediate surroundings. But, slowly, you are settling down emotionally and that is a welcome sign.

24 March: New Moon in Aries

The energy and determination return to you in a big way. You will put in sincere efforts to achieve your targets. There will be a lot of work and you won't shirk it. But ensure that you and the family are not neglected; you may be caught in a wave that transforms into a tsunami. Family interactions are necessary; and they are solid. On the other hand, the wave may end too suddenly for comfort, and in the end you may be left with just your loved ones. Work at achieving a balance, try and draw the line between work and home, learn to judge how far you can push the envelope. Your sights are well set now and your ambitions are peaking.

1 April: Moon's First Quarter in Cancer

The family once again comes into strong focus. You will continue to work hard and will be busier than ever; there is achievement and you are pleased. You have been able to make the best use of your potential; and Cancerians, though sensitive and emotional, are achievers too. They are extremely creative and respect money as it helps them become good providers and carers. They love logging that extra mile, especially if it is for someone they love. During this period, you are moving ahead resolutely and with force.

8 April: Full Moon in Libra

Once again, the good life beckons. You should get down a bit and become less intense in your reactions. You want to take a breather and savour the joys of hard work. Home and family beckon and you make time for friends, as all this makes you happy and fulfilled. This is an important period. You can now be realistically hopeful of success in your ventures, in all that you have striven for, hoped for, and planned for. You can safely go all out for success and achievement! There is a chance that you may realize a major ambition, or have a long-held wish fulfilled. In fact, I wouldn't be surprised if it's already happened. It could be in the area of love as your compassion for near and dear ones overflows.

14 April: Moon's Last Quarter in Capricorn

You look at a more comfortable life now. You have to make decisions with far-reaching impact but, somehow, you are not able to. You have to be practical and pragmatic. Travel and money matters are in sharp focus. You look at funds, loan, insurance, joint finances, land and other sources of boosting your income. There is pleasure too and occasion for the good times. It is certainly not all work. You are never the fiercely ambitious sort and like the bull, you refuse to carry the plough forever. So you often retreat into your shell and ponder life's journeys.

23 April: New Moon in Taurus

You look at a fresh approach to life. Finance and business are just one parameter, but certainly not the only one to measure your worth. You are fascinated by progressive ideas and new discoveries, and interested in projects that expand your mind and stretch your capabilities. You are almost out of step with reality; you look ahead like a seer, a visionary. You may embark on new ventures suddenly, quit uncharacteristically, but don't get despondent if things don't work out the way you want them to. You are inquisitive and curious in this phase and step out of your comfort zone to look at the world with new eyes.

30 April: Moon's First Quarter in Leo

Ganesha says you stretch yourself in all directions. You reach out to people and they response favourably. Your plate is full to overflowing with events and activities. Family and loved ones expect much from you in this phase. Work takes a back seat and you quite like – and do justice to – all the socializing. There is travel, expenses of all kinds and some stress. You find cracks developing in some new-found love and this disturbs you. You find solace in quieter retreats and may visit a spa or place for healing for rejuvenation and treatment.

7 May: Full Moon in Scorpio

Your sojourn with fantasy is short-lived; you are back to the material world. You will look at money and its joys and grab all financial openings with both hands like a fielder at first slip in cricket. You also do up your home and office and refurbish your personal wardrobe. You could indulge in major shopping and I dare say that it is not window-shopping. Expenses will mount naturally but you are in that sort of a mood. You are confident that you will find new ways of revenue generation. So, you splurge on yourself and the family. The theme this week is money and how you can spend it. You will be indulgent and happy about it too. You somehow feel that you will never be broke. Ganesh will ensure that, don't worry.

14 May: Moon's Last Quarter in Aquarius

You fuse work and pleasure and there is no letting up. You tap all avenues and are all geared up for fun and work if you can balance that out somehow. You will find time for hobbies, other interests, sport and leisure activities. You will also accompany the family on a happy outing. It is an enjoyable time. You love the planning and preparation, and the advancement in whatever you do. You think big and look at the large picture of life. You want more and you will move towards it. Nothing and no one will be able to satisfy you now; your appetite is giant in size.

22 May: New Moon in Gemini

You set a scorching pace in this week. There is the successful completion of projects and a flurry of activity at all levels. You are in total communication mode, and are on the go with intensity and purpose. You are also emotional at this juncture and work a lot with your heart, which is not a good thing, if I may add. You see infinite possibilities in whatever you aim to do and your attitude undergoes a transformation. But once emotions cloud your judgement, there will be mistakes. You can get very subjective in your thought processes. Keep your eyes open to guard against both failure and regret. Ganesha guides you through tough times!

30 May: Moon's First Quarter in Virgo

You will get more philosophical. Several personal issues come to the fore. You are called upon to solve family matters, which can get tricky. You may be mired in quicksand and don't know how to proceed; sometimes it can be a lose-lose situation in life and this can well be how it is for you, if you're not careful right now. You look within for answers, re-examine options, and search deep within your psyche. Relationship and people will hold centre stage; there will be profound social interactions, an interaction of feelings and not just casual meetings. You look for answers but they are elusive, and you may need to go by your gut instincts and feelings. This is an emotionally explosive phase and stress may also make you succumb, health-wise.

5 June: Full Moon in Sagittarius

There will be a flurry of relationships; you will be reaching out to all corners. There will be indiscretion and errors but that is the mood you are in. Although money issues play at the back of your mind, you will be drawn to nothing in particular but to people as a whole. Your affections are diluted and you could get into a mess. You also look at various money-making opportunities but it may be getting you nowhere right now. This is not the right time for it, says Ganesha. This is a phase when you do a lot and yet feel you're achieving and doing nothing. You are easily distracted and all your efforts lead to naught.

13 June: Moon's Last Quarter in Pisces

You are a bit steadier and more focused now. There is some work and housekeeping to do which is good in a way as it keeps you occupied. Your mind needs to be tethered now to something or the other and this preoccupation will help a lot. You spend on the good thing of life whenever you are at a loose end and this is one of those times. You may thus renovate and refurbish, acquire a new wardrobe and accessories. You also look for a new love, someone to cherish and indulge; it is also a way to get rid of the boredom that is eating into you. Your mind is everywhere, running wild, and you need to do something to tether it.

21 June: New Moon in Cancer

A full moon and in eclipse; what a time! The permutations are endless with interactions, conferences, meetings, collaborations, travel and meeting and doing new things one after another as though it is all a roller-coaster ride. New studies, research, new techniques, new discoveries will all lead you to faraway explorations. If America hadn't been explored, you would be in the mood to do it. Since you will meet new people, there will also be the forging of new bonds, warmth, good times interpersonal relationships. Honesty is the best policy but take care not to shoot your mouth off at inopportune moments.

28 June: Moon's First Quarter in Libra

Your ego is all pumped up and you work with new energy. Now, says Ganesha, the time is right for you to make a fresh start. You overcome all obstacles and embark on new ventures which will take off and proceed smoothly. You are filled with enthusiasm and are on the go throughout this period. The mood is update and nothing can get you down, but put safeguards in place because such speed needs caution. Luck is on your side and so you needn't worry too much. Yet it is always wise to keep the seat belts on in a fast car.

5 July: Full Moon in Capricorn

Once again, your emotions will dominate your activities. You will try to initiate happy, supportive relationships. You will also look at grooming, beauty treatments and couture to look physically and emotionally ravishing. You are much friendly, outgoing, giving and generous. Bonds and ties can never be far from your mind and loved ones will again dominate your attention and time. They will crowd you and make demands and you will savour every moment of the cuddling and pander to their desires. The new moon is in your sign and there are new beginnings at so many levels. Your intrinsic nature comes to the fore and you are as happy as can be!

12 July: Moon's Last Quarter in Gemini

Ganesha gives you a lot to do this week. You shuttle between work/business/love/family, and you also look at how best to balance both achievement and happiness – not always possible. You also continue with your shopping, and the desire for goodies doesn't seem to lessen. Watch out or you may be overreaching yourself financially. But work will be good and productive and that is a great help. Love will also blossom and, on the other end of the spectrum, i.e., money, you will be deeply involved with insurance, joint finances, mutual funds and accounts where concrete financial matters are concerned. This is a good trend to have in your birth month. All aspects of your life are greatly energized. Family bonds will be vibrant and you give and get love easily. You could be one of the world's happiest persons right now.

20 July: New Moon in Cancer

Once again, this period is all about ambition and money. You find the energy to live big. You reach out, and full of plans, life, gusto, go unabashedly for what you feel is your due in life. There will be once again money issue like loans, legacies, legal matter and inheritance to deal with. You are also a big draw at parties, seminars, gathering. It is an exciting time for you socially. You meet new people and are drawn out of your customary shell. There is no reason to be inhibited; just go and seize the moment.

27 July: Moon's First Quarter in Virgo

Once again, you are losing track of expenses and these will mount hugely. You might go on a buying spree and you have to check yourself before your bank accounts run out of the last rupee. On the other hand, you are making new associations with promises of more rewarding work. So, finally, it may all balance out. There is a desire for action and/or the genuine expansion of your interests. The work and play areas will be enticing and you make the most of the opportunities that come your way. It is an active and fulfilling period and you are on the upswing in more ways than one. Despite this all being so busy and involved, this is a very fulfilling period in personal and emotional terms. So it's good going all round.

With the new moon, you have entered a powerfully intense phase. You are creative in all your undertaking and you love it. There is an ego boost too, but you may have to curb your tongue. Cancerians are normally mild but you can lose your grip and turn harsh and even nasty. I suggest you don't! You appreciate beauty and will adorn yourself with all the beautiful objects you have bought and feel good about it. You find loads of appreciation and just love all the compliments and flattery coming your way. Your life is rich and you are riding the wave. Enjoy! This is a period of many fortunate new beginnings as well. A time to hope and gladness is what Ganesha calls it.

2 August: Full Moon in Aquarius

You are in the eye of the whirlwind. Your social life is packed with outings and visits. There is growth and travel, even higher studies, and many new spiritual bonds. You are moving ahead with intensity. There is smouldering passion, too, eagerly awaiting you and you are not one to dither when the right opportunity presents itself. It is a hectic period and many contacts need to be established and worked out for the future. A new and passionate love affair may also sidetrack you a bit.

11 August: Moon's Last Quarter in Taurus

Your growth at all levels is happening at double the time. You will be mentally stimulated and loving every moment of it. There is no room for despondency, though at times there is a tendency to slip into a kind of depression. There is a chance of developing new relationships which may be to your advantage. This is also a good time to network and meet up with the old associates as well as make new ones. Your life is vibrant and there is an intensity of emotions in whatever you undertake. You are never one to take life lightly, but this time undertones are even more serious. You are filled with empathy and understand people as they really are. Ganesha has given you some really fine insights.

19 August: New Moon in Leo

Travel and love are the twin themes this week. You want to care for others; it is a deep-seated need. Partnerships and collaborations will be highlighted and there will be success at interviews. You may also attend rituals and ceremonies. Movement and growth/progress will be highlighted and all your travels will be successful and pleasurable. Your kindness and genuine warmth will go far ahead of you like a benign aura. Ganesha has blessed you! You will also earn and spend a bit more than necessary. After all, what is the use of money if it is not in circulation? Try telling you anything to the contrary in this Taurean phase!

25 August: Moon's First Quarter in Sagittarius

You would have been moving forward at reckless speed and there will have been a lot of stress. You also fill as if time is running out and want to do many things at the same time and all too meticulously. But this is no time to speed away in all the directions. Your health will suffer. You don't have a strong constitution, and will probably need to take recourse to alternative therapy as it is easier on the body. It may also be the time to watch your eating habits as you have been gorging away during the high phase of the earlier weeks. You put on weight easily around the middle. All this can have a debilitating effect on both your health and image which you are very conscious of. Some time-out will be good. Learn to relax and go with the flow. Take to yoga, pranayama and do some deep breathing to conquer the stress that is overtaking your life. This is a good time to start all this.

2 September: Full Moon in Pisces

You feel like a star and it is good for you as, once again, there will be many attempts on your time from family, friends, loved ones, colleagues, subordinates, superiors, everyone and cousins and even pets, dependents, stray animals and so on. And, of course, you can never say no. Your kindness and helping hands win applause and you feel good about yourself. You will rave and rant against injustice and have a natural empathy for the underdog, but no one can doubt your sincerity. Helping others is your true calling. You are the good Samaritans of the zodiac.

10 September: Moon's Last Quarter in Gemini

A sensitive period for sure, but you are reaching out and there will be many interactions. Foreign connections, collaborations, tie-ups in one form or another will work well and lead to success and prosperity. You will also travel and make contact with different types of people. I quote from my previous book (it's a quote I use all the time) 'Astrology – which reflects life – is a continuous and continuing process and no work stands in isolation, just as "No man is an island", to quote the immortal words of John Donne.' You are working at full throttle and in a continuum of interactions; and success and glory come in no small measure.

17 September: New Moon in Virgo

The family can never be far too behind in your mind and thinking and once again they will be making demands on your time and energy. In all the travel and achievement, you have kept the family at bay, but no long. They are both your strength and your weakness and you can never be far from them. There will be an improvement in domestic affairs and there will be a much-sought-after or much-needed settlement in family affairs. Older people may need your attention, as well as your sibling and children, as you are the one they all love to take refuge with. While focusing on home, house and property, make time for them too, and Ganesha will bless you even more. Remember, charity begins at home. If you can't be with your loved ones, it makes little sense spreading yourself thin for the whole world.

24 September: Moon's First Quarter in Capricorn

You have tasted success at so many levels these last few weeks. You are well on a path to even more glory. Nothing is always smooth sailing. Ganesha reminds you, and there could be some upheavals. You will adapt a more conciliatory approach which really helps in getting things done. You will also like to immerse yourself in beautiful things almost like an escape mechanism from all the troubles which may bother you on this road to glory. There will be tremendous work pressures but you manage to cope well. You also spend a lot, and the goodies you buy make you happy; shopping too, as we all know so well, can provide emotional release.

2 October: Full Moon in Aries

The quest for achievements doesn't stop. You have also found some breathing space and have chalked out newer horizons to conquer. You manage to take a few outings, probably to a health farm, to get recharged for the final assault, to attain the realization of all your dreams. The year is in its final months and a lot has been achieved, but the spur of the ambition goads you on without respite. You work out strategies and the funds needed and will discuss details with collaborations, colleagues or perhaps your partners in enterprise. You are on a good wicket, and you don't want to get out without heaving a mighty six right into the stands! It is the IPL season of your life and you certainly don't want to be out hit wicket!!

10 October: Moon's Last Quarter in Cancer

The mood is upbeat and you continue with the trends of last week. You work hard, meet people, travel, get the money organized and reach out to newer benchmark. You clean up your image and tidy up the home and office. You get new clothes, possibly a new hairstyle, and get into shape with the right food and medication, possibly with visits to spas and health centres. The results are visible and there is a new you breaking all barriers and moving ahead like the wind. Success is all yours, dear Cancerians, and it is not just because of Ganesha's blessing; you have put in your mite and the rewards are just!

16 October: New Moon in Libra

You taste the fruits of all that you have put into your life in recent times. You are successful and have managed to achieve most, if not all, that you desired. You are happy to be alive and basking in the comfort zone of a job well done, thanks to your own untiring efforts. You enjoy it all with friends, family, children, partners, in-laws and all your near and dear ones, as we say in India! There is felicitation all around and you are the toast of the moment. Let the bubbly flow! Enjoy your time in the sun and leave all your cares to take care of themselves.

23 October: Moon's First Quarter in Aquarius

The mood is grand and not just good. Your work is going well and your relationship is easy-going. Financial targets have been reached and friends from all over want to celebrate with you. You balance it all like an expert juggler. You meet all sorts, and have exceptional encounters with a wide cross section of people. You are learning and growing all the time, and what a way to be! This is a good time for embarking on new ventures.

31 October: Full Moon in Taurus

You are filled with new ideas. There is a tendency also to get despondent, but stay away from any negative thought processes. You look seriously at more work avenues. You are filled with courage and daring. If you know what you are doing and where you are going, this is a very blessed state to be in. Your mind is in a whirl with many different thoughts and ideas therein. You may move house, or just be shifting your base, relocating to a new city/town. There is some romance too but, more than anything else, it is a period of innumerable thought processes almost on a collision course. Restore a sense of balance in yourself with prayer, spiritualism, tantra and mantra. You are fiery right now, not calm.

8 November: Moon's Last Quarter in Leo

There is a lot of thinking to do. You also feel genuinely for the world, the poor and the downtrodden, and want to donate to charities. Your heart strings will be tugged. You are fine professionally and the home life is also stable, and so you reach out of the world at large. This is a happier phase at the emotional level but expenses will mount and you will have to work hard to meet them. There is also a great need for family bounding. So there will be many diverse pulls and pressures and you have to sort out what you want. All this confusion will certainly inspire you to greater efforts. But many of your ideas may belong too far into the future. You will need to be more practical and face the realities of today head-on.

15 November: New Moon in Scorpio

You are filled with confidence and security in your abilities and assets, and enjoy the stability. Family ties are important as also investment of all kinds. Finances will be on the upswing and you will enjoy the good life. Of course, nothing comes free or easy. You will slog for every extra bit. This could take a toll on your time and other associations but that is the way it is. You need to demarcate your priorities both clearly and well in order to achieve true and lasting success. As they say, you are either born rich, or you marry rich or you work for it. In this case, I suspect, you will work for it, if the other two possibilities aren't true for you! Mario Puzo said, 'Behind every fortune is a crime,' but I hope this won't apply to you!

22 November: Moon's First Quarter in Pisces

There is expansion in all your activities. There may be a few delays and confusions, but these are minor glitches. The larger picture which you are framing in your mind, and in the world, will be pretty wonderful. The pace is hectic with many demands on your time and resources. Be steadfast, hold firm and don't abandon faith. You will be travelling and meeting people, spending more and grabbing with both hands. There is a lot on your plate, much more than usual or what you are used to, but it's good to go all out. You have nothing to lose and a hard-earned victory is on the cards, says Ganesha. There is, without doubt, an upward swing in all your activities despite the expenses and the heartache.

30 November: Full Moon in Gemini

You work hard with grace, dignity and determination. There is travel in the offing, and many new associations that may prove beneficial. You will expand your horizons and, possibly, embark on new study. But love will never desert you despite all the upheavals. Old relationship are as strong as ever and there are also new ones. Knock at the door; all you have to do is to let them in and get closer, more intimate, more loving. You will be very outspoken and extroverted, pumped up by adrenaline and new dreams. You will be spot-on in many fields, even love, Ganesha tells you with a smile.

8 December: Moon's Last Quarter in Virgo

The last month of the year begins with a contemplative state of mind. You will be energized with ideas and want to do many things at many levels but are yet quite withdrawn and contemplative. The focus is also strongly on property matters, journey and creative work. There is suddenly some intense bonding too and you may even get a brand-new image. But you will also need to make the necessary adjustment and do some rethinking of your personal and professional interest which may clash hard at times. Emotions will have to be reined in, and some self-control exerted. You need to keep your extra-sensitivity in check too. Deal with matters with the head, and not always with the heart, counsels Ganesha. You are liable to make mistake that way and you must guard against it, by trying for greater rationality.

14 December: New Moon in Sagittarius

Lots of things change now. You are working in many directions. Even your approach to life may change. There will be hectic parleys, communication, even engagement or marriage; several possibilities exist. Some travel is also thrown in and you will certainly reach out to larger audiences one way or the other. Your people skills will be greatly tested, and tie-ups, collaboration, compromises and negotiations will draw on your management skills and bargaining power. You will be flying in many directions and need to keep steady to manage it all well and happily – which you will do in the end. You do work very hard now even though the gains will not be visible for some time to come. The groundwork, however, is well laid.

21 December: Moon's First Quarter in Aries

A slightly intense phase is setting in once again. There are many challenges and you need to be better equipped to achieve whatever you have set out to do. There is a lot of running around and a flurry of activity and communication at all levels. There could be higher studies and more training to help you handle all that you hope to surmount. You don't really worry about this tense period; in fact, you may even enjoy it as it brings in achievement and success in all your endeavours. Who doesn't like to sit on top of the pile, and you could well be right up there! The intensity of this period can also tire you out to bits; it is more than what you had bargained for, so a little rest, relaxation, unwinding will all be necessary, says Ganesha.

30 December: Full Moon in Cancer

This is certainly a great way to end the year on a truly high note. You are a natural lover of your life and a great rock of your family to lean on, but now money and funds will be vital issues. Bank issues, real estate, bonds and anything that deals with money will be in sharp focus. It is the final week of the year and there is merrymaking too and you are, undoubtedly, enjoying yourself to the hilt. You are also ambitious and see yourself as an important part of society or the community you live in. Work will be fulfilling too, and you walk the fine balance between office and home, as we all know one can't exist without the other. On the contrary, you are brimming with energy and looking forward to new challenges, in the year ahead, secure in the knowledge that Ganesha is watching over you, as always.

LEO

23 July–22 August

Symbol: The Lion
Ruling Planet: The Sun
Fire-Fixed-Positive
The Sign of the King, the Lover.
Special Note: Ganesha says that generally life has a particular pattern, rhythm and cycle. In the same way planets also have it. Therefore, sometimes repetition of what I have said before happens. I just want to inform you about it.

All the annual forecasts cannot be of the same size very obviously.

Ganesha says, the smoking gun, the main reason for your success, dear Leos, will be the formation of Jupiter (money), Saturn (limitations), and the electric planet of sudden events, namely, Uranus (spirituality). Simply put, this trio leads you to fame and glory. How?

JUPITER

Let us first call Jupiter on our astro-radar. Jupiter will be in your sixth angle from 2 December 2019 to 18 December 2020. You will be interested in cosmo-biology, the study of the living universe. This will make you a caring and daring person – a true Leo trail.

> 'Work is not a curse, it is the prerogative of intelligence, the only means to manhood, and the measure of civilisation. Savages do not work.'
> – C. ALVIN COLLIDGE

Work, work and work – don't you love it! You will be great at it, especially handling your public relations with both flair and sincerity – and it pays great dividends. Dealings with bosses/employers/superiors are as good as your vibes with colleagues, subordinates, employees, children, pets and dependents. There could be some tension and health hazards to reckon with around this time. Play down the self and ego angle in conflicts and confrontations, and you should be able to come out on top. Try and put your own personal interest temporarily on the back-burner. There is an astrology reason. Jupiter is in your sixth house of income, profession, service and livelihood, honours and rewards from higher up. You have a lot going for you.

Future gains and added prosperity could sum up the financial angle. You can well afford to take a short trip/holiday/or make a weekend getaway and come back with your batteries recharged. Domestic bliss, much more harmony in home and family, romance, love and marriage are added benefits. Friends are both numerous and sincere and add greatly to the quality of life. The actual time span for all this is from 2 December 2019 to 18 December 2020.

Here are a few extras. Loans and funds, health and hygiene, exercise and workouts, the recovery of important goods and items. Please also add relationships with servants, employees and colleagues; recovery from disease and injuries, and being in fine fettle; and above all, the ability to communicate. Wow! What a list! Ganesha says, loan, funds, taxes, colleagues, servants, promotion, perks have all been mentioned. I deduce, therefore, that as a result of your creative energy, you will get a promotion, or if unemployed, you will get a job, and if you have been down in health and energy, both will definitely improve. In short, Jupiter in your sixth angle will act as a pep pill and energy booster. It will give you push and go.

Let me update you with more information about Jupiter. Jupiter will lubricate your intellect, pep it up with all sorts of pills and goodies, so to say, and thus your brain will send messages which will galvanize you into great action! True, I might have mixed my metaphors. True also, I might have gone medicinal in my approach. But there is no doubt about my meaning. You will sizzle with ideas. And you will carry these ideas out, the latter being as important as the former. Let me specify the goodies from Jupiter in your sixth angle till 18 December 2020.

a) Health, pets, relationships with colleagues and subordinates; if you're the boss, hiring and firing of staff.

b) Focus on the services you and your company give to the customer; in this I also include after-sales service.

c) Different systems and techniques of working.

d) Top-notch performance, and results will be targeted and handsomely achieved.

e) Lost valuables may be recovered.

f) Loans can be taken, if necessary.

g) The maternal side of the family will have much to do with you.

h) You will be extremely conscious of diet, exercise, food, flavour, aroma, the right way to prepare and serve food.

i) Fast recovery from injuries (and there may be hospitalization or a medical check-up).

SATURN

Saturn will start a sojourn in your sixth angle of health and work from 21 December 2017 to most of 2020. Yes, it does mean that responsibilities will be piled upon you with avalanche ferocity. But an avalanche does not happen every day! Neither does it mean that you will be completely overwhelmed or submerged under it. It only means you will have to work hard and be reasonably regular in all that you do and undertake. It will be difficult to play truant. You will have to be in good health to face challenges and opportunities.

This is really good way to get going, says Ganesha. You've decided to leap headlong into action, chasing success, and achievement, pleasure and joy; and this gives you the opportunity to do so – in both love and money. Exciting new opportunities for gain and progress come both in spheres. Finances are handled well but it is your career/profession that you handle with inspiration and insight. Coupled with your customary daring, it leads most definitely to new openings, perks, benefits, new projects with a high degree of satisfaction. You may be ready to take some calculated risks too, knowing that you have the guts to see them through and ensure that they will pay off spectacularly. It's a good phase at home too; almost certainly a time of no romantic/sexual conflicts. If they do arise, you see to it that you resolve them peacefully, affectionately, and in a very proactive manner. That is exactly what your brave, action-oriented nature demands. Maybe it's your new-year resolution, but the results are spectacular. You have decided to go far, and you need the stamina. Unnecessary stress or even too much anxiety is bad.

As Saturn will be in your sixth angle from 21 December 2017 to 23 March 2020 let me sum it up for you by informing you to take care of your health, your diet, your relationship with servants, employees, pets and dependents. Finally, it is my observation that you Leos often demand too much from life and your companions as well as fellow workers. Please do not push the envelope as the American say. Also, for elderly Leos it could well be a time for retirement. If this happens, do so gracefully and try to get another part-time job only if you are up to it.

BLUEPRINT FOR THE ENTIRE YEAR

January: Expenses, secret deals, negotiations, trips, ties.

February: Success, projects, ventures, funds, children, creativity, good luck.

March: Money, family, promises, promotion, perks.

April: Contacts, communication, contracts, research, import and export.

May: Home, house, renovation, buying/selling, ill health, retirement.

June: Fine, all-round performance, you strike it lucky and win applause.

July: Loans, funds, joint finance, domestic matters, job, health.

August: Love, hate, marriage, divorce, contradictory influences.

September: Loans and funds, health and pets, religion, spirituality, rites for the living and the dead.

October: Freedom, intuition, inspiration, publicity, long-distance connections.

November: Work, parents, status, rivalry, prestige, tremendous pressure.

December: Friendship, wish fulfilment, material gains, socializing, group activities, happiness and health. You end on a positive, winning, winsome note.

Summary: Cooing and wooing, marriage, collaborations, work and rewards, mind-blowing experiences, creativity at white heat, journeys and trips and immigration, children, hobbies, entertainment, communication expertise at all levels. Well, that's as exciting an adventure as you can hope to have, winks Ganesha.

Personal Message: Leo is light, power, glory, majesty and dignity. So far so good. But now Leo's aim must be to bring together all those who want to dedicate themselves to the advent of a new world with no distinction of nationality, creed, religion or sex.

Your happiness quota is 82 per cent.

WEEKLY REVIEW BY PHASES OF THE MOON

10 January: Full Moon in Cancer

The year has an explosive start. You give yourself the freedom to wander into unfamiliar territory and to explore new possibilities. Your main wish/desire is to have a free and unlimited life and will make all kinds of efforts to make it possible. The thought 'I will be positive no matter what!' will go a long way and there is no need to be ego-driven. You will mobilize your resources and energies to your advantage both at your end in handling your funds. If you are able to keep your cool, you will meet with even less resistance. Work will enable you to grow and develop your needs; and opportunities will change, but you'll change with them.

17 January: Moon's Last Quarter in Libra

Communication and individual responsibility will be the buzz words in this phase. At work and social settings, you will feel powerful and much sought after. Some kind of a social shift or a change in status is on the cards. You will gain in reputation, but you mustn't give in to the dark side of power, or a tendency to misuse it. Remember that power has to be both legitimate and accountable. Ganesha says that you will expand your horizons spiritually and this should counter the dangerous ego drives which you are prone to. You often feel that you are the last word in whatever you do and are God's gift to mankind. Remember, pride comes before fall.

24 January: New Moon in Capricorn

Starting now, luck is on your side. But you have to recognize your thoughts and keep away from negative reactions. The universal synthesizer – love – is in the air. You will feel connected to the people around you, and people will in turn be drawn to you. Parents, elders and in-laws will feature prominently in your life. I must warn you here that there is some danger to their health and well-being and you may have to seek expert medical advice. This is also a period when you will be compassionate and will connect to a higher power. Try to live in gratitude and appreciate all that life has given you in such abundance.

2 February: Moon's First Quarter in Taurus

This will be a good time for you to deal with old accounts, settle scores or check the status of your joint accounts. It is a time for new beginnings. Relocating may be a positive move because all change is ultimately for the better. The universe is in a constant state of change and resisting change can and should be avoided at all costs, since this is not the time to be stuck in a rut. You may need to take a loan for expansion at work, or at home. Funds will make themselves available to you. Life improves and there is a new direction and purpose of life.

9 February: Full Moon in Leo

You will be blessed with abundance. It's time to cash-in and treat yourself to a good time. A vacation with the family may become a real possibility. There will also be profitable travel. You may even see yourself promoting ecological awareness by contributing to an organization that work for the environment. Even in your domestic set-up, you will promote greater awareness, better living habits. Ganesha is pleased with you.

19 February: Moon's Last Quarter in Scorpio

You are going through an experimental phase in order to identify your true strengths. This is cruel to your development. But you are in the process of determining the things that matter most. You have the ability to get things done and don't want to be lost in the crowd. You are determined to be a leader in your chosen field. Travel is a natural extension of the pursuit of knowledge and you will be travelling for work and pleasure. You will get assistance from a different quarter and family life will be comfortable with more than the usual share of happiness.

23 February: New Moon in Aquarius

This is the period during which there will be both more money and more love. The stars align themselves to usher a period of intense passion and love. Your popularity will soar, there will be new romantic interests, and your family, staff and co-workers are left feeling that you are in true value addition to their lives. There is quality travel too on the cards. There may be the danger of fires, accidents or some kind of an unhappy twist in fate but you will be able to negotiate the worst. It may even be a good idea to renew an insurance policy; if you haven't got one it may be time to get it. Take the necessary precautions as it is good to be forewarned. If you can prevent something untoward, do it; it is your advantage.

2 March: Moon's First Quarter in Gemini

Pluto will be there till 23 March 2023. This means that the pay packet will get heavier, the big promotion is lurking around the corner, and you will climb the ladder of success really fast. You may feel all this starting to happen this week. You will multitask and balance a variety of needs and goals. You will achieve much and gain a lot of respect. There will be applause, perks and the goodies of life coming to you in plenty. You relish it all and bask in its glory.

9 March: Full Moon in Virgo

You'll pick up life's little treasures along the way this week. There will be a heightened sense of awareness as you will operate from the soul instead of the mind. You will define and redefine your own life. You are filled with greater enthusiasm and will re-examine the world and open yourself to new experiences with family. There may be some remodelling of the home or office as you attempt to clear the clutter from your life. This significant and profound journey will be spread out over the next eight years.

16 March: Moon's Last Quarter in Sagittarius

You are now experiencing uncertainties and doubts about your future. There are innumerable obstacles confronting you and it is difficult to stay focused. There may be unsettling domestic issues or health problems like a miscarriage in the family and all this can be most upsetting. Take time off to relax and meditate and allow negative thoughts to flow out. Remember that change is the only constant and obstacles are necessary for success, happiness and growth. Obstacles are challenges and as you find ways to overcome them, you grow. Do not be pinned down by negative thought processes.

The three Ps – persistence, positivity and patience – are the cornerstones of your life now. Ganesha's blessings are with you.

24 March: New Moon in Aries

You begin to realize that you are extremely lucky and gifted and thank the lord for it. You will muster the courage to make the sacrifices required to pursue your dreams. You get disciplined and streamlined. For example, if you are a singer you will give up smoking to increase your vocal range. You may even taste international success and will have the guts to be able to make the sacrifices. Don't feel insecure or scared about spreading your wings. Remember that no one has it all and sacrifices have to be made. To get something, you have to lose something else and you have to be prepared for all this. Even your closest allies may not understand you but nothing succeeds like success, and when you do well they will all rally around you. Just remember that it is vital to follow your instincts. Buying and selling, warehousing, distribution, goods and services may see an increase in activity, and may prove to be profitable areas.

1 April: Moon's First Quarter in Cancer

This is a time of love and reconciliation. You are thinking it in a positive way and notice that you are connecting with people who are doing the same thing. There is some misfortune heading your way, but you are prepared to take it full on. There is some exciting travel on the cards, possibly a cruise to an unseen destination, a dreamy boat ride down the backwaters, or even a breathtaking road trip. There will be many experiences and you will gain a lot from it. You may be rearranging your closet or cupboard and end up giving away odds and ends that are no longer of any use. It is good to de-clutter as it makes way for new energy.

8 April: Full Moon in Libra

You have been able to reflect on your past and identify a pattern of behaviour that you know is not good for you. But you are as stubborn as ever and are not willing to change. You let your heart make all your decision and they could be wrong most of the time, as they will be subjective. Your intuition will also tell you to distance yourself from certain people, projects and preoccupations. Pay attention; it is in your interests to heed all warning signs. This is a good time for your individual strength, and leverage them. Don't settle for anything less and don't undersell yourself. Don't also be short-sighted and impractical; look at the bigger picture. There also will be huge expenses as you will make purchases for the family. There will be many pulls and pressures and you may be in an indulgent mood. Look for happy and positive ways to fulfil your needs. Ganesha is watching over you.

14 April: Moon's Last Quarter in Capricorn

There has been tremendous change in your outlook. You understand a little more about the power that you have within you. There will be a lot of entertaining in this phase and you will be making many new contacts. You will gain appreciation for your hospitality, charm and wit and be the soul of the party. There will also be some restructuring at work and you will look at many new areas for improvement and progress. When something doesn't work, you try another tack; it's always been one of your signature characteristics.

23 April: New Moon in Taurus

The three Ps – promotions, profits and prestige – are at the core of this week. You involve yourself with initiatives that empower you to forge ahead. A significant rise in energy levels translates into long, productive hours at work, especially for those in the media – particularly, brand-building, media planning, and profit maximization – these become primary corners. Learn to get along with people of all hues. This is not the time for resentments or anger that has been buried for a long time. Try to open up and express your feelings and you will see that it is also good for your health. This is also the time when you may win an award or be felicitated for your work and be recognized in your community. You are gradually becoming a more influential member of society and it is adding to your aura.

30 April: Moon's First Quarter in Leo

Life takes on a sense of adventure and there are exciting times spent outdoors. You are reliving your childhood through your children or simply engaging in activities that remind you about your youth. It's a pleasurable experience and immensely rewarding. Things may not be on the relationship front but your work is both engaging and profitable. You will also find time for hard work and you may even enrol for a new study programme. There may also be international travel which could be very beneficial.

7 May: Full Moon in Scorpio

You will think and ponder over what you really want out of life. Most people are not working in areas that they are best suited for. They in the wrong job and hang in there out of compulsions. We can say the same thing about marriage but that's a different issue and we will go into that later. Ask yourself in no uncertain terms what you want in your life today. You deserve to have the best. There is only one life and so don't make too many compromises. If you feel that you are unable to go the distance due to limitations that you have created in your mind, it is time to snap out of it! The two Cs – compassion and communication – are also a recurring theme during this phase. Realize that in life, by and large, you are answerable only to yourself. Try to give love and affection practical expression as there isn't enough of it in the world.

14 May: Moon's Last Quarter in Aquarius

The level of conviction in your beliefs will be astounding. You have so many unanswered questions, but it doesn't stop you from feeling this way. Your confidence and charisma will soar. You have realized that it is good to have problems and unanswered questions in order to challenge yourself to find solutions. This is also the time for a new love and you may begin to feel an uncontrollable attraction to someone who has recently come into your life. There is another aspect you may want to look into. This might be a good opportunity to explore the realm of friendship and see where it takes you. Friendship with the opposite gender can be platonic too. This is also an emotional and sensitive period and there could be an upsurge of emotions. Friendship and love will be paramount now and it is up to you to make most of it. This is an important phase.

22 May: New Moon in Gemini

You are counting the day for some kind of a renaissance to happen, not realizing that it has already begun. You can't see yourself changing, but it's apparent by the way people respond to you. It could be a combination of social re-engineering, doing the same things a little differently, or your recent good fortune in the stock market that is fuelling this attraction; there could be any number of reasons. You have always been someone who has challenged the status quo, and yet can handle almost any situation. You also change your wardrobe, look at a new diet and fitness plan and work on a complete makeover. There is a new you waiting to burst out of your shell and take the world by storm. Ganesha gives you a little pat on the back.

30 May: Moon's First Quarter in Virgo

Innovation is the buzz word this week. Technologies outside your industry will force you to learn, to acquire, to adapt, to change. You will be on a learning spree as you incorporate new technologies in your workplace. There will be rapid expansion, and you reap the whirlwind. There will be a reallocation of funds and resources to maintain a sustainable growth rate. You make rapid progress and make the right investments. The home environment may be getting a bit difficult with some nagging and fussing as you are caught up in work and can't devote much time to it. But all this will settle down soon enough as the family see you flourish and the dividends at work shower them with the goodies of life.

5 June: Full Moon in Sagittarius

You are jet-setting, globetrotting and reconnecting with old friends and relatives. It could be that you have been promoted to a position of authority too quickly. You will be hard put to cope with the new assignment but you manage it well in the end. You will learn to develop your people skills and other emotional competencies that come with time and experience. You learn the value of building relationships and dazzle your superior with your talent and intellect. It is also important to connect well with your subordinates. This is a valuable period in life when you learn a lot of lessons and grow as a human being.

13 June: Moon's Last Quarter in Pisces

By now you have established credibility and a power base. You have been judged by your actions and are finally in a comfort zone. There are applause, money, rewards and felicitations. Live in the 'now' and enjoy every moment. Make the purchases you have always wanted to even if it means spending too much. Life is fleeting and you have done well. So loosen your purse strings. It's time for relief, reflection and restoration. Ganesha blesses you.

21 June: New Moon in Cancer

Huge investment and large purchases may become a necessity. You deal with loans and funds. Joint finances and raising capital look at scaling up production. You must commit to only as much as you can deliver. Demand is practically impossible to predict if you are introducing a new product. You are giving people choices they never had. Remember, high quality will always translate into high volume. You are worldly and wise enough to realize that you are a man of energy and drive. You will align your business objectives with other strategies and create markets for your products. There may be the opening of a new plant, a storehouse, or perhaps even a wedding in the family.

28 June: Moon's First Quarter in Libra

You are feeling very entrepreneurial. You will soon be able to place people in key positions so that you can be free from everyday concerns and focus on the development of new businesses. Your family rallies around you and there is greater love and appreciation around the dining table. Expense will mount and there could be travel for work. Family elders may need medical attention. This is a mixed week when you make progress and are, yet, pulled back a bit by a lot of other factors outside your reach. You will take it all in your stride, and cope, with Ganesha's help.

5 July: Full Moon in Capricorn

Ganesha facilitates both material and higher gains. The focus will be on adding value and building your portfolio of assets. The acquisition of wealth, the infusion of capital, joint accounts, loans, funds, an inheritance or perhaps even a lottery, may be round the corner. There is a strong indication of a sudden unexpected gain this week. Money comes in and also leaves your pockets in the form of expenses. Rest assured that the money will come in and that's what matters you. You don't have to worry unduly.

12 July: Moon's Last Quarter in Gemini

You may come across many complex situations this week but you will manage to demonstrate a level of maturity that surprises yourself and manage to overcome all that is thrown at you. You will do whatever it takes to be happy. You have realized that nobody can take that away from you. You will orient yourself, evaluate the situation and develop cognitive maps. You have keen business instincts and a proven ability to deliver the bottom-line result. You may even end up jumping from one organization to another to get ahead faster. You have a very impressive week ahead of you. There is also romance on the cards filling you with passion and excitement.

20 July: New Moon in Cancer

There are many new realization this week. The world is changing rapidly and you are forced to confront that reality. Don't indulge in criticism and learn to accept change, and that people around you are entitled to their beliefs and quirks. Life is dynamic. Learn to forget the past and don't hold on to it or live by it. Every moment changes and you must learn to go with the flow. Most of us have a tough time imagining a tomorrow that is different from today. Learn to embrace change as it is the only constant. Surprising announcements will elevate the week. You'll feel enthusiastic and optimistic about work and will put your heart and soul into it. Work also helps you escape from all that is bothering you. The prospects for next week are also good, and you look ahead with optimism.

27 July: Moon's First Quarter in Virgo

You realize that your own happiness is a by-product of the happiness of people around you. There is a lot of entertaining and you spend lavishly on your family and friends. You use your intelligence, imagination and knowledge to your advantage and make rapid progress at work. You pore over blueprints for the home, office or a home away from home. There are many new interests which take hold of this week. Agriculture, gardening, irrigation and even areas like renewable energy solutions have caught your interest. Spread out, as you have nothing to lose and everything to gain.

2 August: Full Moon in Aquarius

You take a radically different approach to work and the results are all too visible. You move away from old-fashioned practices and come up with brilliant ideas which win kudos from across the board. There is little time for family as you slog away with your new work schedules and ideas. You do outstandingly well but do not let success get to your head and resist being ego-driven. I know it is easy to say all this but if you don't take heed you could get into more trouble with office politics. Your family takes a back seat while you wrestle with issues at work about your product or unwind a bit, or the stress will soon take a toll. Ganesha tells you to slow down a bit without losing track of your priorities.

11 August: Moon's Last Quarter in Taurus

You have recently come out of a long relationship or are thinking about an exit strategy. You feel you have been wronged and feel like you need to go on a shopping spree. You spend on apparel, jewellery, cosmetics, spirits, electronics and dining out. You definitely include far more than you ever did before but it is making you feel good. You are hurting inside and prefer to bond only with your pets. But remember that the goodies you buy might momentarily enrich or elevate your existence, but the physical and intellectual stimulation you receive from nurturing, loving or even talking to someone is irreplaceable. You need to get back to life. Ganesha will hold your hand till you are fit to walk on your own.

19 August: New Moon in Leo

You concentrate heavily on money matters this week. Funds, loans, finances, borrowing, buying and selling will boost your self-confidence and pride. You may take an exotic vacation and may find yourself doing something adventurous, different and exciting. You feel refreshed and rejuvenated by all this and you may even wear your adventures like a badge of honour. But you have to return from it. The holiday has been great and now reality beckons.

25 August: Moon's First Quarter in Sagittarius

You want it all, but are often exhausted trying to get it. You don't believe in debt, but you won't like lack of money to stand in the way of buying what you want. Financial liquidity is both necessary and desirable if your goal has to be realistically achieved. You are driven and determined. But there are many moments of anxiety and doubts of depression. You feel alone, and solitude and loneliness don't suit you. You are the type who loves an entourage and thrives when your praises are being sung. You like to be in command and be the dominant person in a room full of people. But you have been focusing single-mindedly on a work and are now on the verge of exhaustion and bankruptcy in both love and pure bonding. Friends and family members abandon you, in a manner of speaking and let you be. They feel that you will come around when you are done with your work. They know that there is no use telling you to do something because you won't. Listening to others is not your forte. But remember, nothing waits for ever and it may just be too late.

2 September: Full Moon in Pisces

You're dreaming and planning for the future. You're renovating the house. Your kitchen is the primary space for connecting; it is the command centre for family interactions and coordination. Your house has always been sought after for entertaining friends. People show up unannounced because you make them feel at home. You, thankfully, take a break from work and spend time with pets and your beloved. There is good bonding and you are freed from the obsession of making more money. There is health and harmony and Ganesha believes that this is the greatest wealth.

10 September: Moon's Last Quarter in Gemini

You work to improve your spiritual plane by helping the underprivileged and needy. You make donations to causes and offer medical aid to those who cannot afford it. They bless you from their hearts for this gesture. Ganesha too gives you his blessings. You are able to enjoy moments of relaxation and revitalization thanks to all this. You have been spending a lot of time at home with your children and your pets of late and now you begin to see its value in your life; it is truly time well spent. It is good that you are not neglecting your own family while saving someone else's, which is often the case. Charity begins at home!

17 September: New Moon in Virgo

You have embarked on a journey where people are looking at you for answers. You must consolidate your discretionary time. Set yourself deadlines for various activities. Time is the scarcest resource and needs to be managed well. Every aspect of your existence will be galvanized, improved and uplifted. You will be more active at home as well and there will be harmony at work and play. There will be innovations at work and at home, and new strategies. You will see your concepts come to life if you stay the course and refocus on the fundamentals.

24 September: Moon's First Quarter in Capricorn

This could be a challenging week – delays, disappointments and adverse conditions spelling out defeat and even doom. You will have to be careful and not take undue risks. Learn to compromise and don't embark on new projects. Be wary of dangerous activities as the risk of accidents is quite high. There may also be minor illnesses and hospitalization. Money flow at work will be obstructed and so expansion will come to a halt. Keep a tab on expenses as you may have to tap into your reserves even for day-to-day expenses. This is a testing time and you will be challenged every either way. Of course, it all depends on the individual horoscope and this is just a generalization. There may also be unwanted litigation and several other pinpricks. This is a good time for self-discipline, diet control, exercise, yoga and meditation. Relationships and family bonding may also be tested during this period.

2 October: Full Moon in Aries

An engagement or a marriage is strongly indicated. It is very clear that love is a genuine and solid commitment for you. Love and passion are not mutually exclusive. If you have been dating someone you could move to the next level. If you are single, chances are that you will meet someone significant. Romance is the paramount theme now. Work too doesn't suffer and you will be able to balance both areas of your life well. You may also be visiting welfare centres, hospitals, old people's homes, places of healing and learning. You are keen on mental, spiritual and intellectual expansion. There is all-round growth.

10 October: Moon's Last Quarter in Cancer

It is difficult to make future plans because your partner/spouse does not see things the same way. You need to sort this out first. Place your goals on hold and take time off work to discuss over the affairs that have been troubling you. You need to look deep for solutions. Your health improves and you are feeling energetic and healthier than ever before. You start your day earlier and are most energized in the morning hours. You have also probably incorporated a new fitness regimen into your routine which will pay dividends. Focus on family and relationships, and less on work. You need to focus on what truly makes you happy and not disperse your energies in different directions. Happiness is your goal and you are taking the right steps in that direction. Ganesha is with you every step of the way.

16 October: New Moon in Libra

There may be a minor accident in your vicinity. It is nothing to worry about, but it will change the way you perceive life – it will be a turning point for you emotionally. There are new avenues at work and opportunities to explore a different space. You are gathering new information, meeting and interacting with new people and challenging yourself professionally. The more you learn, the more you realize how little you know. You brush up your knowledge skills and check the areas that could use your talents and expertise. Ganesha sees success within your grasp.

23 October: Moon's First Quarter in Aquarius

It's the right time for friendship and new bonds as we revitalize old connections. Your current friendships have a lot to offer, but you have not nurtured them. You have had trust issues and have always tried to push people away from any involvement in your personal life even when you needed them. You will attempt to change all that this week. Career will be on the upswing and there is recognition at work. Travel to exciting, unchartered destinations is also on the cards. There could be visitors from far away who will bring in much-needed excitement. It's time to be surrounded by genuine friends and take everything in your stride with a winning smile. Ganesha knows that you are a winner and what better endorsement do you need?

31 October: Full Moon in Taurus

This is time for romance. There will be lovely moments with your beloved. Try to be loyal and appreciative and true to your love. Dream, if you will, of the moment. True love will help you discover yourself as your thoughts will create a powerful emotional state which you will acknowledge and respond to. The finances are sound and comfortable. There will be buying and selling and you will be inclined to spend extravagantly. There could be good news for those expecting a child. Ganesha promises many good times too.

8 November: Moon's Last Quarter in Leo

You have endured a lot and come out as winner. You now know that you have what it takes to withstand life's hard knocks and punches. There is nothing that can get the better of you. There are expenses and travel and many meetings and collaborations. At one level, it could all be a waste of time but you have to meet people and engage in discussions to test the waters for further business expansion. In friendship you give people choices they never really had before. You have all the ingredients for success and the ability to upgrade your life. All you have to do is make the right choices.

15 November: New Moon in Scorpio

You will be looking at doing something creative this week. Don't be daunted by what the end product will be. If you are a writer and think that your writing won't have a polished feel, for example, it doesn't matter because it will shine with the exuberance that rightfully belongs to you. You will create an individual style which will be very rewarding. Success at something new and different is foretold. You are not limited to any one medium as your imagination runs riot. This is also a period of reflection and re-evaluation. There are many forces and influences at play now and you could be moulded any possible way.

22 November: Moon's First Quarter in Pisces

There will be family issues to solve. There could be tussles between children/parents/spouse/elders at home. It could be tense. Keep your cool and don't say things you will regret later, and think before you voice your opinion. Don't rush into anything, or take hasty decisions. There will be some pressure from an unexpected source. Try to respond with ease and grace even though you feel that the situation is somewhat irredeemable. At work, there will be an increase in buying and selling but your funds are tied up and liquidity affected. There will be a fundamental realignment of your needs. Ganesha is by your side, to help you through, always.

30 November: Full Moon in Gemini

You may go on a shopping spree now in order to feel good and boost your sagging morale. You are looking for an emotional lift now, a 'happy pill' that these new purchases can give. You don't care about the consequences. You don't even want to know how much money is in the bank as you splurge on different things, many of which you may never need. You want the adrenaline charging through your veins; come what may and you are willing to take risks and even pay a heavy price for this mood. It can be a difficult phase and you could lose balance. It may be temporary, but it is there and you wrestle with the demons that are now devouring you. You will come out unscathed in the end, but the mood takes its toll.

8 December: Moon's Last Quarter in Virgo

Someone significant is warm and gracious and sees things from your perspective. There are moments of frustration, but you are in control creating a buzz at every turn. You experience a certain kind of freedom from doing things the traditional way. You have chalked out a series of steps that are sequential and logical, you define and refine the process, and there is a level of maturity never seen before in your handling of both business and domestic issues. Negotiations could be under way in a new industry – possibly fashion computers, education or hospitality. Whatever the domain, you are skilled at creating excitement and interest.

14 December: New Moon in Sagittarius

Someone compelling and charismatic enters your life. He/she has the ability to make you run in circles. For once you will find it exceedingly difficult to assert yourself in a way that is uniquely you and you may have to feign indifference to protect yourself if you want to do that. At work you earn plaudits by refocusing on the fundamentals, producing dramatically better products, and improving the brand's emotional positioning. You will get support from your co-workers and create dramatic breakthroughs. There are ups and downs and some very difficult moments but you display consistency and stability.

21 December: Moon's First Quarter in Aries

You are taken in by new ideas, you play around with them a bit, and then let them be. There are several opportunities but you have to grab them and make them work for you. This is a period of constant rethinking. There is continual travel too and you need to ensure that you don't miss your focus. If you make the right decisions at the appropriate time, your relationships will be more intimate, engaging and long-lasting. Relationships need nurturing and a lot of emotional and physical space is required. Don't get over-possessive of your partner. It will also be a good idea to seriously rethink your diet, wardrobe and fitness levels. Yoga, meditation and other forms of spiritual strengthening will certainly help. Look at the bigger picture and don't burn yourself out.

30 December: Full Moon in Cancer

This has been an interesting year. You have been tested and challenged and, as in a game of snakes and ladders, you have made progress and fallen too. In addition to the work and home fronts you have also earned enormous popularity and won kudos in the community. You are now connecting with people whom you may not have had an opportunity to meet. You're developing skills as a social facilitator that will serve you well in the future; this could even pay off handsomely on the work front. It will also be a good idea to spend the last days of the year with the family, particularly with your parents. It is time to recognize their invaluable contribution to your life and shower them with gratitude and appreciation. You must realize that whatever you are today is because of them and a little token of appreciation will go a long way. Just acknowledge their presence in your life, if nothing else! Ganesha will always bless you for this.

VIRGO

23 August–22 September

Symbol: The Virgin
Ruling Planet: Mercury
Earth–Mutable–Negative
The sign of the Critic, the Secretary

Ganesha agrees that love makes the world go round. Writer Thomas Mann says, 'It is love, not reason, that is stronger than death.' Hafiz, the originator of the ghazal as a form of poetry and also one of the first and greatest Sufi thinkers in Persia, sings: 'Words have no language which can utter the secrets of love,' and that life is like a 'jewelled cup'. But unless there is the wine of love in it, it is lonely and lost. This is how writer Kenko puts it. Yes, I also agree with this wholeheartedly.

Obviously, I have spotlighted the aspect of love, because it will be one of the mainstreams of 2020 for you. The reason why? Jupiter, the planet of good luck, will be in your fifth angle from 2 December 2019 to 18 December 2020.

VIRGO

JUPITER

Across the gateway of my heart
I wrote: 'No thoroughfare.'
But love came laughing and cried:
'I enter everywhere.'
—H. Shipman

Ganesha says, 'enter everywhere' sums up the power of love, especially for you. Jupiter will be in your fifth angle from 2 December 2019 to 18 December 2020. Love will percolate into your life in these ways:

- You will entertain and be amused, have romantic inclinations, which could well be fulfilled.

- You will have the freedom, the free will and the sheer joy of doing what you desire – and that's great in any language. In fact, that is why the fifth angle is called 'the seat of pleasure'. You will be an ardent follower of the pleasure principle.

- Children and loved ones will respond and make it all worthwhile. To love and be cherished is the sure way to happiness and delight, and that's your destiny, says Ganesha.

- Your luck will hold in games of chance. The luck of the draw will be with you. If you are fond of sports and the arts – especially singing, theatre and films – your luck will hold too. Your mate/partner/friend could accompany you on a journey, or you might go alone, but there will be plenty of movement for you and your dear ones.

- Those of you interested in prayer, words of power, tantra and mantra, talismans, religious rites and rituals, will find this period propitious.

Jupiter will be in the practical, no-nonsense sign Capricorn, by Western astrology. Therefore, your love and imagination will be expressed along useful, practical, lines like those in architecture, medicine, teaching, research, doctoral theses, psychology, psychiatry, law, management, production of movies, editing and writing, event management, health and fitness, diet and exercise, sports and hobbies, photography, sculpture and painting, childbirth and forming links with the young.

SATURN

Saturn will remain the same as last year

Saturn will start a sojourn in your fifth angle of health and work from 21 December 2017 to most of 2020.

> May I be like the Sun in seeing; like Fire in brilliance; like Wind in power; like Soma in fragrance; like Lord Brihaspati in intellect; like the Ashvins in beauty; like Indra-Agni in strength."
> —SAMA VEDA: BRAHMANA, 11.iv.14

Let me now go into some detail:

1) Saturn highlights your creative impulses, your romantic and artistic needs, your sense of untrammelled, unhampered, total freedom. Like that, eh? Children and grandchildren give joy. Entertainment and

amusements will be your birthright. You could be moving with the younger crowd, maybe the jet set, maybe students, maybe toddlers and kids or writing about them, painting them, and in any case having much to do with them. That's the bottom line. Do not become involved with the problems of others, not now, please. Also, you could lose the affection of others; yes, that's the flip side. And, there is scope for a suitable avocation.

2) Secret knowledge, journeys, an initiation, travel, spiritual and uplifting experiences – which just dissolve the dark aspects and recesses of life and sorrow – will be yours. Yes, you will overhaul your entire life and make it grand and complete. It's like a vacuuming from within and after that, how can there be any looking back?

3) *Mobile perpetuum* is the Latin for something in perpetual motion, and that means a grand reaching out to people and places, an ability to move, manoeuvre and manipulate, becoming precise and penetrative in letters, calls, communication, contacts and coexistence. You will interface with people powerfully and pleasurably, and that, by itself, is rare and noteworthy.

So strong is this movement and this reaching out that it could result in a house or office or shop or industry move, immigration, contacts with foreign lands, neighbours, society in general. You could almost step out of your body and do some astral flying. I am not kidding! 'Move it' is the glorious and clear message from Saturn

BLUEPRINT FOR THE ENTIRE YEAR

January: You will be off and away to a really flying start, says Ganesha, and as you know, well begun is half done.

February and March: Expenses but also progress; therefore, mixed results.

April: Excellent for finances, family affairs and earned income.

May: Reaching out to people and places by all media of transport and communication.

June: Important for peace, buying/selling/renovating/decorating, a home away from home.

July: Love, romance, the luck of the draw, creativity and children, family and fun and fortune.

August: Health, employment, pets, servants and colleagues and a few problems connected with these.

September: Love and hate, marriage and making merry, but paradoxically, in a few cases, separation and legal cases, and that is why life is so complex, uncertain, full of contradictions and surprises.

October: Funds, loans, capital formation, money matters, shopping.

November: Inspiration, journeys, name and fame, good luck.

December: Power, prestige, parents, profession, awards and rewards, money, home, house and office.

Summary: The word 'joy' best sums up the celebration of life; of daring and caring despite the odds. Ganesha says home, house, work, status, prestige, parents, in-laws, travel will keep you on your 'twinkling toes' in 2020.

Your happiness quota is 85 per cent.

Special Note: From 31 December 2019 to July 2025, Uranus will help you in matters to do with finance, travel, publicity, invention and innovation. You must learn to strike when the iron is hot.

WEEKLY REVIEW BY PHASES OF THE MOON

10 January: Full Moon in Cancer

You begin the year like a person who is possessed. The previous year ended to your satisfaction and you managed to achieve a lot. Now make plans for more work and further expansion and, of course, more money which is the lubricant that drives your engine. You are not particularly ambitious but your insecurities are many and money helps provide a healing balm over them. Those of you who are the meticulous and fastidious types pore over minutest details and this can get difficult for colleagues and associates who insist that you look at the larger picture and leave the nitty-gritty to them. So please take care not to get too critical and over-demanding. Learn to decentralize, apportion work to others and trust your team. It takes all sorts to make the world and you will have to make the necessary allowances. People have blemishes, you do too, so don't expect a perfect world. You are practical but sometimes miss the wood for the trees. With the new moon in Capricorn at the start of the year, you push forward at work vigorously and manage to achieve a lot. There will be pleasant moments with loved ones too as you make quite an enviable start to 2020.

17 January: Moon's Last Quarter in Libra

You are pressing all the right buttons and pushing ahead on all cylinders. A lot will be achieved. You are normally very careful with money but this week sees you spend recklessly. There are power, status, prestige and bankrolls in the offing. You are not terrific with people and so a touching up of people skills will be necessary. There will be a lot of entertaining too and those with indulgences are likely to go over the top. You should also guard against secret deals and involvements and clandestine affairs which will boomerang in the long run. Also, avoid get-rich-quick schemes however tempting they may seem now. A travel is indicated and meetings with many new people which will help broaden your horizon.

24 January: New Moon in Capricorn

The focus shifts to family matters. Your health as well as the health of near and dear ones may need attention. A parent or an elderly relative may need hospitalization and you will be busy with a lot of running around which you hadn't accounted for. There will be emotional moments when you will be tested and there is also the possibility of a lot of family drama. The mood is charged and electric.

2 February: Moon's First Quarter in Taurus

You are chafing at the bonds that tie you down and look for freedom. You feel constrained and locked in and need to grow further. You need a bigger pond and fresh new avenues to find your true calling. You will look at spirituality in a new light and may get ritualistic and religious. You will be startled by the esoteric and for a while, at least, will be rocked off terra firma. You will also indulge in poor feeding and visit hospices to aid the less privileged. You may also donate generously to causes dear to your heart. This is an unusual week and the focus doesn't seem to be on work. If anything, you are looking for answer to many profound question that bother you. You want new experiences to understand life and its meaning. You want to get out of the rut in which you have been for very long and try out new things. Suddenly, you feel adventurous. Watch out for depression and mood swings too. Your mind is in a whirl and you seek out adventure, experience and learning. The monotony bores you as you look, quite uncharacteristically, to hew your own path.

9 February: Full Moon in Leo

You have never been steadier. The first quarter in Taurus sees you working hard and aiming for the stars. You will achieve a lot and make money. There will be applause too for all your efforts and you have the good sense to make the most of the situation and make the necessary investments. Your image in local circles and in your peer group is heightened. Life is good once again. You are the cynosure of all eyes and the purple patch you have hit more than obliterates all the earlier deviations. There is bonding with family and friends too and a glimpse of romance which promises to grow. This is a truly lucky period and you have to make the most of it.

19 February: Moon's Last Quarter in Scorpio

The good run continues. You have a strong, even single-minded focus on work and it reaps rich dividends. There are indications of travel, new collaborations and expenses. You are likely to spend on home and the office. You look at business expansion and there is happiness in the family. The stork could be visiting soon. Ganesha's blessings are with you. You continue in expansionist mode, tap newer horizons and make rapid progress in all your endeavours.

23 February: New Moon in Aquarius

The early part of the year is going well for you. You prioritize your goals and go about the planning quite meticulously. This is a period of expansion and growth and you don't spare the horses. You will have to be careful with the spoken word and also try not to overextend yourself. Try also to keep away from unnecessary altercations. You have been pushing too hard and this could result in stress and illness. Expenses continue to mount and there is nothing that you can do about it. Take care to avoid litigation.

2 March: Moon's First Quarter in Gemini

You risk losing recently found stability. You have the right mindset and attitude but are on fickle ground as you are torn by emotions. You want to move ahead in life and make money and all usual accoutrements of progress but, somehow, you can't. Your mind is a swamp and you are on edge and can't think straight. You are not sure if this is the job you want and may be looking for a change of scenario in your work/career/employment/profession. You are fickle and too fastidious; the moment you get a job you turn it down finding fault with it. You also find deficiencies in your mate/spouse/partner and there could be unhappy times because of this. You seem to be on a fault-finding spree with everything. Curb this to be bothered by tendency and you will move ahead. You seem to be bothered by every little thing that doesn't find favour with you. This mood is contagious and your colleagues and family don't like it one bit.

9 March: Full Moon in Virgo

Not much changes this week. You are still in a limbo. People, work, domestic issues and several other factors make huge demands on you. You try your best to remain on the straight and narrow and find some direction in your dealings but you can't. You have to walk the tightrope and find sanity, which is going to be very difficult. You normally hate instability but nothing seems to be going your way now. You are challenged on all fronts and you strive to wriggle through it all. You are enthused by high finance and happy domesticity in normal times but the balance sheet is empty now and the home front is in disarray. But nothing lasts forever and the situation will change. Trust in Ganesha when the chips are down and you will sail through.

16 March: Moon's Last Quarter in Sagittarius

The situation changes dramatically. You found clarity and move ahead with purpose. You make up for lost time. There will be joy in relationships, bonds and ties of love. Work too will be on more solid ground. You are now steadfast in your desires and reap the rewards. You do well in speculation and in the market and also find time to have fun with the family. There will be outings and many happy moments. Children will be a source of joy. You meet up with parents and elders and there may be a family gathering which will stoke old memories and bring back many happy times. The full moon is in your sign and chances are that it all works your way.

24 March: New Moon in Aries

The stable run continues. Work moves smoothly and you start making good progress. There is expansion on all fronts and several profitable dealings. There are also collaborations and travel which benefit you. There is precious bonding and, possibly, deep love too. You are on firm ground after a long time and you must make the most of it. This is the right time to make long-term plans. With the focus that you are blessed with right now, added to your inherent business acumen, the chances of success are very real.

1 April: Moon's First Quarter in Cancer

You make steady progress and are tied down at work. There are new ventures on the horizon and you have a new zest to take your work and life to the next level. You ink profitable deals and may even prospect overseas connections which could prove beneficial in the long run. Work has never been better and you love every moment of it. You accomplish whatever you set out to do and meet your deadlines. This upward curve will go a long way in strengthening your finances for the entire year. Also, this mid-year direction sets the tone for all work-related activities. Use this period wisely and I assure you that you will be laughing all the way to the bank!

8 April: Full Moon in Libra

Your profitable run continues unabated. There are some emotional moments with the family too and the health of an elder member may need attention. There will be soaring expenses but you are also making money and so it won't be a problem. There will be genuine progress and you will be able to afford the good things of life. You make all the right moves and are ultra-efficient at work. Home life will be pleasant and children will bring great joy. There may be an addition to the family; if you are a pet lover, there could well be an exotic new acquisition.

14 April: Moon's Last Quarter in Capricorn

While there is progress, expenses also skyrocket and you make many purchases for the home and the office. There is domestic bliss and, if single, a meaningful new romance is in the offing. You refurbish your wardrobe and may take to the gym, yoga or any other fitness activity. You will also look at new diets, alternative therapies and a brand-new way of thinking. You realize that you have to change your mindset and will look at new forms of thoughts and philosophies. You also meet new people in this phase and need to make a good impression. All your projects run smoothly and you seriously look at taking the entire purpose of your life to a higher plane.

23 April: New Moon in Taurus

You are fascinated by new ideas and spend time with those who espouse new philosophies. You look for wisdom and erudition in people and may go shopping for seer. Work continues on a steady footing and family life is also peaceful. So you have the time and reason to get distracted. There is a happy mix of fun and work, peace and bustle, and your ambitions are all about checking out a new consciousness. There could be travel and even periods of solitude when you seek the inner recesses of your soul. You look at living in another dimension without the help of recreational drugs or hallucinogens. It is not easy, but you are ready to move on from the mundane world and its everyday requirements to profound quests.

30 April: Moon's First Quarter in Leo

There are many changes that you will now initiate in your life and work. You overhaul almost all aspects of your life and embark on a new you. There will be new work and new associations and you have realized the value and relevance of genuine bonding and are keen to have the best of it all. Siblings and relatives will mean a lot to you and you will be drawn to intellectual activities, higher studies, even research and information technology. You want to get out of the rut you have been in and allocate time for various aspects of your life which you had so far neglected.

7 May: Full Moon in Scorpio

You find yourself in the lap of luxury. Money flows in from unexpected quarters and you revel in this windfall. You make sensible purchases and investments and, thankfully, refuse to go overboard. You are grounded and know by now that the situation can change dramatically overnight and so are extra cautious, which is just as well. It is a pleasant time in many ways: there is enormous bonding with the family and moments of great joy. Strangely, despite the windfall you also get stingy and count your pennies. Luck is with you and it may help if you are less insecure and loosen your purse strings.

14 May: Moon's Last Quarter in Aquarius

The good times continue and you make resounding progress in whatever you do. The theme is money and you will busy yourself with buying/selling, shopping reality, funds, bonds, loans, markets, speculation and every other conceivable finance. You are less sober and cautious now, are willing to take risk and look for thrills. This is not a dangerous mood to be in because you ride the crest of good luck and so continue making profits. It is also necessary to take risks sometimes; nothing ventured, nothing gained. You are normally in a conservative and over-cautious mode and thus, in a way, insured from both success and failure. It is safe sitting on the fence but you need to step out of your comfort zone and explore new waters. You won't know if it is too hot unless you are scalded, and sometimes one needs that!

22 May: New Moon in Gemini

You are now brimming with confidence and feel that you can accomplish the impossible. A new daring or bravado takes over your psyche and changes your outlook to life. You have been insecure and almost timid for long but now, this new-found success instils tremendous confidence in you, and you march forth into the arena of life with the aggression, temerity and invincibility of a fully armed and cocky gladiator. From a calculating middle-level accountant, metaphorically speaking, you have been converted into a financial whiz who believes in and deals only in high stakes. You are in the seat of power and work like a demon because you see clearly the results of the upward trend that has taken over your life completely. The upswing has been in your favour for long and chances are that it may continue. There is more work and more responsibility, the stakes are getting higher, and the gambler in you just loves it all.

30 May: Moon's First Quarter in Virgo

You are on a fantastic run. You shine at the workplace and there is no stopping you. You are inspired to do great things, and once the self-belief is in place, success is yours for the asking. There will be beautiful moments with your loved one this week; an interlude to the heart-stopping work that you have been engaged in. There are candle-light dinners and stolen moments of pure unadulterated love. It is great to work and make money, but isn't it even better to share it with a loved one?

5 June: Full Moon in Sagittarius

You now look at expansion of your work. There is recognition and you are being well rewarded for your efforts. Success breeds friends and suddenly everyone rallies around you and believe that you can do no wrong. You like the adulation and can see through the pretences but you are watchful and yet shrewd enough to go with the flow. There could be international travel, work-related collaborations and even domestic issues to handle. You will be hard-pressed for time, but every moment will be well spent. If in the media, you will strike a purple patch and will be much in demand for your ingenuity and creativity.

13 June: Moon's Last Quarter in Pisces

You are slogging away and continue on firm ground. Your life seems well balanced and in harmony with all the usual irritants removed. You are finally being rewarded for prolonged periods of sustained hard work. You have also seen life at close quarters and realize that success can be very fleeting. You make several investments to secure your future when the chips are down. You realize that the family comes first and they have to be secured from the vicissitudes of life and you go about that in right earnest. There is time for partying too, but that is not a priority now.

VIRGO

21 June: New Moon in Cancer

Work increases and expenses mount. There is sustained travel and collaborations which could be profitable. There is a fair amount of risk-taking in the new deals and you don't have the soul of a gambler, but you are human and can get greedy and swayed by what is on offer at the end of the rainbow. You can be sold dreams and false promises in the mood that you are in and so be careful or you may be caught off guard. You may also want to be unethical and turn a blind eye to several clauses which don't pass legal muster. At the risk of repetition, let me add here that nothing lasts forever and that the stars impel but don't compel. Also, a lot has to do with your personal horoscope and such generalizations could well be off the mark. But these are trends you have to watch out for and they could come true too. You are doing well and are on a high-growth trajectory but there are pitfalls you should be careful about. It is said that everyone has a price, and now you are being tested!

28 June: Moon's First Quarter in Libra

This is a rewarding phase as you continue making money and earn applause from peers and the society at large. You may be publicly felicitated too. There is social advancement and you grow from strength to strength. You are positive, pleasant, inventive, creative and inspired. You are going great guns. There is progress and plenty and you have the good sense to make the most of this flourishing season. I must add though that you must read the fine print and take all precautions to avoid litigation and any unsavoury fallout in your new endeavours. Team members will have to be carefully scrutinized for their credentials. The pie is getting bigger and creamier and the flies will naturally want to feast on it uninvited! I must warn you against lies, deceit, sabotage and back-stabbing.

5 July: Full Moon in Capricorn

You will be spending a lot of time with the family now. A parent may need hospitalization and you may be called upon to help. You have been neglecting family ties for long and, in a way, you make up for lost time. Expenses mount and this is also an active phase but for entirely different reasons. The overall thrust and focus of all your activities will definitely be money as you are practical enough to know that nothing moves without money, but this is not the time for new deals and work-related issues. The family gets together and there is bonding of a very high order. The homes may be filled with relatives from afar and there could also be bereavement in the family. Life is many-splendoured with all the colours and facets of a grand soap opera. In fact, life is the grandest soap opera. So you will have to be prepared for all the shades it offers and be ready to receive whatever the lord has in store for you. There are good times and bad times and you have to learn to accept whatever is on offer without cribbing too much.

12 July: Moon's Last Quarter in Gemini

You try to multitask and juggle several things simultaneously much to your discomfort as your schedule gets even more frantic. Work, family, socializing, partying, networking, lobbying, etc., will swallow your time and your peace of mind. You need rest to prevent burnout and there are chances of illness. You take to prayers, meditation, religion and rituals for solace. Luckily, there is also love on the cards and this provides a welcome relief from the dour schedule of work and more work. You feel light and happy and spend time and money on the object of your distraction.

20 July: New Moon in Cancer

The flirtation of the previous week was just a mild distraction. Work pressures mount and your complete focus is necessary now. Your plate is full and overflowing with journeys, relationships, meetings, collaborations, associations and acquisitions. You cope brilliantly with rare zest and enthusiasm. You have learnt lessons from life and have decided to make the best of the moment. There could be minor altercations at work and depression too. Take time off and sort it out before it snowballs into something that you can't handle.

27 July: Moon's First Quarter in Virgo

The pressures keep mounting and you decide to redefine goals and priorities, rethink and plan the future in a different way. You just can't keep moving at the frenetic pace you have been in. You have been pushing yourself over the top and it's hurting now. Expenses skyrocket and there are all sorts of emergencies to cope with including hospital visits. You realize that something is wrong with your lifestyle and it is taking its toll. You need to cut down on your indulgences and get more disciplined. A medical check-up may be necessary and you need to trim the fat out of you and your lifestyle or you are heading for serious trouble. Ganesha advises you to heed the writing on the wall.

2 August: Full Moon in Aquarius

You make the changes and step on to a higher level of activity and achievement. There are joys of all kinds to experience. Work is well organized and the home front is harmonious. You concentrate on increasing your influence and status as well as your bank balance. You have made separate time for letting your hair down and now work is not life's sole obsession. There is a chance that you may get involved in shady deals and so keep away from tricksters and fraudsters who will be in plenty. You don't need to lose your hard-earned reputation and wealth for an unnecessary indiscretion. You are continuously being tempted and need some sort of equilibrium.

11 August: Moon's Last Quarter in Taurus

Your life is turned on its head now from finances and achievements; your focus shifts to quality interactions and bonding. This is a period for the cementing of old and new associations and you indulge in parties, ties, collaborations, ceremonies and functions. Money is not the focus of your life now and you are seriously looking at holistic growth. There will be many new influences and you will get off the beaten path and pursue a new dream or vision.

19 August: New Moon in Leo

You have come a long way this year. This is a peaceful week in which you relax and try to forget all your worries. There is a new development on the romantic front as you are pitchforked into a heady romance. Nothing makes sense to you any more now and you are head over heels in love, lost in the afterglow of a new affection that has taken you by storm. You will have to strive for objectivity as it deserts you completely and you refuse to listen to any kind of reason. Friends, associates, colleagues and family get a whiff of it and try to bring some sanity to your life, but you will have none of it. You are swept by the fragrance of love and worship it. The mood is overpowering and until it lets go of you, the noose just tightens. If you are already married, it goes without saying that this could create a lot of problems leading even to a separation or divorce.

25 August: Moon's First Quarter in Sagittarius

You manage to extricate yourself from the clutches of the new paramour with great difficulty thanks to a new moon in your sign. The affair isn't over by any means but you manage to find dry ground to steady your feet. New ties and bonds have been reinforced, and there is a shift in your thinking and focus. Domestic chores and work commitments now are less of a burden and you manage to handle it all well. You will be dealing a lot with home, land, property and issues relating to there. Whatever you embark on now will bear fruit soon. So make the rights choices and decisions.

2 September: Full Moon in Pisces

Your house is in some order now and you can look back with satisfaction. You are happy and relaxed and spend on the good things of life. There may be a holiday with the family or with friends. You enjoy the love, warmth and companionship of close associates thanks to a changed attitude in which you hold relationships important in your life. You have tasted success in the material world but the taste of true love is sweeter and lingers longer. Ganesha advises you to make the right choices as this period can be a tinderbox and highly inflammable.

10 September: Moon's Last Quarter in Gemini

You are in for a radical transformation. You are imbued with zeal, self-belief and confidence and feel a surge of power. There will be family functions to attend including religious ceremonies. There will be several demands on your time from friends and well-wishers and since you don't want to displease anyone, you remain at their beck and call which can be a nuisance. But your priorities have changed now and people and their interests are your primary concern. Love will remain the presiding deity of your life, and as long as it runs smoothly, you are on a high.

17 September: New Moon in Virgo

You are called abruptly to a wholly different professional and social scene. A wide spectrum of business and professional transactions, deals and negotiations will have to be handled. You will be entertaining, attending or giving parties, being a good host/hostess, and will be the soul of every gathering. You are meeting many new people and trying out new things, possibly even a new dish. That is the mood you are in. You need to savour something new now as the old has become stale and gives off a rotten stench. The waters are turbid and you need to infuse fresh life to it.

24 September: Moon's First Quarter in Capricorn

Your life is full of surprises and this disquiets you. There is no uniformity or steadfastness in your life and you try your best to give it some stability. You are feeling rattled by the continuous turn of events and long for some peace and predictability. But you have also been having crazy mood swings. You find yourself at the door of an extremely busy, involved and perhaps occasionally even confused phase. There will be many personal and professional issues to address. Relationships of all kinds and at all levels will be the focus this week. You love to keep your word and make it a point to honour all your commitments. All this takes time and energy and you can be left feeling depleted and drained.

2 October: Full Moon in Aries

You are fighting against all odds and it is an uphill climb. Nothing is working according to plan and you don't know what to do now. At times, there are marvellous flashes of genuine inspiration/ intuition/ perception and at other times there is only a void which is difficult to plug. You keep oscillating from triumph to despair. You are realigning goals, priorities and your image to find the key that fits. There are religious rituals to undertake and several journeys, as you try to fit into a world that is not making much sense to you right now. You may feel lonely, lost, solitary and isolated, belonging to no one and nothing in particular and this is not a pleasant state to be in.

10 October: Moon's Last Quarter in Cancer

You have the right intentions and you back the right horses but the rewards are not as expected. There are new opportunities and a chance at true peace, plenty and prosperity. You take a break and spend time with congenial companionship. You try to let your hair down and laugh, play and relax, but it doesn't help too much. Deep down you know that your plans are not working out as you had hoped they would. You need to look ahead with hope. You look at the metaphysical aspects of life and seek answers. It is a time of deep introspection. There could be marital problems and several indulgences that trap you and throw you frontally into a downward spiral that is, in a way, of your own making. Your mind is not rock-steady and is the cause of all your problems.

16 October: New Moon in Libra

There is some confidence and self-belief in your efforts but they are still not bearing fruit. You are in debt and could take to gambling and other excesses. It is high time that you pull up your socks or it could get too late. The family is pained by what they see and you also refuse to listen to the sane counsel of friends and well-wishers. You know they are right but you are adamant and refuse to listen to your inner voice which tells you to change in no uncertain terms. Your mind is warped at the moment and you are being swayed by new-found associates who don't mean well for you. You need to extricate yourself from the quicksand of life right now before it smothers you completely in its slush.

23 October: Moon's First Quarter in Aquarius

You are trying your best to make the most of the rotten situation that you find yourself in. It will help if you take to self-disciplining through yoga and meditation. Work is unattended and you could risk a job loss and this could lead to further ramifications. You need to steer your boat to stable ground and make an all-out effort to do it. The waters are now swirling around your neck and you realize that you could drown. Everybody helps you. Family and friends rally around you and, together, you make every effort to salvage lost ground. Suddenly, even total strangers lend a helping hand.

31 October: Full Moon in Taurus

Many aspects of your life will zoom into sharp focus. Your potential is actualized and your performance will be awesome. You achieve a lot and ride the wave. New projects will be successfully completed and you will find many new sources of income. While all this happens, you will also be living dangerously with indulgences, expenses and sexual involvements. There could be marital strife and misunderstandings with loved ones. There may even be litigation, police complaints and a messy turn to events. This is not what you want from life and I suggest that you take the necessary precautions before you live in regret. Your emotions often get the better of you in this period and you need to cool down. It may be a good idea to look at yoga and meditation as alternatives, possibly even a diet change.

8 November: Moon's Last Quarter in Leo

There is progress in your affairs as you wrestle to quell the demons that hound you. You look at growth and advancement and you push hard to achieve your true potential. You make many changes which could even include a job hop or a new line of work altogether. You feel isolated now and need to get back lost prestige. You take time off and spend it at ashrams and with gurus looking for answers. There may even be a pilgrimage to a shrine as you seek divine help. You have slipped off the rails and need to get back on track. Your mind is still playing tricks with you and you strive to quell it.

15 November: New Moon in Scorpio

There is a shimmer of hope as you slowly regain control of your life. You need to get back the respect of your peers and need to start investing is yourself more. You bring in discipline to your life and organize. You put in long hours at work and start from scratch. The dividends start showing almost immediately as though your life was just waiting to be set right and looking for the slightest excuse to stabilize itself. Finances improve and so do relationship. There are other personal gains too but the larger canvas needs to be more illuminated so that you know where you are headed.

22 November: Moon's First Quarter in Pisces

You are pulling yourself from the bootstraps. You have indulged yourself in various ways and feel it is time to return to the daily grind. You make superhuman efforts at your job/work/profession and realize that sincere hard work is the need of the hour. You put in long hours and slowly recover all that you had lost. When you look back at the year, the balance sheet is not so favourable and you need to set it right. There are also domestic issues to be resolved and very little time for partying and entertaining. You have a new realization for success and you want it at all costs. There is no point in living in regret and you realize that the way forward is the only recourse.

30 November: Full Moon in Gemini

Your efforts are proactive and you are charged with zeal and energy. People reciprocate your feelings and the world loves a winner. So, suddenly, you find even strangers and mere acquaintances rallying around you. There may even be romance in the air but take your time before you begin to be swayed by all this. You make stupendous progress as you pan out new targets. You are on an achievement spree as success breeds more success. You make money, pay off your creditors, and enter the last month of the year on a high. You have been in a rocking boat for long and now you are riding the rainbow. You have plugged the leaks and hope to put the past behind. You thank the lord for this change in fortune and push ahead towards more achievement. You are living in gratitude and that is a good way to live, says Ganesha.

8 December: Moon's Last Quarter in Virgo

As I have said many times, nothing remains stagnant and change is the only reality. The species that manages to survive is the species that adapts to changing circumstances. You are now oozing confidence and there is travel, romance, marriage/engagement, collaborations, financial gains, festivities, outings, get-togethers, shows, picnics, parties, operas, plays, and family reconciliations. You have everything to gain in this period and so push ahead with some risk-taking. You go turbocharged and hog the limelight. You will do well in any sphere of activity – from politics to corporate affairs the world is suddenly your oyster.

14 December: New Moon in Sagittarius

You are making big plans and spreading out in every direction. You are possessed by a new zeal and are on achievement mode. There could be overseas travel which will prove very beneficial. Those in the media will win kudos for their creativity. You are inspired and are filled with wisdom and new insights. You find new methods of moneymaking and, if self-employed, strike out in several directions with considerable success. If employed, you are in for a promotion and a raise and several perks which take you to the higher echelons of your organization. You are hugely ambitious now and step on the pedal. Friends, family and domestic affairs can wait a while as you proceed ahead in one-dimensional mode.

21 December: Moon's First Quarter in Aries

The work scene is going well and now you find time for the family too. There is a balance now and you are in full throttle. You are confident and determined to reap the whirlwind. You can see clearly that the year is ending well. As you achieve more and make more money, there is a new sense of well-being You share it with the family and they exult in it. There could be a happy occasion like the stork paying a visit. Health will be good.

30 December: Full Moon in Cancer

You realize that a lot has been achieved this year and you make plans for further expansion in the coming year. Your life has been choppy to say the least and you have, sometimes, plumbed the depths of despair and also reached great heights. Luckily, you have also managed to pull out of the pit. You look seriously at new moneymaking opportunities and also decide to spend time with near and dear ones. If you have been neglecting an illness, this is a good time to seek professional help. Alternative therapies could also be a good treatment choice. But it is advisable not to neglect a health issue that has been bothering you for long. In your darker and weaker moments, there will be many insecurities that continue to plague you and you will have to find an escape from these demons. Money and work are fine but what use are they without peace of mind? Despite these nagging thoughts, you sail into 2021 quite happily filled with hope, joy, wonder, anticipation and enthusiasm.

LIBRA

23 September–22 October

Symbol: The Scales
Ruling Planet: Venus
Air-Cardinal-Positive
Libra in a Nutshell
The sign of the Judge, the Ambassador

Ganesha points out the world's most expensive dress – worth $2,000,000, embellished with 2,000 carats of emeralds and 200 carats of diamonds – was shown off by a model at a fashion show held at the National History Museum. In addition, the Kohinoor diamond, which can financially support and sustain the entire world for two-and-a-half days, could well come your way. Libras, beauty is your birthright.

Ganesha says, it is your destiny to deck yourself in style, enjoy the goodies of life, entertain and be amused, and possibly continue with renovation/decoration/investing/buying/selling/mortgaging of land, property, building, shop, office, godown, warehouse, farmhouse.

JUPITER

From 2 December 2019 to 18 December 2020, Jupiter will swish away in your fourth angle, emphasising

a) Buying/selling of house/office/shop/godown/warehouse.

b) Renovating/decorating/altering; adding a room or so.

c) Better health and more cheerful ambience/surroundings.

d) Improving your entire base of operations, and that, says Ganesha, is both extremely important and necessary.

Taking an active interest in all your surroundings, as we Indians say, but that does not mean that you must be nosy and interfere in the affairs of others, though most of us do it in India!

You will say '*Mi casa es tu casa*,' which means, my house is your house, to all friends, as you Librans are exceptionally smooth and gracious hosts. To Adam, Paradise was home. To you home will be paradise. As Edwards has said, 'For a man, his house is his castle.'

The fourth angle is normally associated with the later part of life, old age, retirement, and paradoxically, with a few new activities which do not require sinews and muscles. Major streamlining of the home and house, office and shop, also come under Jupiter in the fourth angle.

You will demonstrate considerable managerial skills and artistic excellence in anything to do with property. Property is a broad, all-inclusive term for your assets. Land and farming are included in property. Finally, Ganesha points out that all matters which have not been resolved will be solved, at least to some extent. But do not try for a showdown, and have a masterful yet pleasing and positive attitude. Modern astrology believes that heaven or hell is in your mind. You may agree or not, it is entirely up to you.

SATURN

Saturn, the planet of limitations and perhaps of suffering and sorrow, duties and responsibilities, spirituality and humanity, will be in your fourth angle from 21 December 2017 to mostly 2020. Strictly speaking the fourth angle stands for house, home, property, family, land, building, godown, warehouse, farming. In short anything to do with parents, in-laws, buildings, gardening and property. Here Saturn will blow hot and cold making things sometimes a bit difficult for you. Farming and mining, elders, guardians, the settling of outstanding matters, improving your environment, saving for the future will be some of the most important matters ever for you. If you are attached to elderly people, do look after them wisely and well. That is my strong advice.

According to Indian astrology the ancient acharyas call the fourth house as *sukha bhava* or *matri bhava* i.e., House of comfort or House of parent, and the following subjects fall under its jurisdiction:

1) Parent or step-parent; mutual relationship between parent and self.
2) Death of natural parent/step-parent/adopting parent; events and developments from it; subsequent impact on the individual and matters/problems of inheritance/succession therefrom and their settlement/solution or quarrels and litigation/violence, etc.

3) Acquisition by purchase, hiring, lease, contract, etc.; of property or premises for own use or by other members of family or by partners, on responsibility or liability of self and the question of relations between landlord and self.

Breeding and maintenance of cattle, cows, buffaloes, horses, donkeys, ponies, camels, goats, sheep, dogs, cats, elephants, hares, pet animals, birds like parrots, poultry farms, pigs, bulls, oxen, deer, antelopes, fish and fisheries; problems and disputes relating thereto, and using it as side or sole means of income.

BLUEPRINT FOR THE ENTIRE YEAR

January: House, home, family.

February: Romance, children, creativity.

March: Work and health improvement measures.

April: Marriage, relationships, contacts, trips, ties and opposition.

May: Loans, funds, health, taxes, accidents, legal matters.

June: Publicity, publishing, fame, religious rites, matters to do with parents and in-laws.

July: Parents, in-laws, work, rewards, family, the effort you do put in.

August: Contacts and group activities, gains and joy.

September: Expenses, health, but also God's grace and success in ventures and fine connections, collaborations.

October: Confidence, success, charm.

November: Finances, family, food, fortune, the four Fs.

December: Communication and contacts at all levels.

Special Notes: From 31 December 2019 to July 2025 Uranus will be in your eighth angle of finance, investment, public trusts and anything to do with money. Ganesha says this applies very specially to you Librans in 2020.

Your happiness quota is 79 per cent.

WEEKLY REVIEW BY PHASES OF THE MOON

10 January: Full Moon in Cancer

It is a rollicking start to the year that Ganesha gives you, and you really can't complain. The new moon in Capricorn is just the ideal launching pad for you, most auspicious for new beginning. Its fine placing in Capricorn stirs you to put in your best. Work will be top priority and you will be setting your sights high. Ruthless ambition will be on display right at the start of the year. Way to go! Money will also be a priority. But don't work and money go together anyway? You will be looking seriously at investments and every means possible with which to augment your income for the grand plans you have in mind. All avenues of revenue will be closely scrutinized and you will look at making improvements wherever you can. At the same time, and quite uncharacteristically, you may not be overtly expressive of your emotions and this may lead to misunderstandings with loved ones. Your focus is on work and money right now and you will have no time for the finer, softer emotions. This can lead to some misunderstandings at home. Don't ruffle too many feathers, but at the same time don't make too many compromises. You have to tread the middle path, carefully and cleverly.

17 January: Moon's Last Quarter in Libra

Quite an unusual year for Librans! You will be on the go with meetings and the reviving of old associations too. You love company and never like being left to yourself; a mood that suits your natural temperament of being with like-minded people. You will be the life of the party and the centre of attraction wherever you go. Librans usually take time in decision-making but this time, you will be all over the place like a battering ram, full of intent and purpose. This is an aggressive start to the year and you will profit from it. You make your intentions very clear right from the beginning and brook no opposition. 'Well begun is half done,' nothing could be truer as far as you are concerned. This is a period of progress and you move headlong from one achievement to another. Again, you are ruffling feathers in the process but you are in no mood to bother about such trifles, unlike your normal self. You mean business, and nothing will stop you from achieving what your goals are.

24 January: New Moon in Capricorn

The busy, determined trend continues. You will continue making progress and will be quite content with whatever you have achieved so far. You will find time to pause awhile and savour the fruits of hard work. Now you will also make time for loved ones and will gently take your foot off the pedal. Librans love the good life, and now is the time to celebrate with loved ones. You will make up for lost time and all will be forgiven. You have set a scorching pace so far. Now you will slow down and look back with some pride. You will spend time with family and will love creating harmony and mending broken fences. All will be well in your relationships – especially personal ones like marriage. Librans are pacifists and do not flourish when misunderstandings and quarrels are rife. So you go out of your way to make peace.

2 February: Moon's First Quarter in Taurus

You are calm and composed this week. You have achieved and are content, you turn to prayer, spirituality and meditation. You get contemplative and look within for more profound answers. You are in a mood of thanksgiving and contentment. On the flip side, there are mounting expenses and other worries. But you have the mental strength and the money to overcome these minor hurdles. You ride the wave with aplomb. You will turn to the higher self now and tap your spiritual reservoir. You realize that there is a power above and will pay obeisance to it. This is a unique phase in which material and spiritual progress will be linked. There is all-round growth at many levels.

9 February: Full Moon in Leo

In this phase in an earth sign money matters will be paramount. The strong theme during this period continues to be finance, property acquisitions, possessions and buying and selling, especially stock and commodities. But you need to protect your rights as well. Don't succumb to get-rich-quick ideas, however tempted you may be. People may ride roughshod over your principles and you should take care to guard against this. More money is definitely enticing but the means is as important as the end. Family matters and personal affairs also take a lot of your time and attention. There is a good chance of being pressurized and exploited and you need to guard against this. Forewarned is being forearmed and Ganesha is warning you not to be tempted by gains or by unscrupulous or dubious means of progress/earnings. Librans know what the good life means and come into their own when there is peace and harmony. Don't sacrifice mental peace for monetary and material gains, however tempting they may be.

19 February: Moon's Last Quarter in Scorpio

This is a grand phase. You feel good about life and about yourself and will be able to follow your heart and your true inclinations. Moonlight and roses, love and storybooks, romance, leisure and pleasure are what this week has in store for you. Financial pressures ease and there is luck in dealing with funds and investments; you may even take risks in speculation and gambling, with some success too. You are empowered in this phase to take both your money and your emotions. But Ganesha warns you that it would be wise not to play too fast and loose with someone you cherish. Keep a handle on your euphoria and don't go overboard. There are pitfalls; tread carefully. As we all know all that glitters is not gold.

23 February: New Moon in Aquarius

You are now back to the nitty-gritty of day-to-day life. It is a drain on your creativity and a grind, but you handle it gracefully. While in this mode, you are also drawn to spiritual pursuits, meditation and the higher truths. You will seek a deeper meaning to life, far higher than the daily toil. There will be the demands of family, work and your own inner life. Ganesha also says that there may be short journeys which are both productive and relaxing. You will get work done and also make contact with people both socially and professionally. You will reach out, display awesome skills and achieve a lot. Very little can hold you back in this phase. You feel energized and empowered and nothing can hold you back. But it will be in your interest to hold your own tongue; why hurt others when you can avoid it?

2 March: Moon's First Quarter in Gemini

This is a period when you learn a lot about life and from life. You realize that though your personal progress is more or less assured, there is a great need for self-restraint in order to get truly ahead. Confrontations and showdowns will be counterproductive, and may even be dangerous, especially in personal relationships. The going will be far from easy and you need to control your temper and strive for emotional balance, and try to meet people halfway. Ganesha warns against betrayals and let-downs. You have to be on your guard and to act slowly and with deliberation, lest you make a risky move and it boomerangs. Treading the middle path gets things done and ensures success, productivity and a pleasant home environment. There will be a tendency to overreact, but this is the time to be rational and sensible. You cannot look at life through tinted glasses any longer. Several matters must be dealt with proactively and at the same time.

9 March: Full Moon in Virgo

This is a taxing, tiring and demanding time of highs and lows. There is probable wish-fulfilment, but also much anxiety. A lot of involvement with your work and professional issues will also include a fair amount of socializing and running around. While there is much love in your personal and family life, there could be some animosity too; you will be hated and loved in equal measure. Your introspective and detached tendencies will, quite naturally be activated. It is a rigorous and taxing phase in which you may have to take a back seat temporarily. But it is not all bad. There is fun and pleasure too. Maybe Ganesha is just testing your mettle in this really paradoxical week with pulls from several directions. You will be headed in different directions and only time will tell you which is right.

16 March: Moon's Last Quarter in Sagittarius

You pass all Ganesha's tests with flying colours. You pull out all the stops at work in terms of both fresh ideas and their execution. At home and in the area of love too you are generous. But you are overextending yourself and will need to take care of yourself both literally and figuratively. Look after your health. There will be a strong emphasis on social service, larger issues, productivity and work, which you will handle with flair. You have great social skills and charm and you will manage to keep people of all kinds at ease. In the process, you will also achieve your goals with little or no acrimony or hard feelings. It is a good time for loans and funds and your relationships at work; everyone at the office will be pleasant and productive. Despite the various pressures you will sail through thankfully and achieve a lot.

24 March: New Moon in Aries

Your vision of your future is clear. You work hard, making all possible efforts to convert your dreams and hopes into reality. You will try out many new avenues of work, you will also be aware of the great need to deal with financial issues.

There is much buying and selling ahead and also the signing of lease documents, contracts, instruments of negotiation, promissory notes and such. Fashion and food will also grab your attention. This is a period of better health and better prospects. You have been striving for some time to achieve this and now, finally, it is within your grasp. There is a distinct upward momentum in your affairs.

1 April: Moon's First Quarter in Cancer

The scope of your activities, especially professional ones, will narrow. This phase is all about money and money matters. Income, assets and all sorts of monetary gains are your major pursuits. The desire to have a larger income overshadows all your other considerations and activities. Your working life will hover around business issues, acquisitions, capital, funds and so on. Yes, this is a good time to launch a project, finish pending work, take on new assignments. Lending/borrowing/investing/buying/selling/shopping will all continue to be very important. You are motivated not by greed but by the practical common sense that has realized that material success is also necessary for true peace of mind. You need to keep the family happy and there are mounting expenses to reckon with. Money does sweeten life, and who doesn't want a sweet life?

8 April: Full Moon in Libra

Life has taught you, in recent times, to assign realistic goals and priorities. Once again, the focus is on the material plane. You are looking at providing comfort, security and protection for both yourself and your loved ones. Many issues need to be resolved. Real estate property, renovation and family matters are uppermost in your mind. You also need to get your way without hurting others and that is a tightrope walk. Family matters do get resolved, but with the usual strife and turmoil. There is no getting away from domestic bickering, whatever you may do. Sometimes, you feel as if you are being taken for granted and it's difficult to conceal these emotions as no one likes to be undervalued, especially by loved ones. Don't allow this feeling to grow. Nip it in the bud and get on with your work as though all is well. It is the only way to combat domestic strife. Without being rude, pretend that all is well and go ahead.

14 April: Moon's Last Quarter in Capricorn

This is a very good period with the full moon in your own sign. This interesting and reasonably profitable phase is all about money and honey (my favourite phrase). The highlight is personal and shared finances. Love, passion, romance, partnerships and trade also flourish. Ganesha says that you have a very hectic time ahead and your plate will be full of professional and emotional demands. But you are determined to enjoy it all and give your very best to the situation. I assure you that in the long haul this will pay dividends. There may also be a short journey in the offing and some legal issues or law courts to deal with, as there may be settlements and compromises to arrive at. You will be in the thick of negotiations of various kinds. Yet, what matters most will be the feelings of sharing, togetherness, bonding and warmth. You will aim for harmony in all aspects of your life and will achieve it. There will be parties, old associates dropping in, and a lot of wining and dining.

23 April: New Moon in Taurus

You change tack. Pretty dramatically this week you will also have more time to pursue hobbies and interests that are close to your heart. Here, love needs to be mentioned in particular. This is where you register your greatest and most pleasing gains. Loved ones, your spouse/partner in particular, will get special attention. There may be more than one person who falls in the ambit of your love interests. Thanks to this mood, there is a greater joy and it is more enjoyable too. You are in great form. There is money in hand and you are emotionally happy. You are fun to be with and therefore immensely popular. Again you are the life of the party!

30 April: Moon's First Quarter in Leo

Watch out for new developments. You will be looking at true growth, comprising your own assets and your larger role in the community. You will look inwards at your own limitations and will also spend time with welfare activities and charities. You move positively from the worldly affairs that occupied you till recently to more self-analysis and introspection. Your main criterion is personal growth and you will do all that you can to progress in the right direction. Ganesha gives you blessings. You look at the larger picture and look at growth in several areas of your life.

7 May: Full Moon in Scorpio

The highlight of the week is a true and genuine reaching out to people. This week sets the trend for a sudden and pleasing shift of interests. Communications – whether phone calls, the media, or just dealing with correspondence, building up fresh contacts – will be the highlight of this period. You are satisfied with concrete gains and there will be pleasing fellowship with those you meet, especially with other Librans. You excel and triumph in good intra- and interpersonal relationships. You love the cordial interactions with friends, relatives, neighbours, colleagues and co-workers. You may even reach out in friendship to complete strangers! The year has almost reached the halfway mark and you have been living at full throttle.

14 May: Moon's Last Quarter in Aquarius

This will be a great week. With your money worries and issues resolved, you turn to the arts, theatres, music, fun, and enjoyment at parties, find occasions for happy times with children and pursuing your own interests and hobbies. Leisure is at the forefront; you are not slogging away. You are also more resolute in all your domestic affairs and make some important decisions now. You have the resources and style to make a success of anything you enter into, even if it is falling in love. But Ganesha warns you against complacency. When the going is easy, it is even easier to get too sure of yourself. This can lead to crucial errors of judgement. Don't be impatient or resentful or inconsiderate in your dealings. Sometimes, you may make heavy or unrealistic demands on others, which may not be realized, and could cause sorrow. Ganesha bids you guard against this. Look before you leap.

22 May: New Moon in Gemini

This is not the phase of flight of fantasies; it is certainly not the phase for light romance. You focus more on the physical. You plunge headlong into love, passion, the pleasures of sex, and yet remain firmly entrenched in the more pragmatic pursuits of funds and loans, legacies and money matters.

This is a very interesting month. You will also be captivated by meditation, and religious and spiritual practices. You will plunge into this world and the next. This is a phase of immense possibilities. Remember, this is a Gemini phase and so has to be intense and passionate and nothing holds you back.

30 May: Moon's First Quarter in Virgo

There is a natural and logical progression from last week. But there is a chance here – you will seek spiritual solace, metaphysical truths and deeper insight into life. After the frantic pursuits of the previous week, the mood is sombre, even meditative. Work issues will have to be resolved during this period of introspection. You are interested in genuine and strong bonding; the pressure of work will create an equally strong contrary pull. Try to be flexible and keep an open mind. Don't burn the candle at both ends as you will be worn out, restless and pulled in different directions. By a strange quirk of fate, you will find yourself drawn strongly to seas, water sources, lakes and rivers and places of worship situated near water. There are also strong indications of foreign collaboration. Go for it! You won't sink, for sure.

5 June: Full Moon in Sagittarius

You have somewhat lost track of your priorities or perhaps focus, with all the thinking and introspection of recent times, and it is now necessary to get back to what you love best – people and your interactions with them. You will be bonding with family like never before. They will be your strength, solace, comfort and, above all, your inspiration to get ahead in life. The new fool moon indicates the trend for the coming month and the focus will be on the family. You turn back to your roots. Loved ones and the family take centre stage and you are more rooted in domestic matters. On the career front, you are not headed in any direction, but it is also a good time to take a step back and look at life more holistically. Life can never be all about work, can it?

13 June: Moon's Last Quarter in Pisces

Your family will be the centre of attention in every way. But it may not all be hunky-dory; there will be negative trends too. You will continue working hard but are drawn into family and property matters, house and home and renovations of all kinds. Librans are great at diplomacy and your special skills will be called upon to resolve differences and create a pleasant and harmonious atmosphere between differing and diverse groups. Ganesha says that family and work are the twin themes that will require probably twice as much involvement and effort. But you love all this, and it is not a drain on your temperament, and, in the end, you do marvellously well. Librans are non-confrontationist and it goes against their grain not to try to mend broken fences.

21 June: New Moon in Cancer

You carry on and make the most of all your powers and skills. It is an action-packed time. The focus is on research, discoveries, inventions and new fields of study. There will also be meetings and conferences, interviews and committees. You will be on the move, reaching out in every conceivable way. A journey may also prove rewarding. Travel for both business and pleasure is almost definitely foretold and it will be productive, lucrative and rewarding – both financially and intellectually. You will be enriched in several aspects of your life now and will certainly make the best possible use of all that Ganesha sends you. To paraphrase Shakespeare, the tide, if taken at the flood, leads to fortune. Make the most of this period and you won't repent.

28 June: Moon's First Quarter in Libra

You need to curb your ego and get more tactful and diplomatic if you want to relate better with people, which is actually the need of the hour. This is a welcome realization. And it is not difficult for Librans as they are committed, tactful and diplomatic always: it is their second nature! Your sense of self-image intensifies and diversifies to include not only how you see yourself but also how others see you. While reviewing both your public and personal image and persona it is also time to weigh, evaluate and what you have achieved. You may be worth your weight but there is always room for improvement. Please don't get complacent, says Ganesha. You will work on yourself. Your physique, wardrobe, manners, make-up, behaviour, every aspect of your life, will be reviewed and improved upon. It is your advantage as you present a fresh and new face to the world. You want to be a new person and Ganesha backs you to the hilt.

5 July: Full Moon in Capricorn

You gain in credibility, popularity and authority. People look up to you. Creative pursuits, be it the cinema, television, the performing arts, every aspect of the media, hobbies, even speculation and playing the market, will be indulged in. You have an open frame of mind leading to greater ingenuity as well as better, brighter ideas. Bonds and ties of love will give you knew focus. You will be putting a great deal into a new relationship, possibly even more than you are getting from it. Success will come to you easily. There will be professional and personal recognition as a result of your soul-searching. Be more flexible and savour the deeper joys. There will be plenty to be happy about both at home and on the work fronts. You are full of confidence; the new you is working, and how!

12 July: Moon's Last Quarter in Gemini

As a result of your involvement with family and domesticity, your handling of people is marvellous. Anyway, as I have always said, Librans have a genuine fondness for people, among the entire human race. You have reached a point in your personal growth where there is no room for hurt, acrimony, false expectations or acquisitions in all your interactions. Ganesha says that this has also been achieved in the professional sphere. Attachments and ties continue to be important and are constantly strengthened and reinforced by you on both personal and professional fronts. But all this is to be expected. There is success at the workplace and in relationships and you develop emotional poise. You experience the joys of love and bonding and are really happy with life. The gains you make will be long-lasting and more pleasing too because they will be profound and deep-rooted. Others will also wish you well and what greater joy can there be for Librans? Ganesha empowers you.

20 July: New Moon in Cancer

This week is a period of quality interaction. There is gain at all levels; you make money and also powerful emotional bonds. You know that being adjustable and adaptable makes for greater happiness, peace and contentment. Ultimately, that's what we all desire. You are more relaxed and responsive to others, and there are gains in the offing. This phase brings home in a fresh new way the methods of getting the most out of life, of using time and resources to your advantage and, in turn, giving the best of yourself. You stand on solid ground and there is no dilly-dallying. You make sustained progress, and impressive results.

27 July: Moon's First Quarter in Virgo

Money and the people in your life, though not necessarily in that order, will be the two main themes in this period. You will reach out to new and old friends and acquaintances and make good profits from business as well. You will be moving at great speed in a bid to improve both these areas of your life. But Ganesha warns against too much socializing and also mixing business with pleasure. You may just get bogged down in the professional or personal spheres and could find yourself losing out. It may get too risky and out of hand. You will take care of finances and career, and be friendly and sociable too. Hold your horses on the pleasure front. Though I've said already, there are good tidings, says Ganesha, and there will be enhancement of work and pleasure coming to you soon.

2 August: Full Moon in Aquarius

Ganesha makes this phase in Scorpio truly challenging and have strange and tough week. You probably feel that you have been pursuing the wrong goals. The focus will be on loans and funds and, strangely, on passion and sex. There may have been and also be some neuroses, anxiety, minor ailments and an unsettled feeling to contend with. You may turn to prayer and meditation. This is testing time and you will tap into the spiritual nooks and crannies of your being, and your soul for answers. Librans are lovers of the good life but looking deeply at the spiritual aspects of life will help you regain a sense of peace and calm within you which is equally important to you. You will seek serenity over material gain as it will be far more valuable at this juncture of your life. A lot has been happening and much too soon. You need to take stock of life and to slow down.

11 August: Moon's Last Quarter in Taurus

Your good spirits will be restored. There will be success with people, and you want to have fun and enjoy the limelight. You seek out good company, good friends, good food and all the good things of life. This is what I mentioned earlier. Being sociable, amiable and outgoing, you will be partying and socializing. Ganesha has given you charisma and charm, even good looks and a deceptively seductive manner. You use it in all your interactions with disarming effect. You are caught up at several levels of social life – both meeting people and even renewing old acquaintances and friendships. The entire family will draw closer, and surround you with warmth. Suddenly, even distant relatives will get in touch. Ganesha says that this is the time to ask for favours, to indulge in social and family activities. There will be joyous times. Yet Ganesha also warns against excessive socializing, which may lead to either offending your well-wishers or neglecting those dear to you. The unique essence of the week will be a coming together of different people, making you feel happy from the bottom of your heart. You will be the catalyst for a sort of communal harmony.

19 August: New Moon in Leo

Money and the people in your life will both be in sharp focus this quarter. You will look at new avenues of business and sources of income. Ganesha warns against too much socializing and mixing business with pleasure. This may lead to situations you don't want to get into and are better off without. You are friendly and sociable and also keen to get on with the overhauling of your both career and income. Leasing, rentals, business deals, taxes and funding will be part of the theme this week. There will be a grand fusion and enhancement of work and pleasure, thanks, once again, to Ganesha's generosity. But, when all is said and done, it is finances which will guide you by the collar.

25 August: Moon's First Quarter in Sagittarius

Your life is moving at a certain pace and in the right direction, and you will be filled with a sense of satisfaction. Ganesha sends you your due rewards in several ways. This is a joyous phase filled with good tidings. There is a welcome twist too with travel, journeys for fun or for work, partnerships and ties, whether new or old, romantic ties and attachments, even greater joy in matrimony and other bonds. There is a change in the momentum with new interests, new pursuits and a new slant on life, powering you on. You are taking off on a whole new journey and enjoying it too. The journey of life certainly has fewer potholes and roadblocks, right now.

2 September: Full Moon in Pisces

This is the time for the expansion and extension of your mental horizons. New inclinations and predilections, a new focus, are even more likely to emerge than they were last week. You move towards spirituality and the higher issues of life and are concerned with justice, law and order and the higher consciousness. More than just acquiring knowledge, it will be a widening of the vistas of your mind that interests you. Travel, publicity, visits, interviews, meets, conferences, collaborations and networking (including even in-laws, kin, and distant relatives) within and outside the family, will add to the quality of life. Greater intensity and depth are felt in all your actions and interactions. You live intensely and with a definite purpose. You are raring to go. You breathe fire and are not your normal shy, reserved, slightly introverted self, despite your undoubted charm.

10 September: Moon's Last Quarter in Gemini

At one level, you are at the crossroads. You need to make strong decisions. You don't want your success/popularity, good interactions to slip and falter. It is also a great time to help the community at large, to share resources, give charity or monetary help. You work with purpose and want to get your act together professionally in the larger social context as well as within your immediate social circle. Money will also be an important consideration, and better planning and effort will be required There is a need also to streamline relationships with colleagues and subordinates as well as superiors at the office. You seem to have slipped into the easy-going approach and need to shake yourself out of it. Don't go to extremes. Stick to moderation and all will be well. Remember, balance is your hallmark.

17 September: New Moon in Virgo

You will look at changing your lifestyle and priorities. You need to get your act together and need to do some hard rethinking. Ganesha tells you to look deep within yourself. You have had too much of a social life, been a party animal, and your expenses are also mounting. You need to guard against arousing animosity in others as well. People get jealous of you. You think and act big and are breaking new ground in a number of spheres, but don't forget that even ordinary ties are important and need to be nourished. Take the necessary precautions and you are in line for the four Gs: gains, glory, good times and genuine companions. What more does one need?

24 September: Moon's First Quarter in Capricorn

This phase in your own sign brings many unusual aspects into the light of day (or rather, month). The year is slowly coming to a close and it is a good time for reflection. You started off with ambition and grand plans on the work front and then saw a platter full of goodies coming to you. There have been twists and turn ranging from strange esoteric pursuits, to flights of fancy, the supera-natural and even the supra-natural, interest in spirits, life-after-death, and occult phenomena. But back to the drawing board now and it is time for investments, finances (loans, funds, buying, selling) and raising capital. The material plane keeps you grounded and Ganesha says that it is for your own good. Charity begins at home!

2 October: Full Moon in Aries

You have put in a lot in terms of ideas, effort and commitment and this is the time for reaping the harvest. You like the sweet sound of good money in the bank and the social standing and perquisites that come in the form of pleasing symbols of success. You enjoy it all without a second thought, and why not? They bring joy to you and your family. You look back on the year and even seek to expand on the good fortune coming to you from time well spent. The health of an elder in the family can cause grave concern, but all will be well, and it is a time of contentment. You have earned it, and you know it! But this is also a period when you refuse to rest on your laurels and are constantly looking at ways of getting ahead.

10 October: Moon's Last Quarter in Cancer

You are in an introspection mode. You even look at parapsychology and/or psychic insights and ability. Nursing, healing, welfare interests, medical care, healing minds and bodies, charities will take your time and energy, and quite happily too. You have many desires to be fulfilled and are filled with a new mindset of inquiry. The full moon phase brings a sense of completion and direction to the growth of the past several weeks. Sometimes there is a low phase before the birth month phase. Right now Ganesha gives you a time of calm, introspection, thought. There is a good chance that you will also be involved in trade and travel. Another bustling and hectic period is on hand.

16 October: New Moon in Libra

You are pressured by will commitments to work and family. Both will need hard work and effort. There will also be investments and outlays, both financial and with time. You will have a lot of coping to do as they are all linked. It can be a heavy burden, so guard against overdoing it. But, whatever you do now, the results that follow will be pleasant. I must also tell you now that this is a special time and is filled with favours coming your way. It will be almost ideal for getting things done. You will reap the fruits of all your efforts which will be tangible now. No more guessing and hoping for the best. You will be holding the results in your hands and enjoying the sensation.

23 October: Moon's First Quarter in Aquarius

You are enriched and Ganesha's blessings are with you. Happy times are finally here and you are certainly on top of the world. Go for whatever you need but remember the saying: 'There's no such thing as a free lunch.' But don't let this deter you. Take your chances and plan for the future. Ganesha also tells you to read the fine print. There could be hidden clauses that could be less than favourable in the long run; watch out for deceit. You are now on the go, keen and active, no longer introspective and withdrawn like you were in the recent past. You will be filled with positive energy I don't have to say more; the results will speak for themselves.

31 October: Full Moon in Taurus

It is time for Ganesha to reward you with gifts. Your life abounds with genuine love, romance and laughter. You are not slogging away as you were at the beginning of the year. You seem reasonably well settled and it is the time for a little bit of fun and frolic. There is relief, respite and relaxation and you will revel in it. Librans are ruled by Venus and love the good life. As I pointed out last week. Your family life and personal interactions will also get a boost as you are not anxious and driven by ambition now. The trend is pleasing since you are now able to enjoy life, laughter, love, and all the good things that life has to offer. You are in an enviable phase, and thank Ganesha for it!

8 November: Moon's Last Quarter in Leo

You are enthusiastic and energized with all that is happening in your life right now. You will be a human dynamo, a powerhouse of energy, ready to attain targets you've only been hoping to achieve. You make glorious plans for the future leading to great success and joy. There is new zest in your attitude to life itself, and you work exceptionally hard. You will achieve success in all spheres of life and will ride the wave. The world is your oyster, right now.

15 November: New Moon in Scorpio

There is free time and also a strong inclination to indulge in all kinds of mental activity. It will be back to mind games for you Librans, but of a very different sort. Once again, you look for fresh avenues of self-expression and of exploring new areas at both knowledge and experience. The family and work angles are both energized but there is a certain restlessness that might prove dangerous if it is not channelized properly. Despite all this, you do make sure that you manage all your commitments to the people who matter in your life. Ganesha tells you to convert your enemies into friends and boost your own poise and self-confidence. You also want to beautify your home and office and will make some tasteful and stylish purchases. Expenses will mount but will be well worth it – always so for Librans, who love beauty and aesthetic surroundings.

22 November: Moon's First Quarter in Pisces

The trends are encouraging as the year draws to its end and you have had material rewards. Now you reach out for greater warmth in relationships and are appreciated, valued und cherished. Family life will be on a high and your children will give great joy. There is a good chance of an engagement or marriage happening in this period. It could be either yours (if applicable) or that of someone dear to you. Physical activity, sports, fitness and exercise also stir your imagination. You look at more imaginative work rather than coping mechanically and almost mindlessly with life. You are in an adventurous mood and would like to try out new things. Nothing ventured, nothing gained.

30 November: Full Moon in Gemini

The year may be approaching its end, but your energy remains undiminished. You are on the go all the time and are filled with a sense of fulfilment and self-realization. Family and marital bonds are honoured with deep commitment and genuine caring. You have introspected a lot and have arrived at this point in your life after a great deal of soul-searching. As it stands, nothing seems unattainable, with the kind of mindset and attitude you have created within you. You'll be full of energy and activity, working at a lively pace, getting things done and enjoying every little thing you do! Expenses continue to mount but you are not complaining, as you are confident you can cope.

8 December: Moon's Last Quarter in Virgo

The tide changes here. Once again, from all the gusto and go, you get meditative. You look at the spiritual and the meditative areas with both sincerity and much commitment. Life's meaning and, strangely enough, law and the social order, research, philosophical pursuits and even questions of justice keep you busy through the remaining weeks of 2020. All in all, you will now experience an interestingly different week. During this time you may find your dormant energies and spiritual powers either awakening or getting stronger. You will still mesh beautifully with others (relationships are always the forte of Libran) and make gains in other spheres of life. An exciting week for work too. Your ideas and ingenuity will set the stage for stupendous achievements.

14 December: New Moon in Sagittarius

Your confidence and charisma – the two great Cs – will be at an all-time high. They will be reflected in your interaction, and your attitude to friends, colleagues and family. Having achieved your targets, you look at the lighter, more pleasant side of life. You decide to have fun, relax, let your hair down. You dabble in the creative arts and make more contacts. Expression is the key word here and you also go all out to reach out to others. Ganesha decrees that it is truly people time. The year in ending, the winter has set in, and you look back with satisfaction. You also look ahead with faith, confidence and hope. Your life is filled with an assortment of activities and you are enjoying them all.

21 December: Moon's First Quarter in Aries

You consciously go slow but can't escape the intensity of the month. Finance and family will be well looked after, but there may also be a new love interest that takes a lot of your time and energy. Don't overstep the line and hurt loved ones in the process. Tread softly, says Ganesha. It may just be a passing fancy and overindulgence may cost you dear. Don't rock the boat where family harmony is concerned. You will have visitors and a lot of merrymaking, you will be the force behind the social whirligig. Enjoy!

30 December: Full Moon in Cancer

You are filled with self-belief and hope for the future, and you look forward to 2021. You make firm resolves to go all out on the career and money fronts. You will make steady material progress and be enriched in the mind and spirit too. You may sometimes feel inhibited, but it is all in the mind and can be overcome. There is no need to get too serious. You are rooted and firmly entrenched in terms of self-belief and have a solid base from which you can leapfrog into many new ventures. You start this new period with vigour and optimism and can make spectacular achievements. You have had an unusual year, and it ends well, filled with great promise for future times! Ganesha is with you all the way.

SCORPIO

23 October–22 November

Symbol: The Scorpion
Ruling Planet: Pluto
Water-Fixed-Negative
The sign of the Mystic, the Investigator

In the beginning, we have said that yours is the sign of the mystic. We Indians can talk about void or *shoonya*. This is how I explain void/shoonya.

You Scorpios have the range and the power to understand what shoonya is in this one line: 'Void/shoonya is an immense unimaginable space of nothingness.' This is perhaps the greatest compliment I can pay to you.

JUPITER

Ganesha says that from 2 December 2019 to 18 December 2020, Jupiter – the planet of great good fortune and mighty achievements – will be moving in your third angle. It promises tremendous potential, which can and must, be converted into actual performance. You Scorpios have a chance to show the world just how good and great you are. It is time to come into your own. Connectivity, collectivity, consciousness make the three Cs. The fourth C will be contracts. If you learn to be good at it, the years ahead will hum and glow with promise and achievement. Ganesha says, you Scorpios are achievers and love perfection; therefore, it should serve as a great motivating factor for you.

How come I have singled out communication for you? Jupiter, I said, will zoom in your third angle from 2 December 2019 to 18 December 2020. Jupiter stands for good luck, success and expansion.

The additional goodies of Jupiter will be courage and valour, physical fitness, hobbies, talent, education, good qualities, siblings, longevity of parents, tolerance, capability, quality and nature of food, selfishness, sports, fights, refuge, trading, dreams, sorrow, stability of mind, neighbourhood, near relations, friends, army, inheritance, ornaments, cleverness and short journeys. Wow! What a list!

The additional highlights are:

- the right time to take a crash course in matters which interest you, develop self-expression, cultivate opinions;
- play chess or bridge, enter quiz shows, Sudoku contests – in short, all mental games;
- learn to get along with relatives and neighbours;
- try not to have mental strain, because this is where you are weak and therefore vulnerable; be ready to listen to others, though I know you are able and discriminating;
- enrich your knowledge.

Let me quote because major changes are happening, with dire consequences, on our planet Earth. Jupiter in the third angle shows research, intelligence and the thrust to help people realize that we are a family of man.

Ganesha says, Jupiter in your third angle could help in shrinking the size of the microelectronics packed into silicon chips. It could help enhance memory and processing talks. More accurate weather, climate and geological predictions could be made. Perhaps even artificial intelligence could be the final gift of Jupiter in the third angle. All this could be the brainchild or handiwork of Scorpios.

Let me summarize what the third angle is all about. Mainly, it is about outlets and/or media of expression and ideas. Trips and ties form an integral part of it. News, views, messages through faxes, mobile and the latest technology are the modern ways of achieving this. The writing of books, pamphlets, flyers and mental gymnastics in games such as chess and bridge are good illustrations of it. Every salesman knows that creative listening is a pivotal part of selling and marketing, and advertising. The third angle has much to do with all of it. Improving the vistas of your knowledge and information through books, trade, travel and interaction with people also comes under the sway and domain of Jupiter in your third angle. Jupiter also has reference, very specially, to brothers and sisters, relatives and neighbours.

As a former professor of English, I have a theory about how the word 'neighbour' came about. It came from the neigh or cry of a horse. The cry or neigh of a horse can be heard from a distance. Therefore, the cry or neigh could be heard in the neighbourhood. This explains how the word 'neighbour' came about. I wonder how far I'm right! A neighbour is the person living next door or near us. I could be wrong about my interpretation of the world 'neighbour', or I could be right. It is up to you to take it or leave it.

SATURN

Saturn will zoom in your third angle from 21 December 2017 to around 2020 and will be important for trips, communication, computers, correspondence, contacts, signing of important deeds, papers and documents. It is a good time to appear for a test/competition/interview. The birth of a child is also possible, or you will have joy through your children or grandchildren. Most importantly, you will have the confidence so necessary for success. Saturn will help you to expand and enhance your image in the public eye, and film-makers will be in fine fettle. Saturn, in short, favours creativity, partnerships, productivity.

According to Vedic astrology, the third angle has to do with courage and valour, physical fitness, hobbies, talent, education, good qualities, siblings, longevity of parents, tolerance, capability, quality and nature of food, selfishness, sports, fights, refuge, trading, the army, dreams, sorrows, stability of mind, neighbourhood, near relations, friends, inheritance, ornaments, cleverness and short journeys. The third angle is also reaching out to people and places by all media of transport and publicity, namely, TV, posters, pamphlets, mobile, telex, fax, Bluetooth technology, gizmos, even by bus, car, plane, helicopter and so on. It is also about relationships, improving the vistas of your mind, the marriage of minds, so to say! It is bonding on the physical and mental level, on the plane of ideas! Contracts and deeds will be signed. Partnerships will be essential to progress and prosperity. In short, communication is the key to it all.

MARS

Mars is the mover and shaker of all your actions. Mars motivates you to deliver the goods. The period from 19 November 2019 to 2 January 2020 marks a landmark in your life. It means action time. That from 16 February to 30 March is for wish-fulfilment and that means practically everything. From 26 June 2020 to 6 January 2021 is a straight run of practically everything you wish for. It is possible I may be excited and praise you a bit too much. But the hard and open fact remains that in these six months you could well be a superman and a mighty hero. Use it wisely and well, says Ganesha.

BLUEPRINT FOR THE ENTIRE YEAR

January: You will begin on a positive, winning streak, and journeys, ceremonies, good relationships should be the happy events.

February: Changes on the work and personal frontiers will start and they must be tackled with tact and skill.

March: Socializing and friendship and gains, and a wish-fulfilment.

April: Expenses, secret deals, looking after the sick and the needy; also, you must safeguard your health.

May: A progressive, go-ahead month as pointed out in the preceding forecasts for the planets.

June: Finances, food, family, contracts and comforts.

July: Meditation, the domestic scene, renovation and decoration, excellent rapport with people; travel and communication will be highlighted.

August: Home, house, family, immigration, buying/selling/renovation; a continuation of July.

September: You're on top of any situation; children, hobbies and creativity are emphasized.

October: Job, health, pets, projects, colleagues and your relationship with subordinates and servants.

November: Love/hate, cooperation/competition, collaboration/separation, trips and ties, signing of documents and drafts.

December: Loans, funds, capital formation, buying/selling; do take care of your health and lowered vitality.

Special Note: From 31 December 2019 to July 2025, Uranus – the planet of evolution, revolution, inspiration, new ideas, technical perfection, brain power – remains in your seventh angle. But very specially in 2020, sudden partnerships, collaborations, marriage, affairs, creative juices, new hobbies will be of paramount importance. For whatever it is worth, my advice is go ahead full speed.

Your happiness quota is 83 per cent.

WEEKLY REVIEW BY PHASES OF THE MOON

10 January: Full Moon in Cancer

This is the time for action and you are never one to run away from the good fight. In fact Scorpios love hard work, and the desire for recognition in the world is also deeply embedded in them. You are full of zest and make marked progress with determined effort. Power, prestige, perks, pelf and property are all yours for the asking. You are ruthless and merciless at the start of the year and nothing has the gumption to even get in your way. You bulldoze your way past all roadblock. You are an achiever by any account. No wonder, all the Ps come to you. The year starts well. You long for love and bonding, but achievement comes at a price and you need to choose to work hard, which will reward you right now, over love, in which you believe and will come to you later. You are driven by ambition and will enter successful collaborations. You could be quite ruthless here to, in the larger interests.

17 January: Moon's Last Quarter in Libra

You continue with gusto; in fact, you pick up more speed and move like a rejuvenated Brett Lee. You mean business and get things done with frantic speed and efficiency. Property matter, inheritance, new acquisitions and high-end real-estate deals come into sharp focus. You are fiery and brook no opposition. There is travel and collaborations, and many new vistas are reached in your professional life. Your personal life will take second place and wait patiently in the wings. There is enough time for them after you achieve what you set out to do.

24 January: New Moon in Capricorn

You finally make room in your life for emotions and feelings. Your first needs are money, recognition and a position of control, and once they are in place, you look for love. All your feelings are neatly compartmentalized. The family comes into play here. There is love and bonding. You try to include them in your plans so that they understand you better; it is also so much easier to trust family and include them in all your new schemes rather than put your trust in strangers. There may be outings with relatives, family and dear ones; there will certainly be happy times spent in beautiful surroundings. Your plans are going well and it is time to go soft on the pedal. Enjoy the bonding under the full moon!

2 February: Moon's First Quarter in Taurus

There is a lull after the storm. You need to communicate with people and slow down a bit. There are many new ideas to grapple with and you need to discuss all this. There is a chance of new and meaningful relationships developing. There is closer and more intimate bonding as you want to communicate your feelings, grand plans and work ethic. There is travel thrown in and you meet people from many different walks of life. There is a lot of social intercourse and you are happy that it is all working out well for you – personally, professionally and socially.

9 February: Full Moon in Leo

Somehow, all at once, this is the phase when everything gets more hectic. There will be skyrocketing expenses and new sources of income too. You go on a spending spree and buy the best brands. Money is coming from all your ventures, and so you are not unduly bothered. Money wields its own power and you love the feeling. There will be family outings, meeting up with old friends, visits to sanctuaries and parks and many fun times. The year has begun well and you are happy to enjoy it. Your collaborations too are working out, your investments are giving dividends, and your confidence is sky high. You feel that you are on the right track and feel like plunging into the world of high finance even more. There is romance too. Don't sow your oats indiscriminately – is that the sound advice always. Right now, it comes from Ganesha.

19 February: Moon's Last Quarter in Scorpio

There is a lot of waste and extravagance that you have to guard against. As you know, a penny saved is a penny earned. So you need to rein in your expenses. There will be other preoccupations too as you will also have to look into domestic affairs and little details like children's education, parents'/in-laws' health, schooling and the other mundane details and demands of everyday life. Ganesha believes that you will manage to do it all, despite your grand plans. You understand fully that life is all about managing the details too, and there is no getting away from it. Success lies in micromanagement. Be tactful and diplomatic in your ways. Try to gain a little serenity to help you cope with life's passages, and to handle people gently too.

23 February: New Moon in Aquarius

You are reaching out in a big way, in all directions, to all you meet. There is expansion not only in your work but also in your consciousness. You bow down before a higher power and are drawn deeply towards spiritualism, philosophy, moral and social issues, and even religious rites. There will be meetings with old acquaintances and you enjoy happy times with them. Friends mean a lot to you and you realize, in your quieter moments, that life is not all about achievement and money and fame. When the chips are down, it is your friends you can fall back upon and they will bail you out without conditions. This realization spurs you on to make the most of meeting up with old associates and the reunion will be soul-satisfying.

2 March: Moon's First Quarter in Gemini

The new development in your life makes you very emotional and sentimental. Spiritualism, prayer, tantra and mantra, a lot of meditation and contemplation, the higher values and social questions of law, order, balance and justice will become a part of your psyche. Your realities get subjective and you look at all-round growth. There are strong shifts away from the worldly plane and the new values you are toying with get deeply ingrained in your personality and life, leading to very intense bonding. Love means a lot to you, and you feel you may have betrayed someone and regret it immensely. But there is no use crying over spilt milk and you have to move on. The point is to learn from your mistakes and not repeat them. You experience love at this time too but with the heart, and it is more lasting.

9 March: Full Moon in Virgo

You are communicating with both favour and fire. You meet up with new collaborators and discuss grand plans. There are many expenses and you are a bit confused: should you move ahead full steam or slow down a bit and smell the roses. Expenses will grow almost unmanageably and there is no respite from them. You feel that you are at your wit's end but Ganesha sends down hope. There is enormous potential for growth and your spiritual interests help to calm the mind. You face many obstacles and will need to find a balance between the demands of your creativity and hard work. You visit spiritual masters and imbibe as much as you can from them. There may also be rituals and other religious ceremonies or occasions to enable you to find peace. This is a move in the right direction, assures Ganesha.

16 March: Moon's Last Quarter in Sagittarius

You are not one to be knocked down easily by life's blows. You are tough and get back on track fairly quickly and well. Scorpio isn't called one of the most powerful signs of the zodiac for nothing. The office and home need your attention along with many domestic issues. The health of family members and even pets will need looking into and you get down to handling it all. But you will definitely be pulled in many directions. Due to all this, your own health may suffer too; you need to take the necessary precaution. But you are well armed in terms of attitude and approach and sail through well, watched over by Ganesha.

24 March: New Moon in Aries

New opportunities keep knocking at your door. There is more work, and more money is to be made, along with journeys, legal matters and lawsuits to keep you busy and involved. There will be heavy expenses to meet once again, but you find the strength and finances to cope and that too with great dignity. You realize that worries and troubles are bound to be there and that life has its thorns. The whole point is to manage them with both strength and determination which Ganesha provides you at this moment. There will be many demands from several quarters and you are truly stretched. There is enormous tension, but you somehow find the resources to manage it all.

1 April: Moon's First Quarter in Cancer

The new moon highlights several aspects in your life. You learn a lot from all your recent tribulations, and worries, which streamlines your life on all fronts. You cut down on extravagance and unnecessary spending and realize that, with the right attitude and some fine-tuning, you can cope well. You learn to be positive and will introspect on why and how all this is happening. There are many pinpricks and you must cope, as there is no choice. You can't sink now. So you gather close friends and family and share the issues facing you and enlist support which is very forthcoming. You win them all over so that you stand united now as a team of force to be reckoned with. With this approach and mindset, your obstacles also get obliterated.

8 April: Full Moon in Libra

All the bonding experienced over the past two weeks gets you very close to family and it is a very emotional period. The problems are slowly working themselves out and the family is taking the load off your chest. All this goes a long way in dealing with future issues too. Once all this is put on the back burner, you are aware of the need to look at some fun too. It has been a rough time and you have to balance it all out with some entertainment and diversions. There is respite and you have handled your crises well. Ganesha is pleased with the way you have gone about solving your problems and your affairs.

14 April: Moon's Last Quarter in Capricorn

You look for beauty now that you have emerged from the depths. You have battled the odds and are now happy with the achievements you have made. You feel much more confident and also positive, and ready to embark on a spree of partying, entertaining and enjoying yourself. Money matters ease off, new deals are on the anvil, and there is respite, despite the warming up of the planet! You will make many purchases and do up the home and office to reflect your upbeat mood. You need a happy environment to work and live in, and you spare no effort and money to realize that.

23 April: New Moon in Taurus

You put on your thinking cap and make more plans. You play a more proactive role in family matters and in the community. You like to be listened to and your orders obeyed. Don't get too aggressive or autocratic as it may meet with opposition and resentment. You have a tendency to want to get your point across all the time and these tactics could be interpreted as bullying by others. While you like to have your way always, try to be more gracious about it. Learn to take a few steps backwards sometimes to score a point. Your work proceeds smoothly and you present a bright, clean image to the world. Sometimes, it is necessary to go slow on the 'leader' image that is so inherently a part of your psyche. It makes no sense to gather enemies as circumstances change all the time in life and you never know whom you will need and when. Life is like politics – it makes strange bedfellows!

30 April: Moon's First Quarter in Leo

This is a very good period in which you are in a positive frame of mind and also display great style. You emerge a winner at both work as well as play. You manage to overcome everything that is thrown at you in every sphere of activity. You also display a spiritual bent of mind. This will hold you in good stead in all your relationships. You are able to unwind and look at every situation with equanimity. While you do all this, you also embark on new projects, which promise to do well. Luck is on your side and it is up to you to grab the opportunities and seize the moment.

7 May: Full Moon in Scorpio

You are moving ahead with many plans and projects, making the most of the full moon phase. Cash in on it, says Ganesha. You are a leader/entertainer/mediator and your financial skills/management and spiritual inclinations will be greatly enhanced in this period. You make huge gains. You will find solutions to mind-boggling problems and people at the office and home look to you for answers. Finances will play a major role. You will be playing the market and making judicious investments and buying and selling. Bonds, funds and all other aspects of capital formation will be in sharp focus. You are confident in all that you do and there will be great spiritual reinforcements coming to you. They will help you solve all the issues that you have been doggedly battling against. You have a fierce determination to get ahead, and you really will, with Ganesha's grace. He makes all things possible.

14 May: Moon's Last Quarter in Aquarius

There will be all sorts of delays and obstacles in your path. You have to generate more money and you look around for new ways to do it. You earn much more than you had in the past, but money is still a great need all the time. You look at other avenues of income generation as many family issues come to the fore. It is getting hotter, in more ways than one. This strenuous period could also be dogged by accidents and ill health. While you do extend yourself to the hilt, adequate precautions and preventive care will also be very important. Take to yoga, meditation and antioxidants: in short, de-stress. Don't overextend yourself, and wait out the stresses and strains.

22 May: New Moon in Gemini

The new moon in your sign is propelling you ahead very strongly making you work very hard indeed. There is no let-up in your busy schedule, but you relish every moment of it. There is progress at all levels – recognition, more money made and gains of all kinds. It is a very rewarding period. The home front is also happy and relaxed as a result and there is joy and bonhomie all around. You strike a purple patch in all your affairs. Health is good and there is a possible windfall to cheer you up further. You are sitting pretty and Ganesha is smiling away! A marvellous phase in your own sign!

30 May: Moon's First Quarter in Virgo

The family re-enters your life in a big way now. It could be parents, in-laws, spouse, children, even distant relatives whom you have never met or heard from for a very long time. They all need your attention and this will be time-consuming. Your social life and work time will be curtailed by the numerous domestic demands, but you can't say no to family. This is a frenetic and hectic week and you have to make many compromises. But you get through it well and even manage to see the brighter side of things. In a way, it takes you away from your one-track rat race of work and more work. There are duties and commitments to be met, and why not do it all cheerfully? You will realize that there is a limit to work and money; after all, they are a means to an end and not the end itself! It is in your own interest that you realize this, and the sooner the better. Ganesha's words, not mine.

5 June: Full Moon in Sagittarius

This is a positive and pleasing week with many triumphs which you may not notice until much later. You have been learning many of life's crucial lessons, and will now find time to party. The past few weeks have been a hectic and demanding period and you need to restore the balance. Let go of all trifles and look at the bigger picture. If you don't, life has a way of making you do it, and it will be on its terms and not yours. You go out of your way to entertain friends and play the perfect host. Work and money take a back seat and you decide to just let loose, hang out and have fun. Way to go!

13 June: Moon's Last Quarter in Pisces

Health concerns crop up. It may not be your own health specifically but that of someone dear to you and you have to take care of them. This will also eat into your time, both at work and at leisure, but this is a duty you can't avoid. Nor do you want to; your caring comes from the heart. There is also some travel and a change of plans. You will be in a positive frame of mind despite the disruptions. Somewhere, deep within, you know that this will also pass and you bide your time.

21 June: New Moon in Cancer

You have done well and now the good times seek you out. The clouds have passed and the sun is shining brightly on your life and affairs. There are also several matters to attend to – from family/personal relationships to secret deals, legal or tax/investment complications. But don't worry! You will sort them all out satisfactorily. All this is a part of the evolution of your soul; you have to get across the hurdles and setbacks to realize your true self which is what your earnest quest is.

28 June: Moon's First Quarter in Libra

The difficulties of the past have been well and truly surmounted. You find time to recharge your batteries and decide on some uplifting human interactions and good socializing. You are loving caring and warm in your interactions with people and are a big draw. You are more relaxed and also equally focused on your dreams. You taste the finer things of life and indulge your love of beauty and style. You surround yourself with art, lovely though not necessarily expensive decorations, and many little luxury objects that give you pleasure. You are enjoying life king size and may make expensive purchases too. Ganesha says, even acquiring a Rolls Royce may not be out of place, in the mood you are in right now. So be it then, go and splurge.

5 July: Full Moon in Capricorn

Family issues crop up again. If you are single, you may find a partner as the time is opportune as well as favourable. If you are married, there could be an addition to the family or closer bonding than before with your spouse/mate/partner. There are also new avenues at work and you will maintain your focus on earning and business. The family needs attention and there may be domestic expenses too, depending on your marital status and needs. You may become a bit laid-back and throw yourself heavily into leisure activities. There could even be a family get-together, and you should have a grand time. Children, if any, are also a source of joy and you will delight in their activities.

SCORPIO

12 July: Moon's Last Quarter in Gemini

There is a lot happening now on the career and work fronts and you are on your toes. You cannot back off now. All projects and ventures that you initiated several months ago are on a roll and you need to be in the driver's seat. It is important to make the right decisions which will go a long way in paving the future. Money also comes to you and there will be deeds, documents, agreements and letters of intent and so on to deal with. You have to be alert and clear about what you want. It will also be necessary to keep all these monetary developments and the signing of documents to yourself. This is not the time to share financial confidences, or be too trusting. No need to discuss, or disclose says Ganesha.

20 July: New Moon in Cancer

There is a lot of joy as well as excitement in your life right now. Work, domesticity, family and money – all come together very happily. There will be reorganization, or a revamping at the workspace, to keep you busy, and there will also be many financial demands from all quarters which you will meet without much trouble. This is the time for new ideas, new ventures and new challenges. It is also productive and progressive and you make many new inroads into newer areas of investment and opportunity. Funds and your income will be in sharp focus and you use them wisely with your creativity and imagination.

27 July: Moon's First Quarter in Virgo

You need to remain calm and positive in this phase as a lot will be happening in your life. You will be wondering which direction to take, when and how. There will be changes as well as new challenges at both the work and home fronts. You may even look seriously at relocation. You will need to plan it all out carefully as both expenses and responsibilities increase many times over. This is not an upsetting period per se, but certainly a time that demands a lot from you. You could be pulled in different directions and made to sweat it out. So, I suggest that you remain composed, and work out the focused problematic issues slowly. You have the stamina and the intelligence to wriggle out of corners and also to make good moves.

2 August: Full Moon in Aquarius

This week your life takes on much more and new intensity. You have accomplished a lot and yet make no bones about more plans and ambitions. You want to make more money and embark on new ventures. Like many before you, starting from Alexander the Great, you want to conquer the world. Along with all this, like the Buddha, you are also on the threshold of a great spiritual conquest.

11 August: Moon's Last Quarter in Taurus

As though to unwind or to break free, you will tap your spiritual side and there will be tranquility and inner joy. You are energized with new chakra energy. This is Ganesha's true reward which you may not understand just now. The feeling is one of profound peace and joy and you become a fountain of happiness.

19 August: New Moon in Leo

Now that you are rejuvenated and restored in body and mind, you will sparkle and even exhibit signs of genius. You will focus on work, family, children, and be in total harmony with your immediate environment. You will also explore new horizons and be keen to tap newer sources of knowledge.

25 August: Moon's First Quarter in Sagittarius

You have a new belief in yourself and are very happy for it. You meet and interact with new associates and will love and be loved, care and be cared for. There may also be marriage, fun, laughter, glamour and joy, to add to the happiness quotient. You are a big draw and very popular at parties, gatherings, ceremonies and group outings.

2 September: Full Moon in Pisces

Life is indeed a yo-yo. You never know which string is pulled when. And we are like puppets being manipulated. Just when you have achieved a degree of inner security and belief, thanks to your spiritual grounding, you swing back to doubts, anxieties and worries. What is the reality in you, you may wonder – is it steadfastness or is it instability?

10 September: Moon's Last Quarter in Gemini

You put in sustained effort and work and achieve a lot. In addition to all the hard work that you have put in, there will be many moments of sustained entertaining too. You will find ways to rid yourself of undue worries. There will be heavy expenses, clandestine affairs, secret deals, surreptitious movements, moneymaking opportunities.

17 September: New Moon in Virgo

As the year slowly enters its last quarter, you move closer to home and family, which will be your strength, solace and support system. The world throws out many challenges and you need to retreat to congenial surroundings to face it all, as well as find and manage solutions. There will be meetings and collaborations.

24 September: Moon's First Quarter in Capricorn

The family and new aspects of spiritual progress will play a prominent role in your life now. People play a vital role and there may be love, romance, perhaps an engagement or wedding, hobbies, fun, gambling, speculation and much more on the cards. You will also explore higher planes of consciousness. There are different types of Scorpios and I am sure that whichever type you are, you are on of the mysteries of the universe.

2 October: Full Moon in Aries

There are several deadlines, commitments and targets to be met and you are slogging away, burning the midnight oil. You manage to meet them all successfully, however, and the rewards will be there for you to see. It is a busy, action-oriented week and you will be working at a scorching pace.

10 October: Moon's Last Quarter in Cancer

You will be productive at work and will achieve much once again. Your self-image gets a boost and you get kudos from family, friends, colleagues, co-workers and associates. You are optimistic and positive and work with efficiency. Try not to get an inflated ego as everything is working out the way you wanted it and it will be difficult not to get overconfident.

16 October: New Moon in Libra

There is a lot of satisfaction to be had. You bask in the magic of love, true contentment and peace. A lot of it is thanks to the family who rally around you and share with you the very joys of existence. All this relaxes you and you enter new ventures, projects, collaborations and partnerships.

23 October: Moon's First Quarter in Aquarius

Your birth phase period is setting in. The results are spectacular and you are 'the man of the match' more than once. You are the toast of the season and win praise, adulation and applause from everybody. You are glowing and growing, emotionally and spiritually, and it's happy days once again. You see and realize the power of money and are aware of just how real and tangible it is.

31 October: Full Moon in Taurus

The intense phase resumes and you are charging like a bull at the matador's cape. You have created a balance in your personal and professional life, and now you move ahead to seize the opportunities that come your way. Your achievements are all well deserved and you bask in the glory of a job well done. There is also some fun and partying and even, possibly, a new romance. Don't lose your head and overdo it. There is passion and, possibly, great intimacy, but watch where you are going. Keep away from romance at the workplace as it will only backfire.

8 November: Moon's Last Quarter in Leo

There is greater joy in life for you now, Scorpios. You are sorting out the money angle and even moving headlong and with great speed and determination on that front. There is happiness and contentment. Family life too brings joy, and if you are a parent there will be even greater happiness.

15 November: New Moon in Scorpio

Your birth month phase has the right ingredients for happiness. You are calm and contented and find marvellous emotional balance. You are amiable and understanding and can work through problems well. There are many intellectual, spiritual and physical gains as Ganesha crowns your efforts in almost all directions with splendid success.

22 November: Moon's First Quarter in Pisces

You have to make the right choices now as there will be many things to choose from. While it is fine to focus on the material world, several other issues have to be worked out in the other areas of your life. Mutual funds, shares and stocks, raising of capital and all other money matters come to the fore and you will have to work hard to see them through satisfactorily.

30 November: Full Moon in Gemini

You taste the good life again. There are new acquisitions and add-ons, which can even be gems and jewels, gold and luxury goods along with genuine accomplishments, achievements and true love. Ganesha also gives you the joy of greater bonding at home.

8 December: Moon's Last Quarter in Virgo

The theme this week is marital and close family relationships. It is an emotional period with loved ones and you get a lot of joy from the new chemistry that you now experience. There is fun and gaiety and many enriching associations. You love all this and it is a welcome respite from the hard work that you have put in most of this year.

14 December: New Moon in Sagittarius

The action continues with many challenges in store. The year-end seems to be packed to the brim for you. But this is a pleasurable phase as you get a chance to showcase your skills, talent and determination. There is success as you surmount everything thrown at you. You will thrive in the use of the last word in technology and will invest in the latest gadgets, gizmos and software.

21 December: Moon's First Quarter in Aries

This is an intense phase and a lot will happen. The end of the year could be quite dramatic. There is money to be made and success will beckon on the work front. Health is also good and domestic matters are in control. But, more important, you could be in the throes of a sizzling romance. It is fine if you are single, but I don't have to add here that if you are married a third person will spoil it all.

30 December: Full Moon in Cancer

You ended last year well and began this year on a positive note. You worked hard and spared no effort to achieve whatever you wanted to. There have been ups and downs this year but, once again, you end on a positive note. There are good times at work and at home and you feel very content. There are perks and windfalls and your hardwork has paid off. The bubbly flows and you usher in 2020 on a high note. Life is never just about money and achievement; it is many splendoured and multidimensional.

SAGITTARIUS

23 November–22 December

Symbol: The Archer
Ruling Planet: Jupiter
Fire-Mutable-Positive
The Sign of the Lawyer, the Sage

'Money is round. It rolls,' it has been said. Ganesha points out, in 2020 it will run and roll your way! Ganesha requests you to pay heed to Vic Oliver's discourse on money:

> If a man runs after money, he's money-mad; if he keeps it, he's a capitalist; if he spends it, he's a playboy; if he doesn't get it, he's a ne'er-do-well; if he doesn't try to get it, he lacks ambition. If he gets it without working for it, he's a parasite; and if he accumulates it after a lifetime of hard work, people call him a fool who never got anything out of life!

The reason of heeding this is that you are going to get money, lots of it. You are most welcome to come to me to help you spend it in a full and happy spread! Together with this money trend, another trend also runs almost parallel for you. According to the Buddha, 'Not to do any evil, to cultivate good, to purify one's mind,' is what life is, or should be, all about. This trend will also come into full operation for you Sagittarians. Normally money and spirituality do not go together. Your special duty and dharma will be to reconcile these two. That's what 2020 is all about, points out Ganesha. The results of your activities from 2 December 2019 to 18 December 2020 will start coming in, from a trickle to a stream. Funds and your own vitality will have to be kept intact and protected. Buying and selling, trade and commissions, mutual funds, joint finances, joint holdings, rentals, estate duties, taxes – almost the entire gamut of money matters is to be dealt with. Romance, sexual prowess, physical rather than totally emotional involvements will also hold/attract you. Retirement, a job change, a move away from your regular profession could also happen now. Securities, mortgages, home finances will have to be dealt with too; probably, also a second home. The year ends with you stretching yourself in many directions, hammering out a new deal for yourself, your loved ones and dependents, committing yourself strongly, forcefully, emphatically. Above all, you're believing in yourself, says Ganesha, and that's what makes things happen!

JUPITER

Jupiter will be in your second angle of:

1) Finances.
2) Taxes.

3) Augmentation of income through various sources.

4) Passion and love.

5) Inheritance and unexpected money.

6) Joint finances.

7) Trusts and funds and the use of public money.

8) Taking steps to better your health and your earning potential (these two are very definite).

9) Moving to a new house/office.

10) Looking after the old and infirm in your body, mind and spirit – and as we know, it is all in the mind.

11) Vicarious pleasures, necromancy and the use of tantra and mantra – yes, these are accentuated. A strange assortment. But remember, truth is often stranger than fiction.

SATURN

Saturn, the other main planet, will be in your second angle. It will therefore emphasize food, family and finance. The other salient features will be renovation, decoration, alteration, buying, selling, leasing, shops, office, land, farm, house, in short, property and assets. Architects, builders, contractors, politicians, actors, chemists, pharmacists, horticulturists, gardeners, animal trainers and even newly-weds should perform brilliantly. You will live up to the ideas of Emerson:

> To laugh often and much, to win the respect of intelligent people, and the affection of children to earn the appreciation of honest critics, to endure the

betrayal of false friends, to appreciate beauty and to find the best in others, to leave the world a bit better whether by a healthy child, garden patch or a redeemed social condition, to know even one life has breathed easier because you lived – this is to have succeeded.

What is there left to say?
The two special features for Sagittarians are:

- Development of your personality.

- Anything to do with property, house, home, parents, in-laws, architecture, buying and selling, office, shop, godown, warehouse, land.

BLUEPRINT FOR THE ENTIRE YEAR

January: Legacy, finances, passion, but low vitality.

February: Distant places, research, parents and in-laws, education, children, good fortune through meeting the right persons.

March: Position, prestige, power, parents, home and property, rites and rituals for the living and the dead.

April: Friendship, socializing, gains and glamour, realization of aspirations.

May: Travel, restlessness despite good fortune, expenses, care for health.

June: Good going in terms of health, wealth and happiness; you should thank Ganesha for it.

July: Finances, family, ties, adornment, home, buying/selling, vehicles.

August: Contacts, communication, contracts, crash courses, mental brilliance, new projects, courage, determination.

September: Home, family, treasure, parents and in-laws, work prospects even for the retired, paradoxically, elderly persons will retire shortly.

October: Journey, ceremony, publicity, children, hobbies, creativity; therefore, a lively and lucky month.

November: Job, pets, projects, care for subordinates' health.

December: Love/hate, partnership/separation, but all told, you do gain and can look forward to the future with great confidence. You deserve it!

Special Note: Uranus has changed signs from 31 December 2019 to July 2025. This year Uranus will help you in matters pertaining to job, promotion, pets, social welfare, health and hygiene and support from colleagues as well as servants. Uranus will be your friend.

Your happiness quota is 80 per cent.

WEEKLY REVIEW BY PHASES OF THE MOON

10 January: Full Moon in Cancer

You made remarkable progress last year, and in all probability, depending on the personal horoscope of course, the progress of good trends will only continue in 2020. You are relating better to people both close to you and to outsiders, and you will be expanding your scope of interests/

work in several direction. There is profitable travel foretold, resulting in several new projects that you are keen to embark on and make a success of. Family life and health remain stable. You have a tendency to overspend and it may help to curtail expenses now. I also advise you not to shoot your mouth off too often. Besides, don't trust strangers as there is also an element of deceit and betrayal working in this period for you. Be your guard and all will be well, says Ganesha. Finally, when in doubt, entrust your cares to a greater power and He will take care of you.

17 January: Moon's Last Quarter in Libra

You move along quite well as the year unfolds to its second week. All your financial affairs and other commitments are under control and there is a semblance of peace in your life. You feel that you have finally arrived on the big stage and decide to push further to consolidate your efforts. There are also family responsibilities to attend to and some sudden expenses which may require extra liquidity or just more cash! There may in fact be a cash crunch but you manage to squeeze out of it. You may be strapped for time as there are heavy work demands. You may find that the resolutions you made for 2020 don't stick. You have broken promises to yourself about easing up. Some discipline will help.

24 January: New Moon in Capricorn

This is time for family bonding. You loved your circle of friends and hate hurting anyone deliberately. As a result, there are huge demands of your time and you spread yourself very thin. Your personal affairs suffer as a result. Remember, you can't please everyone all the time, and if you try this, you may only be hurting yourself, and the ones who are really close to you. They may begin to feel that you are neglecting them, but that is not true. Make a checklist of what needs to be done and prioritize your targets. You are highly talented and expressive and love all forms of communication. In fact you are always a big draw for your skills and also your values. There is always an innocence and honesty in your dealings and you trust implicitly. You now turn to the home, hearth, home away from home, domestic and filial duties, the sense of satisfaction that these bring. There is greater confidence, sharing, love and self-belief. Whatever the situation, and no matter how harsh it may be, you smile through it.

2 February: Moon's First Quarter in Taurus

The mood continues to be light. You flirt with romance and light-hearted flings with an I-don't-give-a-damn attitude. You are surrounded by admirers and take care not to hurt feelings which may be far more genuine and intense than yours at this time. You find solace in friendships and social gatherings and indulge in all the joy that can give leisure and pleasure. There are travel and communication at all levels and collaborations and meetings amidst great bonhomie. You will continue with the happy mood of celebrations of good times and festivity. Not a bad way to be, says Ganesha.

9 February: Full Moon in Leo

You have been spending a lot over the past few days and now your attention shifts to money matters and how to conserve your resources. There is some spending too but it is judicious. You embark on new career plans and get a chance to spruce up your image. If in love, you may get serious and more committed about your partner. If not, you look for deep romance that can stir your soul. But, somehow, you find it difficult to fix your attentions on one person for too long. You invest in home and office and prepare the ground for good hard work ahead, with matching results. All the partying has got to you, and the real world beckons you back. You realize that you have to work in earnest now to move ahead in life.

19 February: Moon's Last Quarter in Scorpio

Expenses mount and you will live in expansion mode, making purchases and investments which add considerable value to your life. There is enhancement of property, assets and other such acquisitions. There are also domestic matters to look into including possibly, illness in the family or some such emergency. If you are looking at foreign travel, it may be a good time to process your papers. The work front is opening up and throwing many new possibilities your way, which you should grab with both hands.

23 February: New Moon in Aquarius

The last quarter of this month is in your own sign, and this could be very beneficial. There is a lot of movement, which could well be in your interest. You may shift home or office and there could be huge expansion at all levels. There are elements of some exciting new touch of romance too and a lot of passion and your relationships and interactions will gain in depth. Money flows in but also flows out. You have to plug the leak fast. Ganesha gives you good finances this week and you live well but you are certainly not putting anything aside for a rainy day. Right now, you are living dangerously and squandering it all. You are lucky that the inflow of funds is not obstructed. But this may not be forever, and you have to secure yourself against future contingencies.

2 March: Moon's First Quarter in Gemini

Open displays of emotion are not your forte as such, but this week there are reason for extremes of emotion. There are events at home that get you all tied up in knots and you get extra-sensitive to criticism. You need to go slow and cut the flab out of your life. Ganesha tells you not to be rash and hasty in your decision making. You also have to take a clear stand on all your financial dealings; try and keep borrowings to a minimum. There will also be expenses, trips, collaboration and risks of injury. So all the safeguards should be in place, use your free will with discretion, and beneficial changes can take place. You also tend to react severely against criticism of any kind. Learn to take this in your stride, as it is all par for the course. Life has its pebbles and you must learn to go with the flow. Remember, also, that you can't always be right and criticism often helps you grow as a person, if you take it in the right spirit.

9 March: Full Moon in Virgo

You spread yourself this week and communicate effectively with all you come into contact with. Money is still slipping from your hands but this is not a real concern as you are confident that you will make up what's necessary. You feel, therefore, that you can afford to take it easy a bit and relax and spend time with loved ones and friend. There is powerful bonding with family and that more than makes up for the distractions that could happen on the work front. There is more vibrant interaction with your children/parents and greater peace of mind. You are also in a very helpful frame of mind and are the epitome of generosity as usual.

16 March: Moon's Last Quarter in Sagittarius

There are changes in your life now and you come to grips with reality. Your focus shifts to streamlining the work area and you are highly motivated to do it. A much larger vision is yours now. It is also a good time to travel and make plans for wider communication and mental growth. You plunge into work and want to make up for lost time. You discipline yourself and slog away, much against the grain and the mood that you have been in for the last few weeks. But there are responsibilities to be met and you can't dither for too long.

24 March: New Moon in Aries

The movement you have just initiated is substantive. Many old associates also come to assist. You manage to rid yourself of temptations of fun and freedom and get down to the business of making a living in right earnest. If you are employed, expansion and growth will be the theme of this week. You give a break to the partying and the good times, and slog away. This is a good move, says Ganesha, and you are bound to achieve success.

1 April: Moon's First Quarter in Cancer

You are on an intense work binge. You have changed and now display a great work ethic. You make rapid progress. Associates and colleagues appreciate your leadership abilities and vision and you will make decisions. There will be important collaborations and signing of deals which will benefit you in the long run. It may be wise here to curb your tongue and to go slow on the ego drives. The spell of hard work that you have plunged into is likely to be intensive and demanding but greatly fulfilling. There is bound to be stress and maybe illness but you wade through it all with both determination and class.

8 April: Full Moon in Libra

Hard work is an integral part of your psyche at this juncture. You are full of vision, optimism and faith, and you inspire all those around you to give their best. You gain the support of friends, admirers, acquaintances and lovers. These are good times. There may be the blossoming of a romance with someone you meet, at work, a sort of office romance, I may add. Tread carefully. There are beautiful moments of stolen love and you are on a high because of the same. Life gets a rosy tinge and all is well with your life. If married, your relationship with your spouse gets better, leading to intense bonding. Romance is certainly the focus this week, whichever way you look at it.

14 April: Moon's Last Quarter in Capricorn

You make progress and cover a lot of lost ground. You make purchases and are filled with a love for beauty and all the good things of life. The giant strides you are making now will be the result of the changed mental ethos that you have created within you, caring for those around you, being tolerant and less critical. The softer persona makes for much more happiness and also helps the true cooperation of colleagues/co-workers, bosses/subordinates/employees. There is only one problem now which is that you can't decide on one course of action or could decide and change your mind once too often. This may confuse colleagues/

co-workers and they will wonder what to do. But you seem oblivious of the impact of your dithering on others and will continue with what you are doing, without looking for remedial action. There are expenses and some ill health to cope with.

23 April: New Moon in Taurus

You rise to the challenges of hard work and career advancement and initiate several projects that stretch your imagination, capabilities and skills. Your achievements are impressive and you win applause from all quarters. You embark on many new projects that underscore your ingenuity and creativity. But, despite all this, you are in a thoughtful mood and tend to get depressed for no particular reason. You are fascinated by the human mind and the behaviour patterns of the people you meet. You take time off to lend a helping hand and even mentor and counsel others. You get introspective and search deep within for answers to some fundamental questions. There are no pressing issues that demand your attention but it is the mood you are in: you may feel worried, thoughtful and preoccupied with nothing in particular.

30 April: Moon's First Quarter in Leo

The stage is being set for expansion and recognition. Your self-worth and image are crucial to you and your confidence is surging. Your new career/work avenues are also rewarding despite all the hiccups and expenses. But remember, nothing ventured, nothing gained. The investments made now will bear fruit in the long run. You do spectacularly well in a venture involving overseas business or trade. You are thinking global now. There is harmony, and life takes on a rosy tinge. You are not bothered by trifles and look squarely at the big picture. You may get a bit arrogant, but that is a part of emotional package that you have now.

7 May: Full Moon in Scorpio

There is a new focus and thrust, and you are assured of success in your ventures. Work increases and you have no time to party; even the weekend meetings with friends and loved ones will be taken up by work pressures. This is a really favourable phase in which you make rapid progress. There is expansion in several spheres work-wise, and a lot of money needs to be invested. But this is definitely money well spent because you will earn the dividends later on. There will also be more time for the family and, in the future, for the frivolities of life; but this is the time to get down to hard, sustained work. Opportunity knocks rarely, and it is knocking now. Grab the moment, says Ganesha, and success is yours for the asking.

14 May: Moon's Last Quarter in Aquarius

Work is progressing well and there is also travel thrown in. You are determined to sustain the growth that you have achieved and to even up the tempo. You grow as a person and earn the respect and admiration of your peers. I must add here that in life one always loses a bit when one gains something else and there is no escape from this cardinal principle. Which is why it is necessary to know what you really want from life. Right now, you are on work phase and you are losing out on quality time with family and friends which irks you. But great achievements are possible only with hard work, dedication and sacrifice, and you are willing to enter the slog over with a broad bat. Loved ones understand and appreciate your efforts and aren't quibbling or cribbing about the lack of time. So you don't need to feel guilty about it either.

22 May: New Moon in Gemini

The work phase is in full swing and you are making waves. There is intensity in whatever you do and the stage seems set for passion. Love enters your life and sets it like a wick in a haystack. A new relationship has your heart racing but you are caught in it, and are helpless. Without a doubt, you are overextending yourself. There are possibilities of a burnout and ill health but you are pulled to the flame like a moth. You know that it could be ruinous but you are unable to steer the direction of your life to safer areas. There is danger here. Everything that you have recently achieved may just blow up in your face. But this is life and we need the scars sometimes to remind us later of the recklessness of youth, or even if one is not so youthful, of the dangers of unhinged passion.

30 May: Moon's First Quarter in Virgo

Thankfully, you slow down a bit now and make the correct decisions. There is more sanity in your dealings and you stretch to meet more people. There are partnerships, collaborations and tie-ups at work. You show interest in higher studies, spirituality and faith. You turn to religion and look for answers. You look for a grip on life and spend time with family and friends. It is a welcome break from the smouldering intensity of the last week.

5 June: Full Moon in Sagittarius

You find yourself isolated; in fact your need for privacy leads to long periods of solitude during which you don't even tell your loved ones where you are, which is quite difficult for them to cope with or accept. But you need this 'me' time in which to probe deep questions about life and death and your purpose on this planet in the particular circumstances you are in. You are not really depressed but you are looking for answers not easily forthcoming. You travel to holy places and are on pilgrimage, seeking answers. At one level, you are on the right track. Unless there is peace in the soul, you will not be able to function effectively. Additionally, there are legal issues and some domestic strife but you are far removed from all this to be hassled or worried unduly about it all. You are living on another level or plane now and will be back to earth shortly. Till then of course you cannot be disturbed.

13 June: Moon's Last Quarter in Pisces

You are back on terra firma with many disturbing psychological questions seemingly answered. There is more happiness and contentment. You are cheerful and warm, tolerant and more accepting of yourself, others and situations which earlier infuriated you no end. As a result, there is joy in all your interactions. You are a softer and more rounded person now and you look at life from a different prism and perspective. You finally realize that it all depends on the outlook perspective one has, and that nothing is stagnant or unchanged for long. Ganesha reminds you that life is about change and motion.

21 June: New Moon in Cancer

You stretch yourself in all directions. You reach out to people and they respond favourably. Your plate is full to overflowing with events and activities. Family and loved ones expect much from you in this phase. Work takes a back seat and you quite like, and do justice to, all the socializing. There is travel, expenses of all kinds, and some stresses. You find cracks developing in some new-found love and this disturbs you. You find solace in quieter retreats and may visit a spa or place for healing for rejuvenation and treatment.

28 June: Moon's First Quarter in Libra

People continue to be an integral area of your life. But you need to be objective and dispassionate and re-evaluate and reassess your life and your attitudes. You will realize that you are not centred and are being pulled in many directions simultaneously. The moment you get your teeth into something, you lose interest and move on. This can get disconcerting and irritating to you and the persons involved. Your mind wanders and you are unable to stick to anything for any length of time. You are not particularly disturbed by it, but there is no advantage in being a rolling stone. You also like applause and have a great desire to be popular. But by spreading yourself like this you are pleasing no one, not even yourself. Moreover, it is very unlike your usual Sagittarian focus.

5 July: Full Moon in Capricorn

A lot is on your mind and they will all not be happy thoughts. You are confused, and will be working and thinking at cross purposes. Your income and finances are on the upswing despite your lack of interest in work-related activities, thanks to some inheritance issue that has been decided in your favour. There are domestic pressures too and you are at your wits' end wondering what to do. There is the need to work towards building greater accord and harmony in the home. Discussions with friends/co-workers/partners or like-minded people may give you fresh ideas. Your mind is like a yo-yo and you just can't focus on anything in particular. You need to hang in there and let this topsy-turvy period pass, counsels Ganesha.

12 July: Moon's Last Quarter in Gemini

You try hard to get back on firm ground. Luck is with you and so you haven't lost out on new opportunities. You are back to solid work with new ventures/projects in place, or in the pipeline but there is a hard slog ahead and you are not sure if you'll be able to cope. You like the good life and spend a lot on luxuries. At one level, you are slipping and losing ground. But, at another level, this could be the platform to launch yourself in a big way when the time comes. It is just that you are not motivated enough by the size of the challenges thrown your way. Possibly you want to prove yourself with something more exciting.

20 July: New Moon in Cancer

The tide is thankfully turning slowly in your favour. You are now brimming with energy, zeal and direction and firing away on all cylinders. You will be up to your neck in various activities and just about managing to breathe. You are swimming hard though it's the tide. There are hard work, many new career and work openings, love and romance, expenses and investments. You will be perhaps pushed into corners but you cope well and come out triumphant. You are gripped by ambition and look at reorganizing your resources and putting them to the best possible use. Money matters acquire a vital edge and will call for careful planning. There may be property issues with siblings that you need to sort out and, if married, or in a serious relationship, quality time and attention will be needed to examine issues that are tearing it apart. There is also travel thrown into the mix. You have to take baby steps and wade through all this a little at a time. But you are motivated to go full steam ahead!

27 July: Moon's First Quarter in Virgo

This is a favourable period and you manage to handle your life well. There is harmony in your dealings and disturbing affairs are easily settled. Legal issues come to the fore and require your attention. Health may also need some care. But on the plus side, all these challenges are making you 'match fit' and ready to take on bigger challenges in the future. You also begin to look at the money angle more seriously and think of cutting down on extravagances. You need money for new ventures and look for loans to fund them. A lot is occupying your mind and there isn't a dull moment. But, by all accounts, you are on the upswing.

2 August: Full Moon in Aquarius

You settle down into a regular groove as the year progresses. You are more balanced and look at new ideas and new achievements. On the fun side, there will also be social outings with loved ones and collaborations of all kinds, both personal and professional. You are making rapid progress and making good money too. You will lead the team well and enjoy the full support of colleagues. You mean business and will come up with startling and innovative ideas. You also manage to solve some pending legal issues in your favour and move on to greater success in all your endeavours with Ganesha's blessings.

11 August: Moon's Last Quarter in Taurus

You are brimming with new ideas and there is rapid and genuine progress which will not be short-lived; all your plans are directed for the long haul. You are a sympathetic leader and, as we all know by now, nothing succeeds like success. So all your earlier innovative ideas and plans, which may have been misunderstood or criticized in certain quarters and have now come up trumps cooperation, wins applause and approval. You show your kind and generous side to the world too, and you feel a tremendous hike in self-confidence and self-belief. You feel that you have the magic wand and can make wonders happen. You are happy and will share the joy of a job well done. These are just rewards that Ganesha gives which are very well deserved too!

19 August: New Moon in Leo

You work hard and with tact and diplomacy alongside, and climb several peaks. You have a genial attitude about you, and an easy way of making friends. You are popular at work and are often the soul of the party with your easy-going manner and genuine charm. You love the demands made on you and are happy to fulfil all your responsibilities. Money is not a problem and the family is well settled too. You will make purchases for the home and office and also make wise investments. Good sense prevails, and Ganesha blesses you too.

25 August: Moon's First Quarter in Sagittarius

You will become a stickler for the fine points at work and examine the minutest details with a magnifying glass. There is a lot of balancing to do – with family, friends and work.

There are demands on your time from parents and siblings, as also increasing work pressures which invariably accompany all expansion activity. This phase is a valuable learning experience. You learn to micromanage time and all the demands on you very efficiently. You scrutinize documents with an eagle eye and make plans with rare accuracy and commitment. You are not usually known for this. But you are able to show a side or face of yourself normally kept hidden from the world. You are to have easy-going ways and a happy demeanour. But, during crunch times, you show the world several pleasing attributes, where walking the talk is concerned.

2 September: Full Moon in Pisces

The year is moving towards its final quarter and this phase is in your own sign, which is usually beneficial for all signs. You will rise in the company echelons or, if self-employed, make enormous waves. You travel a lot and strike lucrative deals. There could be business collaborations. There is a tremendous rise in your position, popularity and authority. You take on challenges like Sachin Tendulkar taking on Shane Warne and nothing can stop you from hitting the ball right out of the stadium, i.e., making the most impressive of achievements.

10 September: Moon's Last Quarter in Gemini

You are riding the crest of the wave. Your efforts are crowned by success and recognition at the workplace. There are also joy, satisfaction and true pleasure at home. You are happy with all that is happening and you radiate good feelings which are picked up by those around you. You are deeply loved, appreciated, understood and cherished and, if in a new romance, you live a dream. You are a charmer even when the tide is not in your favour. But now, when things are going well, you lay it on thick without any effort and there are concrete gains in all areas of your life. You are sensitive to others' needs and begin to understand what makes them tick, and are able to see beneath the surface. It is fascinating, and others are taken aback by your perceptiveness and power.

17 September: New Moon in Virgo

You ride the wave in style. Nothing stops you now. The latter half of the year is fortunate. You are flexible and easy-going and don't lose your cool. There is deep, inner joy which works its magic in all areas of your life. There will be travel, collaborations and meetings at all levels. If in the media, you do wonderfully well and get renown baffle your peers and win acclaim. You are the star of the show and win huge amount of praise and attention. Need Ganesha give you more?

24 September: Moon's First Quarter in Capricorn

You are on the fastest trajectory to success. You are lucky and the breaks come your way with ease. There is no struggle as you find yourself at the right place at the right time. There is perfect timing and you have to thank Ganesha for it. Of course, as I keep saying in it all depends on the individual horoscope and the positioning of your planets. But these are the general trends. Your determination to succeed has been mind-boggling and you put in the required effort too. Money flows in and out as you love spending. There is a lot of entertaining too and loved ones draw closer to you.

There is intense bonding and there is spring in your life even though the autumn of 2020 is approaching!

2 October: Full Moon in Aries

You continue making headway and also find inner peace and a sense of balance. This helps you make quick and correct decisions and breast the tape ahead of the competition like Asalfa Powell in the 100 metres. You are ruthless and move with direction and determination, ready for the kill. Nothing and no one can stand in your path. With great achievements come greater confidence and self-belief. You are in no mood for fun and games, and socializing takes a back seat. Your friends and loved ones seek you out but you have other things on your mind. Like Alexander you are at conquering new frontiers and no one can dare to stand in the way. Your mind will be razor-sharp and you will triumph over the opposition with shrewd, calculated moves.

10 October: Moon's Last Quarter in Cancer

There is all-round and sustained growth as you move ahead with a ferocity and determination not normally associated with you. You surprise everyone and zero in on both social standing and advancement at work. Your life is filled with passion and the hormones are raging. You grow at every level, acquire wisdom, consolidate your gains and reap the harvest. There are the usual attendant stresses but they are not enough to distract you from the forward march. You are in conquest mode and like Napoleon Bonaparte, you keep repeating that nothing is impossible. In the phase you are in, yes, nothing is impossible! Ganesha has given you the power to move ahead with astonishing speed, accuracy and strength.

16 October: New Moon in Libra

There is a shift here and you slow down having achieved a lot and mowed down the opposition. You look at doing some concrete inner work and spending valuable and pleasing time with near and dear ones. You are not really in Mother Teresa mode, but you are also not as hell-bent on work expansion as you were earlier. You have set foot on Everest itself and there is no going further up for now. A softer side takes over; you are loving and caring and more able to deal with your emotions. There is a different type of satisfaction that gathers in you. This is a special gift, indeed, that Ganesha gives you.

23 October: Moon's First Quarter in Aquarius

You are going great guns and are active and energized. Your emotional, spiritual and intellectual faculties are pronounced. You look at religion, the occult sciences, philosophy, law, psychology and the afterlife. You have the time and resources now to indulge in these interests and desires. You are filled with passion too, but it is a passion for knowledge. You pore through books, visit libraries and people who are repositories of ancient knowledge and wisdom. You want to grow in different ways and make every effort to do so. There is a new path to your life and you want to examine it closely. You want to appear on the world stage as a person to be reckoned with.

31 October: Full Moon in Taurus

If last week was a bit mellow and easy, this week is quite the opposite, with high energies and powerful intensity in all that you do. You are not one to live in isolation; in fact, you are not at all inclined to be the lone wolf or the intense

SAGITTARIUS

introvert. This week you are not just an extrovert but an intense extrovert (if I may use the expression) as you make contacts and party with a rare enthusiasm. There is nothing specific to celebrate but you are enjoying the moment and that is reason enough. You are romantic and flirt with abandon. There is romance and passion in your life. You are spending a lot, but may actually turn lucky with legacies, windfalls, speculation, gambling, or in the stock market. But this is certainly not a financially prudent time money-wise; your mood is light-hearted and frivolous, and you look at romance and not money with seriousness and desire and intensity You refuse to take life seriously as the fun times roll on. Cupid steps out of the woodwork and strikes you as well!

8 November: Moon's Last Quarter in Leo

Many good things happen to you in an oblique way. There are renewing of social ties and strengthening of old and new acquaintances and friendships. You are also filled with a sense of altruism and philanthropy, empathy for the less fortunate, and you donate generously to all causes. And it is not just for tax benefits. The feeling is genuine. You counsel and mentor those who need it and lend a helping hand wherever it is needed. You also, strangely, feel a sense of guilt which is unnecessary. If you are born lucky, it doesn›t hurt to share the excess at your disposal with those who aren't so fortunate. Learn to enjoy your blessings. This is however a good time to be humble and live in gratitude to the maker.

15 November: New Moon in Scorpio

You have been growing in many profound ways and you are keen on sustaining this growth. You spread out to many areas of study and look for masters and seers. Your interests stretch to the occult, psychology, religion, philosophy and other related areas. There is also hard work to be put in at the office. A lot of diplomacy will also be required in domestic matters to keep the peace at home. You realize that it is not easy doing it all and it may get tiring and irksome. There is genuine love, moments of happiness with children and several other happy distractions to provide some relief and respite. This is an interesting week by any yardstick and there are many lessons to be learnt as the full moon shines on what Ganesha has lined up for you.

22 November: Moon's First Quarter in Pisces

You are living larger than king size, if there can be such a way to live. You gamble with your heart and feelings without discretion and discrimination and no one can stop you. Work takes a back seat and family life could also suffer. Your near and dear ones feel that you have been taken away from them. There may be domestic squabbles and conflicts to handle as well. You may also get arrogant, haughty and inconsiderate and hurt a lot of people in the process. You feel that you are the last word in creation and do whatever pleases you most in a display of self-centredness. You feel you are a power centre and a law unto yourself, but no one can be that – only Ganesha.

30 November: Full Moon in Gemini

You reap the benefits of the start of your birth month and this is going to be a frenetic period in your own sun sign. Your life is action-packed like James Bond. Just like with 007, the fun element will also be thrown into the ring and you have to pick up the gauntlet. You are stretched in many directions and every sphere of your life will be galvanized into action mode. There are all kinds of activities, from romance to adventure, hush-hush wheeler-dealing, new projects and collaborations, travel to distant places and a vibrant and active social life. You will excel at work and surpass all expectations and targets. There are money and love too on the cards, and you feel happy and secure. You are not prone to complain, but you are greedy for more and that, alas is human nature.

8 December: Moon's Last Quarter in Virgo

This is a thoughtful phase and you indulge in some serious planning. You meet all kinds of demand and responsibility and our mind is hyperactive. You get introspective and may even go on a pilgrimage. You want to spend time with the true essence of existence. You want to develop as a complete human being and everything esoteric excites you. Luck also shines on you and throws up many opportunities for growth, renewal, revival, rejuvenation and change. There are new and profitable collaborations and you are no fool when it comes to money. You grab all that is on offer and make a quick buck. You're also kind and thoughtful and understand others' pain and circumstances in a deep and non-judgmental way. You bring solace to wounds and will be much sought after. People look up to you for inspiration, compassion and empathy.

14 December: New Moon in Sagittarius

You are a people's person and look closely at personal associations and interactions. You are friendly, sociable and well meaning and often make sincere efforts to get along with everyone, even with those you really dislike. You are generally bold and upfront and can make enemies, but in this phase, you control your tongue and keep your personal views and opinions to yourself like an professional diplomat. You network, socialize, interact, travel and spend happily. Troublesome domestic issues may surface and need to be resolved with intuition and wisdom. Your confidence in yourself nudges you in the right direction. You enjoy the company of like-minded people and feel secure in their company: suddenly, you start seeking them out, wishing to gain in terms of both knowledge and experience.

21 December: Moon's First Quarter in Aries

You expand your activities hugely and overindulge; there are no limits or boundaries to what you can do. There is travel and there is deep bonding to. You may be on holiday and meet up with a person you want to hitch your wagon to for some time at least. There is palpable passion for some time at least and this person can play an important role in your life. I can't pin-point the exact nature of the association as it depends on your personal horoscope but your heart will beat and bleed for sure! You are in a celebratory mood and the real world and its mundane issues seem totally alien to your mindset. You are not one to be tied down to just work for ever. You are a lover of freedom with a strong ego and individual drives. You want to enjoy, fly! Way to go, says Ganesha.

30 December: Full Moon in Cancer

You end the year well and may even manage to keep next year's resolutions for some time at least, going by the mood you are in now. You are rounding off this exciting and demanding year with determination, performance, achievement, discipline and gains on several fronts. This will serve as a launching pad to greater glory in the coming months. There is added happiness in the form of family support; friends and well-wishers also stand by you in all ventures. Money matters will be good. There is enough in the kitty too for your extravagant ways and you will not need to stop at speculation and other forms of gambling and risk-taking, even when the chips are down. You are fortunate to be blessed with a spirit that never wants to see the downsides of life. You are an eternal optimist and know somehow that, in the end, the boat will right itself. Fortune has the habit of smiling on you and it is up to you to appreciate and value it. Life is all about attitude and you have a sunny disposition that stands you in good stead even in the harshest times. Continue into the new year with zest and verve and Ganesha's blessings.

CAPRICORN

23 December–22 January

Symbol: The Goat
Ruling Planet: Saturn
Earth-Cardinal-Negative
The Sign of the Priest, the Administrator

Ganesha says this is perhaps the most important and truly impressive year for India. Why? By mundane Western astrology, the ruling sign of India is Capricorn. Jupiter is the planet of prosperity, plenty and peace. Jupiter enters Capricorn from 2 December 2019 to 18 December 2020.

Ganesha asserts, this is the year of the Capricornians. Our India, Bharat Mata, is under the influence and impact of the Capricorn sign. Atal Bihari Vajpayee, the late Dhirubhai Ambani, Ratan Tata, Aroon Purie, Pritish Nandy, Baba Kalyani, Salman Khan, Rajesh Khanna and a host of other powerful personalities are all Capricornians. Even Muhammad Ali Jinnah, the founder of Pakistan, was a Capricorn born on the same date as our Vajpayee. Maybe Pakistan and India may have a working relationship this year. I admit I am not God. In other words, this year is the year of India!

What is the real secret of the Capricorn? In one sentence, it is leadership, drive, tremendous organizing ability and objectivity.

> May I be like the Sun in seeing; like Fire in brilliance; like Wind in power; like Soma in fragrance; like Lord Brihaspati in intellect; like the Asvins in beauty; like Indra–Agni in strength.
>
> —Sama Veda: Brahmana, 11.iv.14

JUPITER

Ganesha says, you can take this mantra from the Sama Veda, and make it your ideal in life, because the time has come for it. The reason is that Jupiter, the planet of spirituality, good luck and all-round prosperity, will be in your own Sun sign from 2 December 2019 to 18 December 2020. The spin-off will be that Jupiter will be highlighting your creative impulses, your romantic and artistic needs, your sense of untrammelled, unhampered, total freedom. Like that, eh? Children and grandchildren will give joy. Entertainment and amusement will be your birthright. You could be moving with the younger crowd, maybe the jet set, maybe students, maybe toddlers and kids or writing about them, painting them, and in any case, having much to do with them. That's the bottom line. However, there is also scope for a suitable vocation. Do not become involved with the problems of others, not now, please. Also, you could lose the affection of others; yes, that's the flip side.

Ganesha clarifies that, for us all, your personality is the sum of all your experiences and influences. Jupiter, so to say, overhauls your personality and then galvanizes it, polishes it, makes it more useful, beautiful, and in a way, more perfect, or to be precise, as perfect as humanly possible. Let me put it in another way. Jupiter helps you to achieve, to win the game of life. Also, it elevates your mood, making you an optimist, capable of moving ahead with hope in your heart.

Most importantly, changes in outlook and environment will be very beneficial. That will be your passport to success. You will be the pioneer, the motivator, even if you have not been before, and the key to this will be a strong desire for action. You will take a keen interest in everything and initiate an enterprise, an industry or a major campaign, a political party, an art gallery/display/exhibition. Sales, publicity, ceremony and rites will also be emphasized. In other words, there will be tremendous potential for expansion and enterprise. You are going to be very visible in the public eye.

SATURN

According to Western astrology, Saturn will be in your sign, Capricorn, from 21 December 2017 to around 2020. This is indeed a long run for Saturn. The actual results will be:

- Older people will retire but possibly find new work.
- There will be enormous social changes in the form of new ideas, innovations and inventions, and a mighty struggle with old conventions, rigid customs and traditions and manners and actual way of thinking. In other words, a great change in the behaviour pattern and thought processes of the people of the

world including India. It is a time of transition and transformation but the final result, according to your Ganesha devotee, should be in favour of science and technology, and new as well as different modes of thinking. Thinking leads to behaviour. Behaviour leads to action. Action leads to change. Therefore, like it or not, we are in for a big revolutionary change in our thinking. Finally, it will help us in our own evolution. We often forget that everything in life has a price. Nothing is free. Evolution could be painful but necessary and sometimes inevitable. At the same time, I openly agree that I could be hopelessly wrong. I am guided by my Lord Ganesha, Mother Ganga and Mother Nature. But I openly admit that being a human being, I have my limitations.

One of the salient features will be a very active, positive and well planned move for space travel so much so that we could be preparing for migration within these three years. But for actual migration perhaps, the period from 18 December 2020 to 8 March 2023 will be of the utmost importance. I am informing you about it because I do not believe I will live long enough for you to point out about this to you. This is only an insight born out of Ganesha's grace, intuition and hard, bitter and sweet experience of over seventy years. But let me clarify that in life nothing is final. That is why life is always exciting and not completely predictable. That is the way I like it.

Let me summarize it for you. Ambition + efficiency + drastic changes in climate + human behaviour + structure + technology = a new and wonderful spirituality as well as humanity.

VENUS

Next to Saturn and Jupiter, Venus, the planet of charm and persuasion, has the greatest impact. This year, Venus turns favourable from 14 January to 7 February (communication), 5 March to 3 April (romance and creativity), 8 August to 5 September (partnerships, love, marriage, collaborations), 3 October to 27 October (religion, ceremonies, preparing a blueprint for future action), 22 November to 15 December (happiness for at least contentment with your achievements for the entire year).

BLUEPRINT FOR THE ENTIRE YEAR

January: Off and away to a magnificent start, despite pressures and pulls, says Ganesha.

February: Windfalls, joint finance, legacy, passion.

March: Right contacts, success, travel, publicity.

April: Tremendous drive, ambition honed perfectly.

May: Good news, pressures, delays, but all turns out well in the end. Do socialize.

June: Expenses, losses, extrasensory perceptions and psychic powers, glimpses of Ganesha/God/Allah/the supreme power, pilgrimages, rites and duties.

July: Success, happiness, fun and games, family, victory.

August: Finances, family, the luck of the draw, buying/selling/investing.

September: Fanning out to people and places, contracts and contacts; communication channels buzz.

October: Home, house, in-laws, renovation/decoration in office/shop/home.

November: Despite changes, you do enjoy yourself and are creative, children give joy.

December: Work, health, loans, pets and projects.

Special Note: From 31 December 2019 to July 2025, Uranus will be in your fifth angle. But very specially this year, 2020, Uranus will take a mighty jump or leap from romance to finance. Children, hobbies, love, engagement, executive ability, leisure and pleasure should jump 10 feet in the sky. It will be a hurrah. It will be happiness multiplied thousand times.

Your happiness quota is 87 per cent.

WEEKLY REVIEW BY PHASES OF MOON

10 January: Full Moon in Cancer

You are not a people's person as such, but as the year begins, you would start making contact with as many people as you can. The new moon is in your sign and you begin the year on a high note. Capricornians are decidedly ambitious, and, like the mountain goat, will climb every crevice to be right on top of the mountain to have most breath-taking view and the most delicious blades of grass in the process. You also attract and get the best mates. You are brimming with new ideas of expansion. If you are an entrepreneur and if you are employed, you will be looking at promotions or even a job switch with a far better pay packet and improved prospects. Intimate, personal and professional partnerships will all be generating money. If married, your spouse will also chip in. Your agenda for the year is very clear: you need to get to the top, and you will spare no effort to reach there. There is money to be made and many peaks to conquer.

17 January: Moon's Last Quarter in Libra

The gusto you started the year with will carry over through this week too. Funds, family and finances will be the dominating theme of your life. You are practical and pragmatic and do not waste your time on unnecessary emotion. You are not one for tears and family dramas; you prefer getting on with the job with the least bit of emotion involved. You understand money well and know that it can buy you the status you want. Genuine material security is the prime need and you go all out to achieve it. Money expresses itself in flashy language for you right now – new cars, watches, jewellery, holiday homes and so on. You will look for ways to improve your personal property in terms of add-ons, extensions and renovations. Family, friends and colleagues will help you in your acquaintance; there is no getting off the materialism roller coaster now. They are well and truly on the track for better or worse. Only, to be tempted by get-rich-quick schemes or something similar can be blinding, and you are temporarily blinded by Ganesha will make it pass.

24 January: New Moon in Capricorn

From the first weeks of concentrating on money and acquisition you turn your attention to family and intimate bonding. You are also deeply attached to your family, and your parents and siblings mean the world to you. You know that the family and finance can be well looked after if you earn well and so family and finance go hand in hand. You make extra efforts to secure the financial aspects of your extended family and look for new avenues of investments and expansion. You will tap the markets and indulge in speculations, with some success too. (I must add here that a lot depends on individual horoscopes and these are mere generalizations; and I must also remind you of the fact that the stars impel and don't compel.) If you are in a family business, you may recruit some family members as you feel it is the best way to keep a lid on your activities and business secrets. There are stolen moments of joy with your loved once and many happy moments with children.

2 February: Moon's First Quarter in Taurus

After all the initial expansion and moneymaking, you enter a world of new ideas and inspirations. You also entertain and have fun at social gatherings. It is not that you are not working, but meetings also help you network and make the right connections. You are less driven now and enjoy lighter moments with friends and family. You have to guard against depression though, as there will be minor irritants and they will plunge you into a deep-thinking mode. Your thoughts will get more profound and you will think beyond just money, career and family. This is not a bad thing as it really gets you off your one-track moneymaking schemes.

9 February: Full Moon in Leo

This is a period of consolidation. You will be making contracts with all sorts of people; you will be in a frenzy of communication, reaching out to everyone. You make valuable contacts and your business/work grows. You make money, with the right decisions at the right time and are prudent enough to invest the extra in cutting-edge securities and in purchases that make good sense. There are travel, an upswing in your prestige, more status in your community, and also many finer moments with your love. Everything is going great for you and Ganesha is smiling.

19 February: Moon's Last Quarter in Scorpio

You get encouraged by the good times and pitch in for more expansion. You think big and take risks like a gambler at Las Vegas. You are also in the throes of a new relationship and it is going well. Remember that there is the force of gravity and the higher you go, the harder you can fall. So it's good to spread out and be on a high but don't overextend yourself either physically or financially. If fortunes change (and you never know what happens when), you will fall flat on your face. You also get a tad arrogant and feel that you are the beginning and end of all life. This will provoke others and you will be the centre of a lot of envy, hate and criticism. Learn to be mild and modest. As we know only too well, pride comes before fall. Your love affairs too get over the top and it's time to apply the brakes.

23 February: New Moon in Aquarius

You are moving in many directions and the force is with you. You are doing too much too soon. You are also travelling and meeting people. Sometimes, you get too frank, blunt and outspoken and this will not help your cause one bit. You will also spend recklessly and indulge in all forms of speculation and gambling. There are new romance, attachments and love affairs, and you revel in it. In love you could take it to the next level. All in all, an expensive period in which many things happen to you and others in your close circle. A good period in which life deals you many cards and not all of them are bad. Ganesha helps you to play them well.

2 March: Moon's First Quarter in Gemini

You slow down a bit and think issues over. You must deal with mounting expenses but you are mired in your own doings of the last weeks. You look for more meaning in whatever you do and take recourse to spiritual books, perhaps even gods and god-men. But this is more than an intellectual movement; you move physically too, on business and for pleasure. You look at inner growth and greater knowledge which you realize will help you achieve all that you have set your sights on. This will certainly help, as rounding off your personality is essential towards achieving your goal.

9 March: Full Moon in Virgo

You are communicating frenetically this week. Local and domestic affairs will occupy your attention and set off a great deal of action, though it may not always be to your liking or inclination. There will be intrusions from others which you should guard against. You have been moving fast and in different directions. Prioritize your life and don't scatter your energies like you have been doing for some time now. The home environment needs attention, the office is taken care of, and so a shift of focus is needed. You also toy with new ideas which are quite impractical. Pray to Ganesha for guidance. I do it all the time.

16 March: Moon's Last Quarter in Sagittarius

You are streaming all your activities. You look to others for help in this and it is a welcome move as the world wants to help someone who is keen on doing so. No one likes losers, and you like to be a winner in the game of life and not a whiner. You have many accomplices now who will also, later, want a share in the pie. Capricornians are never whiners. You make changes in the basics and let go of crutches which may have helped you stay afloat in the past. You have a lot of self-belief now and your relationships are revitalized. There are promises of long-term stability. There is domestic ease and you are meticulous in all your affairs done right to the nitty-gritty. All this pays off handsomely and your moves have worked out well. There are sustained progress, domestic peace and an inner and outer balance to your life.

24 March: New Moon in Aries

This last quarter of the month is in your sign. Once again, you seek more avenues for more money as it means recognition, power and security in your lexicon. I do not say that it is not true, but an overemphasis on money may well be your undoing in the long run. You work hard and are motivated to move heaven and earth to achieve your goals. There will be a lot of stress and you need to take care. Family, loved ones, children, parents, in-laws and all the others in your extended family demand your time and you will be walking the tightrope. A tense period in which and you will have to find solutions to the myriad demands on you. Take care of your health and choose your friends carefully; you could go wrong here. There will be many leeches and sycophants who will do your image and reputation no good.

1 April: Moon's First Quarter in Cancer

Outstanding success is in store for you. You are determined and all fired up, and you move in the right direction with panache. You weed out all that you don't need which includes friends who don't mean well and other pretenders. Your attitude is right and you have an infectious optimism which will ensure that you get your point across without ruffling feathers. Family bonding will also be pleasing, fulfilling and there are promises of success and joy in all areas of your life. You make steady progress and squash all rivalry before it turns ugly and disastrous. Since your progress is visible you make the usual enemies who are jealous of your sudden and stupendous growth. But you are well equipped to handle all that and continue with the upward trajectory that you have well and truly charted out for yourself. Nothing can stop you now and you slay forth with Ganesha's blessings.

8 April: Full Moon in Libra

While the work area is moving along smoothly, you also make some personal conquests. You are more creative and attract many like-minded people who will collaborate with you both at work and at play. You have the path to success with concrete results. Your work skills are sharpened and your personal equation enhanced. You have laid the foundations and it is time to work on them and reap the dividends. With the right attitude and hard work that you put in, there is no room for failure. You make steady and sustained progress. There are some family issues that you need to deal with. It will be a diversion – a pleasant detour from your work-oriented strategies.

14 April: Moon's Last Quarter in Capricorn

There is beauty this week and also a reaching out to many people of great value to your personal and professional life. There are many emotions which will surface and there will be an intense love too. Along with all this there will be expenses; you will be making many purchases for the home and office and sprucing up your surroundings with more comfort and glitter. Your heart will rule and there may be wasteful spending too, as many decisions you make now will not be rational and will be based on impulse. It is the time for partnerships and collaborations and bonds of immense value. There are many possibilities opening up in this period and it all depends on how you seize them and utilize them. All said and done, it is the season for love, and love rules. Cupid has struck you, my dear Capricornians.

23 April: New Moon in Taurus

There is steady progress, in fact there has been steady progress for a long time now, but this is a period when you take a step back and introspect. You are filled with ideas and it is not all about work, money and career advancement. You think about the mysteries of life and even get philanthropic. You want to give something to those who are less fortunate and lend a helping hand to those who need it; you want to give back to life in a thanksgiving of sorts. You may mentor others and even turn counsellor. Ganesha has been kind to you and you are aware of it. Now you want to repay society and those who have helped you get whatever you have wanted. You spend time with friends and family and have a great time. You are content with life in this happy week.

30 April: Moon's First Quarter in Leo

Once the finances are worked out, you get to spending the money which you believe is hard-earned. There are many expenses and for a change, your creative instincts blossom. You do well at work and there is recognition. You may even get an award for something you have done, you love the limelight and the appreciation that it all brings. You are the toast of the office, and may get a promotion, if not more. If you are on your own, you make tangible expansion of the business/enterprise. A tremendous sense of aestheticism, of beauty, now grips you. There have been good times and you have worked hard and earned well and now you want to get creative and bring some beauty into your surroundings. You may try new hobbies and may even take to landscaping or get someone in the know to show you the ropes. You want to take your mind off work and look at other diversions, and there are many including a few love conquests. If married, I don't have to add that you need to be discreet and think things over many times before making a move. Don't spoil something beautiful which has taken years to develop for a roll in the hay. If you are single, it is your time in the sun.

7 May: Full Moon in Scorpio

After the break of the last week, you once again are on a high note. You make steady progress and money comes to you effortlessly. I must add here that I use money as a yardstick of success here, but money isn't the only yardstick. Life has many other equally or more important aspects. But, for the moment at least, you have worked for money and you will get it. Ganesha showers you with prosperity and you bask in it. You are creative and charismatic and take the world head on. You are capable of enormous hardwork and your stamina is unbelievable. The results will be marvellous and you move fast and in the right direction. This is an excellent period in which you not only consolidate your position but also make tangible and rapid gains.

14 May: Moon's Last Quarter in Aquarius

You are expanding your areas of interest furiously. Your canvas is larger than life and you are making great progress. Hobbies, sports and leisure activities excite you and you focus on pleasurable activities/pastimes. There are many new ventures, avenues and interests to spend your recharged energies on. You love work and spend with abandon like there is no tomorrow. You live for the moment and the 'now' is all that is relevant to you. It is a good way to be, as long as you don't stretch it. You may also fall in love and have many new associations; passion rules like never before. You have given yourself to what Osho has called the 'core of existence'.

22 May: New Moon in Gemini

Loves rules your life and you move away from the routine of work and money. You may be caught off guard but this moment of insanity will also pass, like everything else in life. You are trapped in the maya of passion and nothing else makes sense to you now. You reach out and bare your innermost self and the response is also immediate and intense. You are riding a tidal wave and hopefully it will take you where it should even if it is the rocks. After all, how much of destiny can we change?

30 May: Moon's First Quarter in Virgo

The mood mellows a bit now and you take a step backwards and manage to observe and evaluate the goings-on of the last few weeks objectively. Love is in the air but you get a grip on yourself. Watch your back and also your health. Explosive emotions can lead to ill health and you have to be careful. You also get a bit distracted with others' remarks and there are all types of little expenses and pinpricks which somehow disturb the harmony of the week. At one level, the mellow mood helps as you show a softer side to war people. It is quite liked and appreciated as they hadn't expected this. You also meet many new people who share your vision of a better tomorrow and a better world.

5 June: Full Moon in Sagittarius

Many people enter your life now. The earlier passion and intensity will fizzle out and there could be new platonic associations which are useful for work and career enhancement. More than the material gains you make will be the reaching out and the establishing of the right contacts. You sow the seeds for future businesses and meet people you can tap when the need arises. And arise it will, says Ganesha. You are strongly determined to move ahead.

13 June: Moon's Last Quarter in Pisces

You now get focused and stable and fire on all cylinders. The insanity of the past is over and now you look at the finer details at work meticulously. You pore over the fine print with a magnifying glass and cover lost ground with a vengeance. All the minutest points will be checked and you make sure that no one can cheat you. But watch out, you can become a nag and get too suspicious of even well-meaning people. You will also attempt to change your lifestyle and get more careful of what you eat and how you look. You may acquire a new wardrobe too. Certainly, you look at life more seriously and get down to the business of life and moving ahead in your career with firm intent.

21 June: New Moon in Cancer

You will spread yourself thin now. You will be meeting people and there will also be some travel. Some religious and spiritual limitations also work their way into your busy schedule. There will be spending and many new acquisitions along with new romance and a lot of entertainment. You want to try your hands at different things and take up new hobbies and interests. There is joy in personal relationships and you socialize a lot. You have your friends and many of them take entertaining to new heights. You are the life and joy of every party; you just sizzle and dazzle.

28 June: Moon's First Quarter in Libra

There is renewed zest and vigour in your professional life and you move ahead as one possessed. You enter the arena of life, throw challenges at all and emerge the winner. Your horizons broaden and there are many new projects on hand. You go for the jugular in both work and leisure. There is an intensity of purpose and you achieve a lot in a very short time. There are also many purchases to be made but they won't bleed you as you have made enough money and also have the good sense to make wise investments. Your purchase, even if they are absurdly flamboyant, will have genuine and lasting value. So in one way, you are still making the right investment and enjoying them too. Money and possessions are never out of your ambit.

5 July: Full Moon in Capricorn

You rope in your associates in your dealing and this proves to be a good move. The attention also shifts from the work front to home and family. There are many domestic responsibilities and joys to handle and enjoy. You also have to invest some time in your housing society or community and you can't get away from all this. Nor do you want to. There are other responsibilities to attend to as well. Plus there may be demands from siblings, co-workers, immediate and distance family and neighbours. Your plate is full and you examine all these commitments with great detail, concern and interest. You realize that you can't live a one-track life and that you also belong to the community at large.

12 July: Moon's Last Quarter in Gemini

Love and money are the twin themes to the week. You also find time to relax, and there could perhaps be a home away from home as a kind of holiday retreat or weekend getaway. There will be loans, joint accounts, bonds, insurance and funds of all kind to deal with on the money front, along with soaring expenses. You do a juggling act and manage it all well. You will also be spending a lot of time with loved ones and that will give you many happy moments. The family is important and you have neglected them a bit. You will realize this now and make up with far more intimate bonding with them.

20 July: New Moon in Cancer

The full moon is in your own sign and you make the most of this lucky phase. Your people skills will be at their best and you will get the support of both colleagues and loved ones. Partnerships and collaboration are vital and most beneficial in this period. You surmount many obstacles and ride the wave to glorious times. You worry about your image and there may be legal issues that could tarnish it. You confide in family and form a strong team to battle these challenges. You find great support and strength in your association and emerge victorious with ease. There is jealousy from your rivals but they are unable to cause you any harm. Ganesha's protection is there for you.

27 July: Moon's First Quarter in Virgo

Money and its appeal to you are more than ever before. You look at finance in a big way, as that is the main theme of this period. Personal and work-related finance hog that limelight. There are tax issues and all sorts of monetary developments that will take up your time. You have to solve it all and spend time behind closed doors getting to the nitty-gritty of your finances and its implications. It takes a lot out of you, but it is time well spent as you avoid the losses and expenses as well as sort out your affairs well. There are meetings galore in this period but they all work out happily in the end.

2 August: Full Moon in Aquarius

You have achieved a lot but you don't want to stop here. You are prepared to stick your neck out like a platoon commander flushing out terrorists. This works as you break new ground and make many startling discoveries.

Your new interests include religion and spirituality, travel and education. You have kept money aside for the family and for a nest egg, and so monetary issues are not the real focus this week. You look for harmony and try to smooth the feathers you have rustled in the past. You are looking to make amends as you finally believe that it is not a great idea to go on adding enemies. You look for harmony at home and in domestic affairs. You extend the hand of friendship to everyone and, surprisingly for you, there are many takers. Everyone, it seems, wants harmony.

11 August: Moon's Last Quarter in Taurus

Your conciliatory moves and work success are highly appreciated. There is enhanced income and prestige. You party a lot now and look at finance in the form of inheritance and legacies. You are a social butterfly and spend time at various gatherings enjoying yourself thoroughly. You are ebullient and enthusiastic and your happy mood is contagious. All this is a welcome respite from the hard slog that you have put in over the last many weeks.

19 August: New Moon in Leo

You are again on the work track. You are confident, pragmatic and determined and will forge ahead furiously. You earn applause for your achievements and decide to expand further and make more money which is never out of your sights for long. You look at holistic progress and make the necessary adjustments to your personal and work life so that both show steady progress and harmony. There are expenses but nothing that you can't handle. You are also, once again, on a shopping spree with family and loved ones. Everyone has a ball!

25 August: Moon's First Quarter in Sagittarius

You give your best to work and your relationship and there is great intensity in whatever you do. You extend your hand towards humanity, undertake social work and spend quality time with your children and/or parents. You are full of commitment and bond well with others. You are endowed now with a new vision and charisma and look at the future with immense possibilities in mind. You are riding the crest of a wave and feel that the world is yours to conquer. Your planning has been meticulous and your sustained efforts are finally paying off.

2 September: Full Moon in Pisces

You have seen yourself in a new light and are empowered by your success. The early part of the year was hectic and now you try to enjoy yourself and ride on the momentum generated in the previous months. There is a welcome change in your perspective and the way you are looking at the world. You are caring and considerate, alert and active. There is a new you eyeballing the world and whatever it has to offer. But, at the same time, while all this is hunky-dory, avoid unnecessary showdowns and run-ins with friends, family, colleagues and the law. There is a chance that you are getting too big for your boots. You will have to work hard on your ego which could be getting in the way of your advancement despite your making all the positive changes in your temperament. You spend and entertain easily and have happy, boisterous times.

10 September: Moon's Last Quarter in Gemini

You are busier than ever before and highly motivated in all that you undertake – and it shows in the results. You spend quality time with loved ones and there are possibilities of exciting travel. But there are pinpricks like unexpected expenses, ill health in the family and lack of valuable resources on issues that are of no relevance to you. In other words, there is highly avoidable wastage of both time and money. There is envy and politics at the workplace and you have to tread with caution. There may also be a brush with the law. Don't put your faith in people without ascertaining their credentials. Look at your finances carefully and put your financial papers/affairs in order. You may also be forced to take a new look at religion and spirituality so that you can derive greater mental strength.

17 September: New Moon in Virgo

There are many distractions at play here. There are partnerships, religious ceremonies, meetings and interviews and several business collaborations/connections, all of which lead you into a profitable, upward spiral. This is a good time to spread your wings and meet as many people as possible. There will be journeys and conferences and you will benefit greatly from them. There is romance in the air and, if married, there will be dealings with close family, your spouse, even your in-laws. If single, there is a chance that you may meet your life partner. There are many positive incidences at work and it all depends how you use them to the best of your ability.

24 September: Moon's First Quarter in Capricorn

Many things change in your life. This can be upsetting as your normal routines go for a toss. There are new work pressures and many changes in the domestic scene which may even include some illness in the family. So expenses will skyrocket. As a result of all this, on the plus side, you make positive bonding with the family. Every cloud has a silver lining, and the home environment is happy bonding. You have to thank the obstacles before you for this happy bonding. You are not one to shirk your responsibilities and you earn the respect and admiration of family and friends to begin with them in their time of need.

2 October: Full Moon in Aries

Family trends continue and you are a source of strength for those who need you. There may be children's education to deal with or the spouse's work could be undergoing an upheaval. You are also automatically involved in it. You are experiencing and appreciating the joys of togetherness and will focus on group and shared activities. These are all pleasant and necessary moments in a person's life and far removed from the drudgery of sustained work and moneymaking. It makes you more human and more well-rounded. You have changed a lot from the inside and it shows. People around you applaud the changes. You breathe easy, metaphorically and literally too, with far better health, and this aids you in your work. You may take up a pastime like painting or music and this helps you unwind. You are ready to take on the larger issues of the world head-on. You use this time to plan and re-examine your priorities and rework them.

10 October: Moon's Last Quarter in Cancer

You have gained some respite and rest and tasted the joys of leisure. Now you look at getting back to work with renewed energy. You feel better equipped to handle setbacks calmly and have greater belief in your own abilities. Your vision is perfect, and as a result, you persevere in your work and achieve miraculous results more than once and have come through with flying colours. You also spruce up your image, get a new look and are rejuvenated in a manner of speaking. You know that you have to strike the right chord now and that all the little details should be accounted for. You strive for greater glory and are on the right track personally, physically, emotionally.

16 October: New Moon in Libra

You are making considerable progress and also have great time with friends and family. Once again, you let your hair down too so that work and pleasure go hand in hand. You allocate time for both and it suits you well too. You find the magic equation of not having to burn the candle at both ends. You can strike the right balance between work and play and yet ensure success. Home life is also better, all your efforts of the recent past have worked in your favour and you enjoy the harmony and balance that you have achieved.

23 October: Moon's First Quarter in Aquarius

There is a dazzling new intensity to your life now as the year is coming to an end and the shadows get longer. You look back and are favoured by a period of growth in every sphere. You have worked hard and made money and ploughed through domestic problems like a warrior. You are visibly proud of yourself. You have a new self-image and glow around you. There is new planning afoot and you want to enhance on the mood that you are in. You focus marvellously. Money is the focus and you also hope to improve your social status. You entertain well and enjoy visibility. There is possible media attention and you revel in it as you realize that it is necessary to be seen, to be heard. With the right publicity, you know that you can stretch the frontiers of your work and career ambitions. So you may go in for a well-planned and elaborate PR exercise.

31 October: Full Moon in Taurus

Your life acquires a new intensity and tempo. You are on the fast track to success and even the fastest escalator is too slow. There may be a few delays and impediments, but you manage to get over all that with some breathtaking risk-taking ability. This is a week of unmitigated passion with your loved one. You find joy in intimacy and you move from physical pleasure to superconsciousness and that, I must add, is quite a remarkable journey, call it what you may. There will be legal issues to deal with, and possibly, a home or office shift. Despite it all, you are on the right track, as you want it, and make rapid progress. You are pedalling hard this year and gaining a lot of ground.

8 November: Moon's Last Quarter in Leo

You are thoughtful at the start of the week and wonder if you are going about it all in the right way. You finalize your plans of expansion and include many new aspects. Finances, funding, raising capital, investments come to the fore and you need to handle them imaginatively. There will also be strong family ties, bond of love and caring, buying and selling of assets, shares, or immovables like real estate. There is a good chance of an inheritance or windfall landing on your lap and you are overjoyed. There is a lot of money to use well, but you are also in a generous mood and spread the greenbacks to all. There are hangers-on but you don't mind. Why should you, when Ganesha has been so kind and showered you with life's goodies with such abundance and grace?

15 November: New Moon in Scorpio

You are flush with funds and the good times roll. You make the most of it and make valuable investments like purchasing land and buying gilt bonds. You also look at new lines of business and investments in which you can optimize existing funds. Along with all this is increased paperwork and minor irritants but you take all this is in your stride. Life is showering its bounties on you with a smile and you have no reason to complain. You entertain well and have a full house. Your generosity extends to family, friends, colleagues and all kinds of new acquaintances. You make many new purchases and live in the lap of luxury. It is a great time and you should be in thanksgiving mode.

22 November: Moon's First Quarter in Pisces

There are romance and passion in the atmosphere and no holds are barred; there is also a balance between home and work and several irons in the fire at the workplace. New enterprises and projects will materialize, but you may be overextending yourself, caught up in a new-found euphoria. You should watch out for possible roadblocks. You also have to guard against a possible display of arrogance, and some relationships and/or professional interactions could turn sour. You are expanding your interests and are generous and in a great mood, but it is still all about project 'me'. This could put people off. Also, your flamboyance may be aggravating others. Either you should take heed or forget about others' opinions and feelings and continue with the way you are. The former may be a better option, says Ganesha.

30 November: Full Moon in Gemini

If money and success mean progress and happiness, you are certainly on the right track. You socialize a lot and fix your sights on higher education and research. You reach out to intangible and genuine growth which you feel is possible only from the inside with more learning. You are on the path of glory, says Ganesha. There are many pleasant times with friends and loved ones, also many expenses and some travel too. You are on a high and nothing can stop you.

8 December: Moon's Last Quarter in Virgo

There is an enchanting, dreamlike quality to your days these days, there is also profound happiness and you truly pleasure with your work, family and every other aspect of your life. You indulge in a lot of social work and reach out to the poor and less fortunate. You make donations to charities and if involved in a humanitarian/charitable concern you expand your area of activity. You are in a giving mood and are also very generous. You are sympathetic warm and caring, and humanitarian efforts, social reform and spiritual growth will excite you. You decide to work less for a change and maybe engage in religious pursuits like helping install a huge idol in your community. For example, there will of course be many expenses and the funds are well directed, and you have the money for it, so you are in a good mood to give a portion of it away, and happily too. This philanthropy makes you immensely happy and, deep within you are consumed with gratitude to the maker for giving you so much in such difficult times.

14 December: New Moon in Sagittarius

You have peace of mind and continue to help others. You have the spiritual foundation for the generosity that has gripped you in recent times. This is an active, expressive and demanding phase and stress levels will run high as you push yourself in different directions. Compromises, negotiations, meetings, collaborations and settlements are on the cards. You meet with seers and soothsayers to unlock the mysteries of life which you feel are opening the pages of a new book on a subject that you have never ever read. You are on the verge of many starting discoveries, both about yourself and the world you live in. Ganesha is goading you on and wishes you every bit of good luck.

21 December: Moon's First Quarter in Aries

You continue to sail through life with great fortitude and determination. You overcome all obstacles with ease. There will be minor delays and confusions, postponements and setbacks but nothing will hold you back. You are capable of both holding your own and also enlisting support. There is intensity to this period despite it being a time of the year when there is festivity in the air. There are work issues, travel and a few disappointments to deal with but you manage to resolve and sort out all that comes your way. The period is strangely intense but also very rewarding. There are many demands on you and commitments to be met but you have the skills and the stamina to overcome it all. It may take a toll on your health, and family matters and romance may take a back seat for a while. But life has never been so engineered by the Almighty that you can have it all; no one can, as it is the way human creation has been made. You understand that well and move ahead with gumption.

30 December: Full Moon in Cancer

This has been a grand year by any yardstick. It is now ending and the last new moon of the year is in your own birth sign. It is also the time for joy, celebrations and fun all over the world. This is a week that will bring out the best in you, and you will be in party mood. Your self-esteem is high, you have society's approval and your work has earned just dividends. The family is also well provided for. Now is the time to party and go wild. There will be partnerships, collaborations and ties (possibly several romantic links-ups) and you are the envy of all. One of these days will also be your birthday. The celebration continues, and you enter 2021 with full energy and enthusiasm and many hopes for the future. It is a propitious phase of the moon and if you start something new now the good time will carry forward to 2021 and even beyond.

AQUARIUS

23 January–22 February

Symbol: The Water Bearer
Ruling Planet: The Uranus
Air-Fixed-Positive
The Sign of the Inventor, the Seeker of Truth
Embracing the world for peace and harmony:

Lokah samastah sukino bhavantu!
Om Shantih, Shantih, Shantih

May all beings in the world be happy!
Om peace, peace peace...

Mata Amritanandamayi is a beacon of hope in our turbulent times. If charity is giving food to the hungry, drugs to the sick, home to the homeless, education to the unlettered and love to the stricken souls, Amma is charitable to the milling multitude around her, Amma's words are magic, and her touch is healing. For the poor, she is a rich source of inspiration to live on. For the homeless, she is the final abode of hope. And for the entire humanity, she is the other word for peace.

It was my dear friend Sheshadri Iyer who made me aware of Mata Amritnandamayi.

I have often said: Life is a bug, without a hug.

Now to the real substance or nitty-gritty.

JUPITER

Jupiter will be in your twelfth angle from 2 December 2019 to 18 December 2020. Jupiter in your twelfth angle stands for secret knowledge, expenses, journeys, an initiation, travel, spiritual and uplifting experiences that dissolve the dark aspects and recesses of life and sorrow, all of which will be yours. Yes, you will overhaul your entire life and make its design grand and complete. It is vacuuming from within, and after that, how can there be any looking back? Expenditure, foreign lands, pilgrimage to holy places, property of parents and spirituality are the other possibilities. All of it will not happen. Only a few of these could occur for you. You must learn from your past mistakes. There will be contact with hospitals, the sick, the suffering, the disabled, the weak, and the helpless. Charitable undertakings and causes are probable. Affairs of the heart and liaisons are also indicated for you.

> O Lord, make my life full of Divine inspiration, that it may become productive only of good. Free me from all pettiness and narrowness. Help me to keep my thoughts fixed on that which is vast and majestic. Expand my heart and enlarge my mind that I may

be able to contain Thee and give myself up wholly to Thee.

—Swami Paramananda

This is your year of spirituality, expenses and possible ill health. Therefore, the above prayer to the Lord will set you free, make you happy, lessen your worries, erase your doubts and anxieties, and keep your relaxed. Jupiter will be in your twelfth angle from 2 December 2019 to 18 December 2020. As a result, a) visits to holy places, b) foreign lands, c) legal cases, d) accusations, e) separations and new unions are possible. You may have much to do with hospitals, centres of knowledge, wisdom, yoga, meditation and charity. You could be initiated into secret knowledge and hidden mysteries. But debts and losses are also possible. It is this unusual mix of pleasure and pain which makes the year unique for you!

Do not go in for liaisons, secret links and relationships, and please try not to exaggerate your troubles, or health problems. In other words, learn to maintain your balance.

You are, as I have always said, completely free to pray to Ganesha, Allah, Zorroaster, Christ, Buddha or any power you like. Amma is only a powerful illustration which flashed into my mind.

I am writing this piece on 26 May 2019 and at eighty-eight years I live only for peace and harmony of the world.

SATURN

Saturn will be in your twelfth angle or hidden angle, mysterious angle or esoteric angle from 21 December 2017 to around 2020. Here I openly admit that even after eighty-eight years, it is difficult for me to predict only about Saturn for Aquarians. Therefore, I am taking help of the Dell Horoscope very openly and informing you about what it says about your twelfth angle.

Emphasis is in your twelfth house, which rules

- personal limitations and problems
- situations of a secretive nature
- investigation, self-analysis
- charitable undertakings

You achieve the greatest success by

- gaining insight into your difficulties
- sticking to a very regular routine
- surmounting oversensitivity
- strengthening faith

You should avoid

- inviting unwise romantic entanglements
- creating tension with your subordinates
- over-magnifying your troubles
- not realizing your faults

My personal solution is that you should pray the mantra of Hanumanji on a Saturday. The mantra is '*Om Praam Preem Proum Sa Sanaye Namah*'. Pray this mantra twenty-one times and give money very specially to lepers, lame

AQUARIUS

people, old people and all orphans. Believe me, Ganeshji, Hanumanji, Shivji and Allah always love those who give charity to others. If you are charitable to others, God will be generous and kind to you also. This is an eternal law which will never change. Uranus
According to modern Western astrology, Uranus is your main planet or you can say the captain of the ship. Uranus has changed signs from 31 December 2019 to July 2025. For this year, the impact of Uranus will be in all property matters, for example, house, office, agriculture, storehouse, warehouse, land, parents and in-laws. Uranus can upset your apple cart and turn things on their head. But this year Uranus will help you in every possible way.

VENUS

Venus, the planet of sex, joy, happiness, parties and socializing, becomes very favourable for you between 20 December 2019 to 13 January 2020. The period from 4 April to 7 August is for creativity, parties, engagement and childbirth. That from 6 September to 2 October is for all sorts of alliances and, as I have repeatedly told, marriage is the biggest alliance. From 28 October to 21 November is for journeys, ceremonies, parents, in-laws and inspiration as well as new invention. Finally, from 16 December to the very end, you will be favoured in terms of promotion, prestige and power.

BLUEPRINT FOR THE ENTIRE YEAR

January: Work and projects could tell on your health unless you learn to relax.

February: Love/hate, attachments/separations, journey/home away from home, marriage/divorce.

March: Funds for work/home, trusts, buying/selling/investing/capital formation.

April: Journeys, publicity, exaltation and exultation, collaborations, a grand reaching out to people and places.

May: 'Work is worship' could well be your motto, and for good measure, add duty and beauty.

June: Love, life, laughter and the law of chances operate in your favour; so if you feel like it, take a few chances.

July: Despite expenses and interferences, property matters and family conditions do give some satisfaction; buying/selling/journeying are emphasized.

August: Go all out for the kill and emerge victorious in whatever you do.

September: Finances and funds will be augmented.

October: Contacts, contracts, socializing, friendships, good news and you.

November: Home, house, family, parents, property, renovation/decoration, buying/selling/leasing/shopping.

December: Plenty of fun and frolic, children and creativity fulfil you; a great ending to a busy beginning, concludes Ganesha.

Your happiness quota is 82 per cent.

WEEKLY REVIEW BY PHASES OF THE MOON

10 January: Full Moon in Cancer

The last year ended with many journeys and new vistas opening up in your life. The trend will continue this year too, at least for some time. You will be meeting many people from different walks of life and, possibly, from different countries and cultures too. There will be a lot of interaction, ideas and energy exchange at all levels, feelings as you reach out and make contact. There may be mood swings and several periods of depression and elation which follow you throughout the year. You are easily influenced and can swing from one state to the other easily. You have wild ideas and never fit into the ordinary, conservative scheme of things and will often be misunderstood. It is easy to see why no one understands you as your ideas, perspectives, philosophies, etc., belong to another world. You are often far ahead of your times. Since you aren't understood and are intrinsically honest, fair, sympathetic, and mean well, this hurt rankles deep within you and results in more inordinate behaviour. You have to work this out yourself depending on your personal horoscope. There is no point in recoiling and cutting your nose to spite your face. Sometimes, there may even be the need to take professional help.

17 January: Moon's Last Quarter in Libra

Since many different moods nestle in you and emerge as and when they feel like it, it is important which mood and which aspect of your diverse personality you take out of the bag. At so many levels, you do not belong to the real world and its mundane demands. You like to live free and fly like a bird.

You can be a creative genius or a social worker or someone who scales the peaks of fiscal triumph. Which one are you? The success that you normally achieve is very different from the typical Scorpio or Taurean struggle and triumph bases on blood, sweat and tears. Your successes are built on whimsy, almost by the seemingly ineffective twirl of your figures. You are pushed to do things this week and there will be many domestic and other social engagements taking up your time. You can be alert, positive, creative and caring and so don't let negativism get in the way. It will be a good idea not to get overtly critical or bad-tempered. You must remember that you have many support systems and will always be bailed out in times of need.

24 January: New Moon in Capricorn

You are filled with love and care for those close to you and even for the large mass of humanity. You are one of the 'carers' of the world and in this moon phase this aspect gets even further exacerbated. You spend time and money indulging others. Some may feel that you have no respect for your time and that people take advantage of you but that is the way you are and there is no escaping it unless you very badly want to. All this could lead to hurt and disappointment and even a feeling of exploitation and resignation. But there is no point in dwelling on negativity and there are many other aspects you can focus on like a home improvement program, renovation, refurbishing, redecorating, etc., which will be useful and also an instant distraction. All your relationships will get a new edge this week and they will flourish. You will also be happy.

2 February: Moon's First Quarter in Taurus

This is a very significant period with many far-reaching consequences. The new moon is in your sign in your birth period on the third of the month which is the number for Jupiter. Every aspect of your life gets heightened. You excel at work and play and are in great demand even to resolve domestic issues. You are a great solution provider and seem to have answers to all ticklish psychological issues. Listen to your inner voice for guidance There will be prestige, social status, promotion, triumphs, awards and rewards. You have a large social circle and the rewards for your efforts will be seen by all.

9 February: Full Moon in Leo

You are moving from strength to strength and this is a period of consolidation. You make great strides at work and make money and do the necessary investments. There is buying and selling and speculation in the stock and realty sectors. Your knowledge grows and several work-related avenues open up. You carry through demanding and far-fetched schemes as you begin to exploit potential to the fullest. It is the start of a wonderful phase and you move ahead with Ganesha's blessings!

19 February: Moon's Last Quarter in Scorpio

There is very little to stop you or halt you in your tracks. You are filled with confidence and begin to think really big. You pursue serious issues and also are in a celebratory mood and there is fun and festivity in your life with a series of parties and get-togethers. Your mood is uplifted and all the gloominess which you were associated with is ancient history.

You examine uncharted areas like discoveries, inventions, research, astrology, auras, magnets, numerology, new diets, macro foods and probiotics, space travel, Scientology, new age yoga, mudras, vastu, feng shui and everything else that spills out of the cupboards of your mind. If you are working in these areas, you do wonderfully well. Is it any wonder that it is called the age of Aquarius!

23 February: New Moon in Aquarius

You are expanding at a rapid pace and meeting all sorts of people. You are signing the dotted line in a series of profitable collaborations. Finances will dominate the week – be it investments, buying/selling, and new acquisitions for yourself, the home and the office. There is money flowing and you use it well too. You are not the type who generally hoards and you like to share your earnings. You get yourself a new wardrobe and add your personal signature to it. You look dandy this week.

2 March: Moon's First Quarter in Gemini

You need to work hard to take a grip on your emotions this week. You will be very sensitive about something and overtly emotional and all this will set you back. You also look at tantra and mantra and spend time in esoteric and spiritual pursuits. You will have close associations and, possibly, the kindling of a new romance. Your sensitivity draws many admirers, and this could well be a time for distraction and rustle with the opposite sex (I understand here that the laws of the land have changed, and gender issues don't come in here). But this will be a highly emotionally charged week and you will have to extricate yourself from it to move on with your goals and plans.

9 March: Full Moon in Virgo

You are distracted by your many associations and spend a good portion of the week at meetings and with friends that, I dare say, will not be hugely profitable. People come to you with their problems and you love solving them. As a result, a lot of time is wasted and more serious work piles up. Domestic affairs also come into sharp focus and you will be attending to the home and family needs. There may be illnesses and unwanted expenses. Be prepared for all that. As we know, being forewarned is being forearmed.

16 March: Moon's Last Quarter in Sagittarius

There is a lot of stability in your dealings and you settle down to the grind. You work hard and see the results easily. You move fast, solve pending issues and lay solid foundations for expansion. Your efforts and endeavours are energized and you are duly rewarded. There are promotion, perks and progress. You are not one to be moved by all this and you take it in your stride. Money certainly buys goodies but it doesn't find a place in your shrine. You live in a world of ideas and dreams, and money, at best, fuels them. You get your high from the origination of ideas and not from the accumulation of money. You know that the greenback is a means to an end and refuse to dwell on its lure too much.

24 March: New Moon in Aries

The concrete and sustained work phase continues. You make steady progress and start new collaborations/ventures/offices. There will be travel and some expenses too. But this is a phase of consolidation and you will be covering a lot of ground. Children will bring joy in sports or in extracurricular activities. There will be family outings, possibly a holiday together. There is all-round growth this week and you are in harmony and sing a happy tune.

1 April: Moon's First Quarter in Cancer

The mid-year is action packed. Even the temperature starts sizzling and you are not left out of the furnace in your dealings. You slog away and make deep inroads into success. At many levels it is a frantic, frenetic and hectic week. There will be scope for the creative expression of your personality, and you examine life with vision, optimism and faith. Your thirst for knowledge gains momentum and you pore over whatever you can lay your hands on. There is remarkable progress too and you are satisfied with the results.

8 April: Full Moon in Libra

You look at bonds, connections, relationships, associations, marriages, engagements, concerts, get-togethers and everything to do with people. You will be in a frenzy of communication as people rally around you. You are in the limelight and much sought after. Your work is going as you want it to and you are supercharged. You are a special invitee everywhere. You are in harmony, living and sharing love. There is a new-found finesse in whatever you do.

14 April: Moon's Last Quarter in Capricorn

You are stricken by beautiful objects. There may be a whirlwind affair that catches you off balance, or you spend time and money decorating the home and office. You are oozing charm and feel virile/fertile. You get away from the pulls of work and look at the other areas of your life which need refurbishing. You widen your horizons and increase your interactions and relationships. You reach out to people and places. There will be many new acquaintances and contacts, ties and bonds that are meaningful. You lay the foundations for the great leap ahead.

23 April: New Moon in Taurus

Your focus at work may suffer as a result of all your other interests and activities. You spend a lot of time with others and, once again, allow mood swings and a fickle temperament to take over your joys. You are very sensitive and emotional and can get buried in the hurts and unsavoury episodes of the past. You get out of this soon but it does take a toll. Watch out for undue stress and possible illness. You give a lot of yourself and are leached on my emotional vampires who find you rare game. Their vibrations affect you. You must learn to protect yourself.

30 April: Moon's First Quarter in Leo

This is a formidable phase in which you push ahead hard and true. You are all fired up to make inroads and are greeted with success in all your activities. You spend on luxuries as if there will be no phase tomorrow; home and wardrobe renovation takes a lot of your time. You also make sensible investments and may buy property. There is money to be made on the markets too. It will be in your interest if you can guard against overindulgence in this period.

7 May: Full Moon in Scorpio

The tide thankfully changes and you enter a phase of hard work. You see the immediate reward and are encouraged to work harder. You put in all that you have. With the work that you have started, on your mind seemingly occupied now, your health improves. You are filled with energy and are set to take off on an exciting, new trajectory. You dazzle with your creativity and charisma. There is domestic happiness and you are relaxed, happy and truly at ease. you win the admiration of your peers and ink projects that take you to great heights. There could also be an addition to the family. The single may also hear the sweet sounds of wedding bells.

14 May: Moon's Last Quarter in Aquarius

Your life is like an unending celebration now. There is better rapport with colleagues, associates, peers and family. You party and entertain lavishly. You are optimistic and are able to fulfil all your obligations. There could be travel on work or a holiday with the family, but the portents are happy moments away from home. You enjoy the good things of life and the sun shines on you in more ways than one.

22 May: New Moon in Gemini

You are not laid-back or relaxed this week but are full of progressive, even daring ideas for future career advancement and financial success. There is a new intensity in all your dealings as you look for innovative methods to make money. There are new responsibilities at home and you are also looking at serious career advancement. This is a good time to embark on new projects. The stars shine on you.

30 May: Moon's First Quarter in Virgo

Watch out for your famed mood swings. This is a volatile period and you could get tremendously emotional about some aspect of your life and it could get out of hand like a soap opera gone all wrong. Your family life is important and it is essential that you work on it. There will be unnecessary misunderstandings and you could be pitchforked into bitter family feuds over inheritance and other issues. It will be prudent to remain calm and let the dust settle as it always will.

5 June: Full Moon in Sagittarius

This is an interesting phase with many contradictory forces at play. You are full of wisdom and caring, exceptionally creative and, as always, willing to help the needy and downtrodden. On the other hand, you may also be rubbing shoulders with the top honchos of business and industry and signing big deals. Many facets of your personality come to the fore here. You don't really care about money, but it comes to you nevertheless in bushels. You also spend time with the family and please yourself with some high-end entertainment and purchases. By any account, this is an interesting phase.

13 June: Moon's Last Quarter in Pisces

The dust settles as it has to and you are back to earth and to the cares, worries and duties of the world. You will be sorting out family issues and work-related problems. It will not be easy and you will have to walk over burning coal before favourable decisions are arrived at. All issues will be finally resolved but it will take its time and toll on you and the others. Money matters will have to be gone through with a fine comb. Family, in-laws, friends and acquaintances, and the community at large also take your time. But you cope well and emerge unscathed. You are full of positive energy, work hard and achieve the desired results.

21 June: New Moon in Cancer

You are moving ahead at a rapid pace now. There is joy in relationships and sustained progress at work. So the major aspects of your life are doing well. Health is also good. This is a period marked by the return of the old associated to the fold and there will be a lot of partying and merrymaking. You are on stable ground and zooming ahead without a care in the world.

28 June: Moon's First Quarter in Libra

The momentum and the pace continue unabated. You are making rapid progress and win laurels for it. There is a surge in your willpower, optimism, vision and aspirations. You are expanding on all fronts and the luck of the draw favours you. Your kitty is full and you can see quite clearly that you are on the right track. You are focused, on a fast-track growth and engage yourself with money matters. You set the house in order which is essential to surge ahead. You also find the time to meet up with those who mean a lot to you.

5 July: Full Moon in Capricorn

You rode the crest of achievements and glory and now your attention shifts to the needs of the family. Children will bring happiness and parents, in-laws, extended family, siblings call for your time. You also retreat from the cares of the world into your private shell. It could be a farmhouse, country home or even a quiet corner of seclusion. But you need to get away and be by yourself. You need to think things over as they have all been moving as fast as a Hollywood thriller. You are doing well and there are no financial worries and, strangely, this disquiets you. You want to seek out masters and seers, good books and music, and look for answers into existence. You wonder if money and its making are all that there is to life.

12 July: Moon's Last Quarter in Gemini

You make big purchases and fill your office and home with works of art. You feel like doing up your place tastefully and that costs money which you don't mind spending. You have new perspectives of life and are faced with a string of possibilities. You have many options and worry which to choose from; this is, of course, a good problem to have. Exert caution against overindulgence and try to maintain a sense of proportion, and balance. There is a lot happening at work and play and you need to make several adjustments to fit in. You enter a period of warmth and luxury, and Ganesha is smiling on you!

20 July: New Moon in Cancer

You need to make strong decisions and steer the boat in the right direction. You are energized and enthused to steer full steam ahead. You achieve a lot and are single-minded and focused. The results are spectacular. You win applause and grow in several ways. There will also be happy times with friends and family. You should, once again, watch your temperament closely. Try not to slip into your dark moods.

27 July: Moon's First Quarter in Virgo

There is substantial growth in the last quarter. You have reached a point in your life and in your career where what you say is of consequence and you are listened to with care. Your innovative schemes and ideas win many admirers and you also make money. There are meetings, collaborations and all types of expenses too. You spend time with the family and there may be minor hospital expenses. Elderly Aquarians may need special care. But once again, luck is on your side and all is well that ends well.

2 August: Full Moon in Aquarius

The bull run in your life continues. There are new associations and, possibly, steaming sex. It may not last but will be well worth it while it does. You spend large sums on the object of your affections and, for a while at least, lose all balance and sense of direction. You throw caution to the winds and immerse yourself in your pet indulgence. Money and emotions remain in sharp focus this week and you also move up the ladder of success and fame. You also grow as a person.

11 August: Moon's Last Quarter in Taurus

This is a very important period with the full moon in your sign. There are many possibilities now but it also depends on how you tweak them. This phase is full of hope and promise. There may be an end to your struggles and mental confusion or they will just increase and blow up in your face. It depends on you in many ways. You have the key. You can either pursue your inner growth and be healthy and more productive or get into needless emotional and psychic dilemmas and drown in their turbid waters. You can have a new and very beautiful kind of advancement or you can get morbid and tiring. Make a wise choice as the possibilities and potentials of this period are immense.

19 August: New Moon in Leo

Luckily, you are brought back to the real world just in time. Several domestic and work pressures are waiting for you to solve them and sort out your affairs. You will have to deal with finances, settlements and legal matters. You have the necessary negotiating skills but all this is a waste of time and a detour from what you really want to do, which is to ideate. There are expenses and pressures of all types and you are pushed to find answers. On the plus side, this keeps you grounded and you work hard for the results have finally arrived after intense deliberations.

25 August: Moon's First Quarter in Sagittarius

You continue on the practical plank and settle down to working hard. There are a lot of finer details that need your attention both at home and at work and there is no time for fanciful thinking. There are appraisals at work and several key decisions to be taken if you are self-employed. This is valuable time and you can't squander it. Money will have to be looked into; children's schooling, parents' and spouse's medical issues and several such matters hog your time and attention. The plough is around your neck and you have no option but slog away.

2 September: Full Moon in Pisces

You will be relating better to people and will be making several long-term plans. There are indications of travel and conferences, gatherings and conventions to attend. All this will go a long way in bolstering your career. You meet up with associates and party. There is the danger of spiralling expenses and some ill health too. You may get into arguments, altercations and unnecessary disagreements and could lose your temper and say things you would be better off not saying. It is a week that is heavy under the collar. You must watch your step and tongue.

10 September: Moon's Last Quarter in Gemini

In many ways, this can be a beautiful period. There will be better health, better prospects and better income, and you will cool off and not enter unnecessary argumentation. There is a lot of entertainment on your plate including a dash of romance. You are in love with love, and so any person or thing that suits the mood will become the object of your affections. If you are a pet lover, you may get an exotic breed home or invest in some quaint pet like a parakeet, iguana, mice, rabbit or something quite different from the ordinary. You will pass through moments of heightened emotions and this can be very beautiful if you dare to share it with someone close.

17 September: New Moon in Virgo

In the third quarter of September you ease off and spend time with loved ones. You decide to take the family out and have some truly wonderful moments. If intellectually inclined, you do exceptionally well. There will be several visitors and some even from overseas. So a lot of your time will be spent socializing and travelling to the tourist spots. Creative pursuits will be highlighted. It is a happy accomplishment or achievement but nothing to complain about.

24 September: Moon's First Quarter in Capricorn

Emotions continue to run high. You are traipsing an electric wire ready to snap. Nothing works out your way completely and several compromises will have to be made in all your dealings. Sometimes you feel defeated, but Ganesha advises you to just hang in there and wait patiently for the tide to change. You do spend time at work and at home solving various domestic issues but you are not all there. You seem distracted and vague about several issues concerning you. There are expenses to handle and several other challenges. You decide to pull up your socks and work at it. This isn't an easy week, and your attitude doesn't help either.

2 October: Full Moon in Aries

You make a conscious effort to handle the situation that is slowly getting out of hand. This results in dividends, and a type of parity is restored in your affairs. There are splendid opportunities for advancement and this is a good time to strike. There is money to be made and new ventures waiting to be started. You are looking at achievements and recognitions. You identify areas of potential growth and go for it. This is a change in the trend of the last few weeks. You are on firm ground now and show determination energy, sense of purpose and direction. You are in achievement mode. There are money problems and other issues to solve and you spend the week seriously meeting all your challenges.

10 October: Moon's Last Quarter in Cancer

The hard-work phase continues. You do well and earn plaudits from your peer group. You are moving ahead uncompromisingly and are meeting all your targets and schedules. There are expenses, wining and dining and affairs of the heart. You could be embroiled in an office affair and this disturbs the peace. You are much more alert, lively and healthy and filled with new-found zeal. You are driven to make a success of your life and your hormones are also flying off in different directions. Charles Darwin would have placed his last buck on you to propagate the species in the mood you are in!

16 October: New Moon in Libra

A lot of quality time will be spent with family and friends in this quarter. There could be weddings, engagements and other family functions to attend, while a lot of time is spent with family. I must hasten to add here that it may not all be happy, there could be illness and some strife in the form of divorce or some problem in an alimony suit. You will either be the mediator or one of the parties needing help; any which way you will be in the thick of it. You need greater income generation to meet all your requirements and you will be hard-pressed to find new avenues of work. You may also involve yourself in social welfare and philanthropy but the need of the hour really is to get your house in order. There us a lot demanding your attention and you need to wear your thinking cap and sort it all out.

23 October: Moon's First Quarter in Aquarius

There is sharpness in your life, an edge that was never there. You realize that you have been procrastinating and postponing the settlement of various pending issues in your life. So, this week, you try to set your house in order. Friends and new and old romance show up, but you are preoccupied with the nitty-gritty. Your life is on the on the verge of an upheaval and if you don't plug the corners now, it may just be too late. So you go about cleaning the stable with single-mindedness. Finally, there is an urgency to your intentions and you manage to salvage lost ground.

31 October: Full Moon in Taurus

Many dark thoughts float through your mind. There will be change in your interests and there will be new ideas and ingenuity at work. You are attracted to the mysterious and to deep secrets. You will also get into the swing of hard work and apply all your ideas to the issues at hand. You are embarking on a new phase of achievement and hard work and you will brace yourself for it. You know that there is no free lunch in the world and you will have to do more than sing for your supper.

8 November: Moon's Last Quarter in Leo

A lot is happening in your life now. You are in the eyes of many cross-currents and will participate in all kinds of social activities. You feel wanted, cherished and loved. You realize that you are really popular and don't have to be the lone wolf any more. You don't have to carry the cross and chafe your shoulders. You are publicly feted and are the cynosure of all eyes. You feel blessed, loved, humbled and also at peace and in gratitude to existence for making this happen.

15 November: New Moon in Scorpio

No lull lasts long, and work calls. You'll get back to business and profession in a really big way now. Work is on an upward swing and you will be actively involved in new business enterprises and undertakings. You make good money and will feel secure. There will be travel too. Collaborations, purchases, comforts, luxuries and vestiges of the good life infuse you with fresh enthusiasm. You display awesome stamina and can move mountains during this period. It is a week of sustained had work and just deserts.

22 November: Moon's First Quarter in Pisces

You continue with a scintillating performance and consolidate your gains. There will be expenses and a hectic social life. Family will be strengthened and you will be busy renovating, redecorating and refurbishing. You will be the centre of attraction at family gatherings and you will enjoy it. Your interactions will be stronger and more meaningful and life will acquire a pleasant hue.

30 November: Full Moon in Gemini

This can be a period of new beginnings both at home and at work. You will make money and also spend it. Lending/borrowing funds, raising capital, loans, stocks, realty and buying and selling will occupy your time. This is the time to plan and strategize for the coming year. There are many new openings on the anvil and a lot depends on how you optimize the chances that come your way. This can be a very profitable phase and it all depends on how you cash on it. This is where you exert your free will and make your own destiny.

8 December: Moon's Last Quarter in Virgo

You spend time helping the poor and the downtrodden. You visit old people's homes, hospitals, hospices, shelters, halfway homes and other such institutions and help out with cash and kind. You have great empathy for the underdog and frequently take this route. Even if you don't have the resources to do this, you spend time helping out family members, friends, colleagues and others in distress. You may not be particularly ritualistic or religious, but appease your soul with such gestures off and on. You feel good about it and the world is a better place thanks to souls like you.

14 December: New Moon in Sagittarius

You scatter your energies and it doesn't result in much. Money comes in through one hand and goes out with ease through the other. You while away time merrymaking and hanging out with friends as though you have no care in the world. Momentarily, at last, your life has lost direction. You look for approval but it isn't forthcoming. You are told, in no uncertain terms, by friends and family that you need to get your act together, and fast. You value their opinion and make amends. But this is just a passing phase and there will be serious issues taking your time in the weeks and months to come. You will brace yourself to face the challenges, says Ganesha.

21 December: Moon's First Quarter in Aries

The end of the year sees a thread of intensity in all your dealings. You are pushing ahead without stops with a new resolve and ambition. You are confident and charismatic, full of magnetism and drive. Your popularity soars and all that you embark on or consolidate lead to success. You don't have much time for the family now but work and its rewards are appetizing. Ganesha sees you turbocharge as you successfully accomplish one task after another.

30 December: Full Moon in Cancer

The year ends well with a strong sense of purpose. You know where you are going and you are treading a definite path. You widen the scope of your life and undertake many journeys. There will be progress at work and you may embark on a new project; you are at the crossroads of major expansion. There will be a lot of family bonding and many celebratory moments. It is a good end to the year and you are all geared up to take 2021 by the horns. You are filled with enthusiasm, zest, energy and new hope for the future. Your friends stand by you and you feel empowered by their support.

PISCES

23 February–20 March

Symbol: The Fish
Ruling Planet: The Neptune
Water-Mutable-Negative
The Sign of the Dreamer-Poet, the Occultist.

Ganesha says, the street-sweeper, a twelve-gauge, twelve-shell shotgun, manifests in a powerful manner. You will also be pursuing your aims, be it money, romance, contracts, children, education, research, funding, home, office and vehicles. This is a good time to show to the world how good you really are. You will 'carpet-bomb' the opposite and win the day! Obviously, I am still enough of a child to enjoy war games. Most men are.

JUPITER

From 2 December 2019 to 18 December 2020 Jupiter will move in your eleventh angle which stands for:

a) wish-fulfilment
b) gaiety and gains
c) promotions and perks
d) socializing and partying and all group activities
e) the realization of dreams
f) children and creativity, marriage, love, socialising

Here is a different way of assuring you that the period from 2 December 2019 to 18 December 18 2020 will be superb for you, says Ganesha. It will make you the top gun. All your efforts, your work and inputs now start to yield dividends in terms of success, happiness, achievements. And that's saying a lot. Creativity will be at an all-time high. Those in the artistic and literary fields, even technology, research, the whole world of academia, will really shine as they come into their own. As if this in itself were not enough, you will have love and laughter, romance, marriage, friends, good partnerships, fruitful collaborations. The deals that you make will work out beautifully and smoothly. All I can say is: render thanks to Ganesha.

SAM GACHCHHADHVAM SAM VADADHVAM SAM VO MANANSI JANATAM...

> Meet together, speak together, let your minds be of one accord, as the gods of old, being of one mind, accepted their share of the sacrifice. May your counsel be common, your assembly common, common the mind, and thoughts of these united. A common purpose do I lay before you, and worship with your

common oblation. Let your aims be common, and your hearts of one accord, and all of you be of one mind, so you may live well together

— Rig Veda

This was chanted centuries ago and holds good even today.

Our New Age is all about connectivity and collectivity. Jupiter in your eleventh angle demonstrates this superbly. Therefore, the quote from the Rig Veda applies very specially to you folks. Yes, that's your destiny.

From 2 December 2019 to 18 December 2020 Jupiter will be in your eleventh angle. The spin-offs will be:

a) There will be wish-fulfilment and hope, and we do know, it is hope that keeps the world going, just as love keeps it passionately alive, and beautiful.

b) Old acquaintances, new friends, sweethearts and loved ones, mate and companions, all form a full circle of happiness for you – well, at least, for the most part.

c) Your income would come from more than one source, and here one of the secrets would be socializing and fraternizing.

d) You must learn not to offend those who love and support you. Not ego, but love, will get you where you aspire to be.

e) Jupiter could also make you spend too lavishly for your own good, or over-reach in business deals and investments, because Jupiter means expansion at all levels, and that applies to your wallet/purse too.

f) Possessions, fusing substance with style, say, in clothes, work, home, renovation/decoration of either new or ancestral property, are foretold.

g) Good news about children and a whiff of romance, hobbies and sports.

h) Pious deeds, charitable acts, the elder brother, paternal uncle, the longevity of your mother, finding lost/stolen goods/valuables, treasures, lotteries and windfalls, recovery from illness and, therefore returning from hospital and medical centres, are the attributes and power of this placing.

Pisces is one of the most developed signs, spiritually. The Great Mother of Pondicherry was a Piscean. The world's greatest scientist Einstein and Yuri Gagarin, the first man to travel in space, were both Pisceans. I am not a Piscean. But I feel Pisceans have something of all the other signs, and imaginative brilliance of their very own. For example, Aamir Khan. Just for the record, the glorious and glamorous Elizabeth Taylor is also a Piscean. In Indian astrology, very specifically, Pisces is associated with both salvation and art. But let me once again remind readers that this book mainly follows Western astrology.

SATURN

Now we take Saturn according to the great astrologer Robert Hand.

Saturn will be in your eleventh house from 21 December 2017 to 23 March 2020. The eleventh house represents friendship. This can refer to your feelings of friendship for each other as well as to friends that you have as a couple.

In the first instance, Saturn in this house does not make friendship between you impossible, but it does somewhat cool your expression of it; you may still have a very enduring relationship. You may be quite reserved with each other, but that may be just as well, for it will permit your relationship to last longer. As the eleventh house Saturn can indicate a very long-lasting friendship.

The eleventh house is also the house of one's ideals, hopes, and wishes. In some cases, Saturn can signify that the two of you have very different ideals and that you don't usually react in the same way towards things. This can diminish your sympathy for each other and make the relationship quite difficult.

Taking the second side of the eleventh house, that of friends outside the relationship, it can be said that when Saturn is operating positively, it indicates few outside friends, but those few will be firm and long-lasting. They may be older than either of you. But if Saturn's influence is not working out well, you may not have any outside friends, probably because of some rigidity in you that makes it impossible for you to share yourselves with others.

BLUEPRINT FOR THE ENTIRE YEAR

January: Open sesame to fame, fortune, children, romance, hobbies, creativity.

February: Health, work, colleagues, irritations over pets, projects and important trifles.

March: Collaborations, partnerships at all levels, journeys with a stopover, reaching out to people, places.

April: Joint finances, insurance, loans, public trusts, low vitality, sex and love in a strange mix.

May: The luck of the draw, knowledge, evolution, wisdom, ancestors and rites, genuine spirituality, long-distance connections, pilgrimages.

June: A high-powered month for work and play, prestige and promotion, parents and in-laws, boss and life mate.

July: A golden harvest for the trouble taken and the seeds planted, and that says it all.

August: Expenses, work, contacts, secret work, affairs of the heart, illumination of the soul, though there could be inflammation of your (foot) sole.

September: Wishes granted, rewards, wish-fulfilment is possible; you will feel wonderful and strong, ready to take on all comers.

October: Finance, food, family, and that does not mean entertainment, amusement, doing the social rounds.

November: Gains, friends, children, creativity, group activity, joy and delight in life.

December: House, home, parents, in-laws, a home away from home, travel, get-togethers and separations.

Special Notes: Ganesha says that Uranus has changed signs and will be in your third angle from 31 December 2019 to July 2025. Communication, contacts, correspondence, consciousness, short journeys, brothers and sisters – yes, all of it will be highlighted as never before. Ganesha says the trick and the ticket is in one-word circulation. That's it!

Your happiness quota is 82 per cent.

WEEKLY REVIEW BY PHASES OF THE MOON

10 January: Full Moon in Cancer

The year starts with a reality check. You realize that your plate is filled with activities and that you are in for a hard slog. You are also ambitious and money is honey. While you are not the flamboyant type and don't necessarily believe in ostentation, you know very well that money sponsors your dreams. So you work hard from the word go and grab every opportunity that comes your way. There is also love and bonding in the family. They understand that work is important to you and they see the tangibles that money can buy. You like a happy home and want to get them whatever they desire. This goads you to work harder. On the flip side, there are also memorable moments with the family.

17 January: Moon's Last Quarter in Libra

The hard work continues. There is travel and collaborations and spectacular gains. Not for nothing are Pisceans called the escape artists of the zodiac. They are smart, polite, diplomatic, shrewd and tactful, and their lives are normally packed with secret meetings, rendezvous, clandestine love affairs, journeys and experiences of all kinds which may startle the average person. They may seem shy and introverted but their lives are generally full of the most interesting experiences and incidents. They know how to get their work done without ruffling feathers and are the masters of patience and shrewd, tactical moves. The intensity depends of course on the individual horoscopes. With all these inherent guerrilla skills you make rapid progress in the first quarter. You simply manage to outsmart the opposition and you do it so deftly that they may not even be aware of it.

24 January: New Moon in Capricorn

The twin themes of progress and expansion continue. There will also be many distractions of the domestic kind; there may be health and money issues to straighten out in the family and, possibly, some altercations which need your sober and mature erudition to defuse. You continue with the momentum of the past few weeks and make good progress too. You take pride in your assets and achievements and even develop an unhealthy ego. This can also be an emotionally explosive period when you fly off the handle for no apparent reason but then, luckily, you manage to return quickly to a placidity normally associated with you. There is no harm in apologizing if you have to; in fact it makes you an even bigger person!

2 February: Moon's First Quarter in Taurus

You are filled with new ideas and your imagination runs riot. You also start thinking of the dark areas of life and get into unnecessary negativity and depression which you have to guard against. You think of unhappy moments in the past and fret about them. Please remember that the past is spilt milk and there is nothing that you can do about it. Learn from your mistakes, don't repeat them and don't dwell on them. There is a change in the earlier trend here and you lose the edge at work. Spiritual, religious, occult and esoteric matters take centre stage and your mind and emotions are in whirl. You know something is amiss but can't put your finger on it. You are like a dog which is looking for its tail and not finding it despite furiously running in circles. There is movement, new associations and many new realizations. You are unsure if money and the mundane trappings of success and achievement of the real world should be your goal or whether a higher calling awaits you. Hold on and be patient, says Ganesha, and the answers will come.

9 February: Full Moon in Leo

You are straightening out and begin to see things more clearly. You realize your role in the larger scheme of things and understand your responsibilities clearly. If you have a family, there are duties towards them from which you cannot run away. There are also work pressures and you begin to understand and accept all this. This is a vital learning experience. Now your focus is clear and there is no stopping you. You shine at work and receive plaudits. There are expenses, purchases, family issues to sort out and many other challenges which ground you. Whether you like it or not, you have to work hard. There is also money to be made and you see the writing on the wall.

19 February: Moon's Last Quarter in Scorpio

This period is full of strenuous activity. You are fully involved in work and manage to make remarkable progress. All your inherent cunning comes into play while signing documents and entering new business deals which work out in your favour. You entertain lavishly and make many purchases for the home and office. You may also consider shifting into a larger, newer and brighter home, or may even shift into an upscale new office. This is a good period for all the ventures that you have embarked on and you ride the crest of success. On the negative side, you must work on your ego management skills. There may also be a tendency to indulge in food, drink and romantic pursuits which you should guard against. Take care of your health. Remember, that it is the only wealth and you must never barter it for pleasures of the senses.

23 February: New Moon in Aquarius

You are racing away like a Formula 1 car. There is tremendous growth in all areas of activity, and some truly interesting and promising offers and opportunities will come your way. You are ambitious, energetic and ebullient and make the most of the situation. You grab everything that is offered and strike hard which is a good thing because fortune is now shining on you. There is passion in your life and you have to watch your step. There is tendency to overdo and step out of bounds. The sheer momentum of the period may just carry you away like a fig leaf in a thunderstorm. Ganesha warns you to be careful and moor yourself till the tempest passes.

2 March: Moon's First Quarter in Gemini

The new moon in your birth sign is propitious. You continue on an upward swing and make steady progress. All that you embark on at this stage leads to success. This is also an expansive phase of emotions and sensitivity and you will react to the slightest affronts which are not really necessary. You are on the boil and steaming away from no apparent reason. There is love in your life and, if married, you enjoy marital bliss. There will be happiness with children, and there may also be an addition to the family. There is achievement and success with new projects/ventures/deals vying for your attention, and isn't this a great way to be when the world is just riding out of a recession?

9 March: Full Moon in Virgo

You spread yourself in many directions and use all the diplomacy and wisdom in your command to emerge trumps. You meet up with old acquaintances and they enjoy your soft, loving nature full of sympathy and empathy for the ills of the world. You bask in all the attention and just love it as you are a non-violent, non-confrontationist sort of person and would rather make friends than enemies. Your ego is fragile and you are easily hurt and so you make it a point to escape ugly situations. Warring parties need you to sort out their affairs as you hear both sides and are non-judgemental. It doesn't mean, even for a moment, that you are a wimp or a coward; on the contrary, you are smart and know where your bread is buttered. It suits you perfectly to sit on the fence in most matters and still worm your way through!

16 March: Moon's Last Quarter in Sagittarius

This is a period in which you make carefully calculated progress. There are many work challenges that require your attention to the fine print. There is some entertainment thrown in but very little time for leisure as such. You count pennies and make wise investments and there will be a lot of buying and selling If you gamble or speculate in the market, chances are that you make substantial profits. There is little room for love and romance in this phase and you lead a sort of Spartan, one-dimensional existence looking solely at work dividends which is not such a bad thing at all sometimes. At least, it keeps you focused and occupied and distracts you from unwanted escapades.

24 March: New Moon in Aries

Your career focus is steadfast, and nothing deters you from laughing all the way to the bank. You enjoy the sound of money and the blossoming bank statements. They fill you with security and joy and you get ambitious and greedy for more money and power. You make purchases for the family and there is happiness all around. Love continues to desert you, but you are not perturbed. Instead, you spend time with old associates and colleagues and let yourself loose in friendship, bonhomie and gaiety. You are steadfast and on one track and it is working for you in this phase; you are not unhappy by any account. If you like the sound of money, there is no reason to dislike this period.

1 April: Moon's First Quarter in Cancer

Your mind doesn't waver and you take risks at work. You gamble and speculate with aggression and believe that risks have to be taken to conquer new horizons. You spend time with bank details, loans funds, real estate deals, financially sound partners and customers, and reap the whirlwind. There is some passion on the cards but not the sort of romance that turns you on. But you are not looking for romance and so you don't miss it. Right now, if anything, you are romancing high-denomination currency notes, and you just love sound and smell of newly minted cash.

8 April: Full Moon in Libra

Life is good and you have no complaints which, I must add, is a rare human condition. You have been bestowed with everything and you thank the Lord and live in gratitude which is certainly a good way to be. This is a wonderful period with beauty and utility, money and deep bonds. Family life is excellent and there is intense romance too. Your work/career is moving along well, and all the hard work has paid off. You will socialize and fuse work and play with pleasure, fun and joy. You are capable of intense love but such intensity and nobility require the right partner and you find it in this phase. A truly lucky period!

14 April: Moon's Last Quarter in Capricorn

This is a good period for intense companionship and indulgences, also many expenses as you will be in a happy mood and will be wining and dining in style. You get a trifle laid-back where work is concerned and entrust a lot of it to associates which you must guard against. There will be a variety of activities and experiences and new projects and collaborations. There will be fun outings with family, and time spent with children. Dependents and pets also provide great joy. Life has many colours and is a rich tapestry of the good times. Enjoy it while it lasts!

23 April: New Moon in Taurus

You continue in a happy mode, with some minor adjustments, in ebullience and enthusiasm. There are journeys, ceremonies, publicity, meetings, interviews, conferences, marriages to attend and all sorts of socializing. You enjoy the attention and make time for pleasant amusements. Work is on the back seat for the moment but you can return to it any time. You use the time to meet old and ailing relatives and spend time with friends and not just for your business acumen but for your charm and inherent people skills. They need you for your humane touch and you are not one to let friends down.

30 April: Moon's First Quarter in Leo

All that you embark on now leads to glory, it is a very successful period and you have to grab the high tide or, to paraphrase Groucho Marx, the low tide can get so low that you don't even see the water, and you don't want that for sure! So, Ganesha is offering you the best of the period and I suggest you grab it for all you are worth. Such great times don't come visiting often and right now you stand to embrace the joys of real success. Family life is fine, but you may not have much free time for loved ones. Your intentions are clear and you realize that the period is good for you. Although you don't show it in your body language, you are shrewd and canny to make the most of the situation and you milk it dry.

7 May: Full Moon in Scorpio

You are filled with expansion plans and have the determination to see them through. It is a fantastic period with a large chunk of luck following you wherever you go. You make spectacular progress whatever you do despite mounting expenses. It is a thrilling period and you are enjoying the ride. If in business, there is enormous money to be made. You have the tactical acumen to seize the moment and mint it. A new love hovers on the horizon and you make time for relishing roll in the hay. The new love may not be significant or long-lasting, but the moments of bliss are too beautiful for you to care about such trivia; at some level this is exactly what you have been looking for.

14 May: Moon's Last Quarter in Aquarius

Busy times reign supreme as you will be on your toes on the work and home fronts. Money will be spent on refurbishing, renovating and decorating your home and office and there could be added expenses on children and illnesses of family members. You will be troubled by all this and will look to spirituality for a way out. You were on a roll, have been pampered for too long, and suddenly there are problems to solve and you don't know how to cope. Family ties will be strong with parents and in-laws coming into the picture. The extended family may also drop in on holiday and the home is full of visitors and the joys and sorrows they bring with them. You are in demand and this leaves you with very little time for yourself.

22 May: New Moon in Gemini

Your work life acquires a fresh coat of paint as you increase the tempo and intensity. There will be many new ties, bonds, partnerships, collaborations and link including distracting romance with many passion-packed moments. If single, there could be serious love on the cards which could lead to the altar. For the married, marital bonds will be strengthened. It can get a bit complicated with relationships within relationships, there may be adultery too, but that depends a lot on the personal horoscope. I am only hinting at the possibilities. But definitely, this is a period of romantic/emotional/marital bonds. Travel is also indicated along with significant new contacts. This is an intense learning period and you have grown in many ways. It is advisable to watch your step!

30 May: Moon's First Quarter in Virgo

You reach a type of completion at home and at work; in many ways, the circle is complete. There is fruition in your affairs and you find yourself in a pool of bliss. You will feel happy, content and fulfilled with life. Your talents win the applause they so richly deserve and you bask in all the attention and glory. Pleasure, profit, joy and contentment are yours for the asking. You take no concrete step forward at work, but there is happiness in sheer acceptance. You enjoy the moment and are in bliss like a Zen master. You are like a lake without ripples and, I must add here that there is no tangible reason for celebration. Some moments in life are pure ecstasy and you wonder why. Please remember that there need be no reason for bliss and it can happen even in a vacuum. This is one of those periods. Just enjoy it.

5 June: Full Moon in Sagittarius

You are filled with new wisdom and ideas and want to share it with the world, or at least with friends and close associates. You may even seem quirky to those who don't know you too well as your imagination runs wild and you come up with innovative schemes. But there will be happy moments with the family and you will take refuse in it. You are also drawn to religion, spirituality, prayer, meditation, rituals, yoga and the esoteric sciences. You may join classes or even enroll yourself in a long camp like one of vipassana, for example. Your mind is charged and seeking answers. Whatever you embark on now has a good chance of doing well. So go for it!

13 June: Moon's Last Quarter in Pisces

There is some sort of reality check now and the material world beckons with its allurements of hard work and its rewards in monetary terms. You can get insecure when your bank account diminishes and you are away from work. So you get down to the task of shoring up your finances.

You find a semblance of happiness, though fleeting. Work has never been the reason for your existence but at least it consumes time and keeps you occupied and distracted from the various dreams that catch your fancy every now and then. Work moors you from the fancies that plague and throttle your mind and consciousness every now and again.

21 June: New Moon in Cancer

The money angle, travel, family, friends and many new diversions grab your attention. You have to cope with funds, joint holdings, settlements, hypothecation, trusts, even alimony and golden handshakes. Many kinds of financial possibilities confront you, and you will be juggling them with some dexterity. This is not what you bargained for but it has to be done. You will also meet many people and there is romance in the air. You get along very well with the opposite sex and sparks will fly. Travel and expenses are also foretold.

28 June: Moon's First Quarter in Libra

You are working at full steam and progress is assured. You may also travel on work and holiday and there could be distractions like illness in the family. Stress levels are high and you have to take care of yourself too. You are loved and appreciated and there is emotional support and happy bonding. It is a pleasant period in many ways as you make progress and more money. It is vibrant, action-packed time and a lot depends on how you react to all that is thrown at you. You even lose your famous cool and so don't look at everything from your perspective alone; start looking at issues from the other person's point of view. You could be wrong and there is no harm admitting it.

5 July: Full Moon in Capricorn

Many new trends are at work here. While you are as busy as ever with work, money, family and several other obligations taking your time and energy, you are suddenly pitchforked into a whirlwind romance that finally leaves you empty, lonelier, lost and dissipated. It starts beautifully and then takes an ugly turn with accusations and counter-accusations. You feel cheated and let down. It may leave you and your faith in the human race shattered. But, remember, that one swallow doesn't make a summer and you don't have to be scalded by it forever. You have to learn to move on. You may feel used, abused and exploited and there is an element of deceit too. Your secrets and confidences may also be bandied about, and it may lead to other more unfortunate eventualities like a loss of face, litigation and so on. Take time off, maybe leave the scene of action, go on a holiday, and come back new and rejuvenated. This is one of life's lessons and we often attract unsavoury people and events to us. It is a sort of shadow self which you have attracted; the desire to connect with the deep within you. Unless you get friendly with it and come to terms with it, this behaviour will only repeat itself out several times in your life. Of course I must add here that such specific indications depend on your personal horoscope.

12 July: Moon's Last Quarter in Gemini

You get back to work and are motivated by money and the good things of life. You need focus as there are many expenses foreseen and you may also indulge in getting new acquisitions for yourself, the family and the office. You will also have to guard against extensive drinking and smoking, if you have these habits. If you don't look after yourself, there could be a serious health scare. You could look at preventive medicine or go in for a regular medical check-up to nip possible problems in the bud. Ganesha's blessings are with you, but you need to, most importantly, help yourself.

20 July: New Moon in Cancer

You are swinging away and are the soul of the office and the party. There is no letting up on the work front though. You may be on the verge of a burnout and you desperately need to de-stress. There are meetings, collaborations and many monetary deals waiting to be finalized by you. This is not the time for romance and friends as you burn the midnight oil and are on the rack. The situation will even out a bit soon but this is a good time to cash in as the dividends will be there to see and relish before the year ends. So go for it, advises Ganesha.

27 July: Moon's First Quarter in Virgo

The bull in the last phase goads you on. There is no slowing down in the enormity of the workload. If anything, it just increases. You have many responsibilities and need to put in greater effort. I must add here that it is all not in vain because success is yours for the asking. You will make money and expand in a big way. Health will be good and you will be filled with energy and zeal to go full throttle. Nothing distracts you and you are on the one-track mode relentlessly and doggedly pushing ahead. This is not your style at all but the phase has a momentum which is incredibly intense and you go with the tide or rather, the tumultuous waves.

2 August: Full Moon in Aquarius

You are on a roll and the phase gets even more intense. All you need to guard against is stress which can take a toll and you don't want to be hospitalized at this juncture in particular. You decide to win the battle in the mind, and it's all mind over matter now. You have renewed strength and purpose. Money matters are handled with flair and intelligence and you will pore over every detail and get under the fine print to protect yourself from any financial damage later on. Be wary of secret deals, unsure clauses and hidden agendas. As you get more successful, there will be many enemies and people ready and willing to topple you from your perch. You will have to tackle them carefully and with dexterity. You should also not get greedy and embark on a mindless expansion spree. Sort out the infrastructure and logistics before making big plans or they could just get out of hand and you won't have the resources to cope.

11 August: Moon's Last Quarter in Taurus

The work phase is ebbing and your mind wanders in different directions. Suddenly, you have time and you don't know what to do with it. You spend time with family and friends and even decide to leave it all and go away from the action for a bout of solitude. It has all been very demanding and you need the rest. Your mind is in a whirl and you need to do a recap of the events that have taken you by storm. You spend time with nature and visit the ailing in hospital. You attend marriages, social and religious functions and meets as distant and remote from your areas of work as possible. You recharge yourself and this is a good way to do it.

19 August: New Moon in Leo

You can't remain from the scene of action for too long and you are back for the slog, refreshed and ready to take on more like Charles Atlas. But there is more peace of mind, harmony and balance now and you don't go overboard with your expansion and moneymaking plans. The short break has been good for you and provided many valuable realizations. You know what you have missed out on and the family suddenly becomes very special to you. You realize that you are a people's person and it hurts when they are not in tune with your feelings or you are not in tune with theirs. The focus this week is on attachments, ties and bonds. There is love, and romance too, and a lot of excitement and true happiness.

25 August: Moon's First Quarter in Sagittarius

With this new focus, you manage to balance work and play well without going overboard in either area. You have learnt your lesson and try, at least for now, for a sense of balance in your life. You will be busy with the home and its myriad affairs like deeds, documents, legal issues, renovation and refurbishing. You are confident and work through all the details to be fully satisfied. The outcome of all this is quite remarkable. You become obsessive with the minutest details and surprise everybody with this behaviour as they never imagined that you had this streak in you.

2 September: Full Moon in Pisces

Many aspects of your life and work are calling for your attention and you don't know which to take up first. Expenses are mounting, and there are travel, collaborations and all kinds of communication. You do not have to show your vulnerable side this week and so it will be necessary to watch your emotions carefully. Please don't wear them on your sleeve as you are wont to. It can be a confusing and paradoxical period ahead and there are several pulls which could weigh on your mind and hold you back from progress. You can be on slippery ground and you swim both against and with the current not knowing what to do or where to go with any certainty. It is an emotionally explosive period and you need to watch your step and your words. Meditate, take to yoga, go to a gym, search for gurus, do anything to divert your mind and your pent-up energies. The confusion will pass but right now it is tormenting you no end.

10 September: Moon's Last Quarter in Gemini

Your emotions are still messed up. You are alienating yourself from the family, friends, associates, and from work. You seem harassed by the demons lurking within you. No one is responsible for this but yourself. It is self-created and it is up to you to solve it. It is difficult to fathom how it all started and what caused it but now that it is embedded in your psyche like an alien it is tearing you apart. If you use this energy carefully, it could work as an eye-opener and you could find the trigger to this mood change. You may take to music and art and spend time deep within looking for answers. You take recourse in spirituality, religion, rituals, visiting seers and god-men and make sincere efforts to find stability. Keep away from recreational drugs and alcohol and Ganesha will help you find the answers.

17 September: New Moon in Virgo

The situation improves and you focus on personal, social and professional relationships. There are many things needing your attention: family, financial matters, work, friendships and all the distractions of the world. There are many deals, transactions and fine interactions in the offing. There are responsibilities and liabilities to attend to and you need to be on the ball. But you are lucky and manage to steer the course. You are slowly bouncing back and friends help a lot. Their friendship means a lot to you.

24 September: Moon's Quarter in Capricorn

New associations now dominate and motivate your existence. In this period your life will revolve around people and relationships. You may also indulge in enormous feel-good shopping. Your feelings will be at a peak and there will be intense bonding and sharing and, I dare say, many copious tears of joy, sorrow, anger, love and repentance. It is a very profound period of great catharsis and you will be reacting from the soul. It is a period that will change you from the inside out. There will be highs and lows, peaks and furrows, and finally, it will all be worth it, says Ganesha.

2 October: Full Moon in Aries

You get out of the trough and start flying this week. There are happiness, fulfilment, gains and achievements. You are filled with new longings, dreams and hopes, and are possessed with a new zest for life and its glorious uncertainties. The tough days are over and you climb the peaks of success from now on. You have worked for it and gone through very difficult times and Ganesha will reward you well. You embark on the path of steady progress and do well at work. You achieve success and plaudits, make money and bond well with near and dear ones.

10 October: Moon's Last Quarter in Cancer

The bubbly flows and the good times roll on and on as if to make up for lost time. Friends and colleagues rally around you and work issues are sorted out together. There is harmony at home and office and a lot of ground is thankfully covered. There is profitable travel and forming new associations will be a good idea to grab what comes your way as tide has evidently changed and you climb the rungs of success.

16 October: New Moon in Libra

You spend a lot of time at home and with domestic activities. There could be reorganization and lot of chopping and changing. You will spend happy moments with your spouse, children, parents, in-laws and extended family. There will be many auspicious occasions at home. Friends will also chip in and add to the harmony. There could be marriages, pujas and various family commitments to attend to. There is peace and contentment in your life is also there. Ganesha's blessings are with you!

23 October: Moon's First Quarter in Aquarius

You continue making good progress. Work issues take your time and you look at expansion seriously. The year is ending, the worst is over and the current is in your favour. You can feel it. All that you touch turns to gold and you know that you are destiny's flavour of the season. Your hands are full with investments, bonds, loans, funds, real-estate deals, stocks and other such profitable issues. Your scope of work expands considerably and you are all set for a long haul of decisive growth.

31 October: Full Moon in Taurus

You are on the treadmill of life in almost all spheres: from work, to family to entertainment. Your self-belief and confidence are at a high and you have the magic touch; there is success in almost everything you do. You may also indulge in religious rituals and go on a pilgrimage. You feel that you are invincible. Power, success, energy and enthusiasm are pushing you forward. In this phase, nothing can go wrong with you. You carry Ganesha's blessings wherever you go.

8 November: Moon's Last Quarter in Leo

Your work does tremendously well and you earn plaudits. You are recognized for your efforts and, if employed, will be rewarded with a promotion and better perks. Your financial condition is stable and there is happiness at home too. You will explore new love and make new friends and acquaintances. There will be quality time spent with parents and family elders and you receive their blessings. Spurred by all the good vibrations, you put your heart and soul into work and continue making remarkable progress.

15 November: New Moon in Scorpio

You have come a long way and are more relaxed, easy-going and fun-loving. You seem to have dropped all your cares and are in great mood. There are love, laughter, companionship and shared joys. There are new trends at work too and they are all beneficial. You don't hesitate to grab every opportunity that comes your way and make substantial gains. This is an excellent period and you are filled with stamina, determination and zest. There are investments to be made and you know that the rewards will be yours soon. Make the most of the situation, says Ganesha.

22 November: Moon's First Quarter in Pisces

The hectic work phase continues without a pause. There are all sorts of expenses but it is not something that you should complain about because it is work-related and it is money well spent. Travel and new associations are there, and your mood and spirits are on a high. You are blessed with energy and are happy too; life is working out well for you. There is joy at home too but what drives you this week is work. You have taken on a lot and there is a lot to accomplish. With Ganesha's blessings, you will be successful in all your undertakings.

30 November: Full Moon in Gemini

You embark on a period of collaborations, companionships and associations. You are in meetings, social and business gatherings, conferences and everything to do with large number of people. You are in your element and this is not the time to be sullen, withdrawn or introverted. You are quite a draw and others seek you out for your charm, ingenuity and inventiveness. You have a way of attracting and regaling people with your soft, non-obtrusive ways tinged with sincerity. You fully understand the need and value of social networking and the contacts you make now will bear fruit in the long run.

8 December: Moon's Last Quarter in Virgo

You enter the last month of the year with a feeling of satisfaction. You have been on an upward spiral for some

PISCES

time now and the money, status and prestige that you have earned are well deserved. Success breeds success and you are full of confidence in your abilities. You sometimes come up with ideas that could be termed 'crazy' by average minds but they are actually strokes of genius. You plan for the future ambitiously and systematically and initiate new projects. You have a tendency to underplay your cards and, in the process, catch the opposition in unguarded moments. You don't have the bluster and aggression of many of the other signs but you slowly and surreptitiously move ahead like a chess grandmaster and checkmate them all. Kudos!

14 December: New Moon in Sagittarius

The collaborations that you have inked bear fruit almost immediately. Your fertile brain is abuzz with innumerable new ideas and you are waiting to pounce on opportunities to give expression to them. You will do exceptionally well if you are in the media, sales, law and other professions where there is people contact and ideating. You have the gift of the gab and can be a versatile writer too. Colleagues pick your brains for new, innovative schemes and you come up with them like a magician drawing pigeons from a hat. Others will execute your plans but you are the ringmaster. If there is a tendency to be overtly obstinate or ego-driven, it will be a good idea to curb it now. A lot of creative people have been destroyed by their giant-sized egos, and you don't have to abort your grand schemes unnecessarily. Keeping your ego hidden is also good strategy and Pisceans are great strategists.

21 December: Moon's First Quarter in Aries

The end of the year takes on a new intensity, a sort of culmination of all that you have embarked on. You scale new heights, come up with brilliant ideas and all your efforts are crowned with success. There is merrymaking with friends and family and the time is perfect for celebrations. Children bring joy, and close family will rally around you and share your happiness. You are ambitious but not crazily driven like some of the other signs. Your strength is your manners and style and in ideating. You are not the type to carry a load on your head; on the contrary, you are the type who has the intelligence to pass the buck and make someone else do the dirty work. You are the ideas person, the imaginative visionary and dreamer. Since it is ideas that make the world go round, you do just that.

30 December: Full Moon in Cancer

You have tasted hard-earned and richly deserved success. You have also, at times, plumbed the depths of despair and come out of it rejuvenated and strengthened. Your trial by fire has been complete: you have passed with honours in your education in the real world. You have entered new territory with all your innovative ideas and have also managed to make money, which is still the mundane and easy yardstick of success; it is the language we all understand without quarrel. Money buys you dignity and you want to lead a life of dignity. The home is also peaceful and you may be blessed with an offspring, if married. If single, a new love that enters your life is serious and you may make plans to settle down with this person for the long haul. Many lessons have been learnt this year and you have been the lead cast in a snakes-and-ladders game. You realize now that you need to keep from getting swayed and need to watch your emotions closely for success. This is a great lesson and will help you in the long run.

Ready Reckoner for All Twelve Signs

Aries	Assertive	Mars	Energy
Taurus	Possessive	Venus	Sex/love/emotion
Gemini	Versatile	Mercury	Five senses
Cancer	Sensitive	Moon	Inner realm
Leo	Rulership	Sun	Personality
Virgo	Discrimination	Mercury	Five senses
Libra	Balance	Venus	Sex/love/emotion
Scorpio	Passion	Pluto	Transform
Sagittarius	Free-ranging	Jupiter	Absorb
Capricorn	Prudence	Saturn	Self-preservation
Aquarius	Objectivity	Uranus	Creativity
Pisces	Intuitive	Neptune	Subconscious

Keyword for every sign:

Aries: Courage
Taurus: Dependability
Gemini: Responsiveness
Cancer: Loyalty
Leo: Exuberance
Virgo: Consciousness
Libra: Charm
Scorpio: Idealism
Sagittarius: Optimism
Capricorn: Steadiness
Aquarius: Friendliness
Pisces: Compassion

I fully agree with other astrologers that there could well be other main characteristics for every sign. Nothing is final.

The Signs and Their Elements

Fire Symbolic Attributes: Energy, faith, enthusiasm, spontaneity, intuition and idealism.

Aries, Leo, Sagittarius.

Earth Symbolic Attributes: Basic common sense, practicality, resourcefulness, management ability and skill.

Taurus, Virgo, Capricorn.

Air Symbolic Attributes: Rational judgement, abstract thinking, detachment, objectivity and perspective, the intellect and the world of ideas.

Gemini, Libra, Aquarius.

Water Symbolic Attributes: Feelings, anxieties, psychism, sensitivity, withdrawal, emotional vulnerability, in-depth perception, mysticism, the world of the intangible.

Cancer, Scorpio, Pisces.

World Horoscope

By Bejan Daruwalla

Ganesha says these are the salient features for our world:

Less is more
Climate change
Robots
Artificial intelligence
Systematizing life itself
Performance orientation
Technology and rationality are kings
Methodology and perfection
Managing men and matters
The best way to get things done
Precision and perfection
Health, hygiene, welfare
Canned packaged spirituality, salvation
Year 2080 is the pinnacle for mankind.

The full potential and power of the brain and neurons will evolve a new world order beyond our imagination and fantasy. It could well be the new God.

AFRICA

Ganesha says Africa is the country of the future. Why? Firstly, my gut feeling is a sort of ESP for essence of something which we know but cannot express. Secondly, by mundane Western astrology Africa comes under the sign Cancer. Many astrologers believe life began in Africa because Cancer is the great Mother of the World. Thirdly, the Tarot card no. 21 says clearly 'The upliftment of the downtrodden and the backward'. Peace on Earth. It is on the strength of this Tarot card that I predicted the success of Obama, the first Black president of America. Now this will also apply to Africa. When? The simple answer is that the next seven years will demonstrate it.

INDIA

For India I have said again and again that Modi was born to purify and cleanse the Ganga. I am writing this piece on 8 June 2019 and the news has flashed 'Wave of 20,000 citizens to clean Sabarmati'. A grand beginning.

ISRAEL

Mr Benjamin Netanyahu is no more the prime minister of Israel. By mundane Western astrology a huge segment for part of the Middle East comes under the sign Taurus. Uranus is right now in Taurus and has seen the end of this Israel prime minister. Next year Uranus in Taurus will be in excellent formation with Jupiter and Saturn in Capricorn, according to Western astrology. Normally I do not go into technicalities. But it is certainly this excellent formation which will draw all the Middle East countries nearer to each other. In other words, a new era begins. On and before 31 December 2019 to July 2025 there is a strong possibility of peace or at least a mutual respect, give and take. This will obviously lead to stability for the Middle East and in a broader sense for our world. Let me put it all in one sentence. As a poet has said, 'The best is yet to be.'

USA

America under Donald Trump will be not loved and respected by the rest of the world. A great pity, and to me a mighty tragedy. But Japan, India, Singapore will be good friends in every possible way. Surprisingly enough, I see that under the premiership of Imran Khan, the former mighty all-rounder of cricket, a glimpse of better relationship is certainly possible. As an astrologer I must be completely objective and at the same time have a vision of things to come. Our world is complex and confused. But I see more than a glimpse of hope. I see a possibility of all of us living together if not lovingly at least in a compromise and balance of relationships. Why? We are right now in the Aquarian age. Strictly speaking, Jupiter and Saturn will be in the sign of Aquarius, and that means good things in relationships and technology will pick up great speed and there will be hope as well as confidence in our heart that we are born to live together and be happy. As I have said many times, this span will be between 2021 to 2081. Lastly, for the sake of new readers of the book, I repeat what I have said in my 2019 book. Let me now reveal the secret of my predictions. We all know that we are in the Aquarian age. In the Aquarian age there will be the marriage of technology and humanity. The planets I personally take into active consideration are

Jupiter, the planet of prosperity and plenty, and Saturn, the planet of duty as well as integrity. Both these planets will come together in the sign Aquarius in 2081. Therefore, intuition and common sense both dictate that it could well be the greatest year of the twenty-first century. The cynics are most welcome to say, 'Mr Daruwalla, you and many of us will not be there to verify the accuracy of this prediction.' My answer is, 'They are more than welcome to their own opinion. To each his own is the guiding principle of my life.'

I am not God. But I try to combine all the above points by astrology and not only find out about it by fusing it with the meaning, purpose and symbol of the planets but by praying to Ganesha to help me fuse it all into one single whole. Let me put it very simply. I try to see life itself steadily and see it whole. This might appear to be a contradiction. But as John Donne the poet has said, 'Contradictories meet in me. What is there left to say.'

Our Future

Ganesha says that technology is king. The main reason for it is we are right now in the Aquarian–Uranian age. Curiosity is the main characteristic of the Aquarian age. Thanks to curiosity, we invent new things and schemes; revolutionize the entire scheme of things and invent, innovate and create a new world order. Group activities is a must for all creative pursuits in our Aquarian age.

In this new world order, we will have to live with artificial intelligence, robotic relationships and lack of human intimacy. These are times of 100 per cent surveillance and no privacy; dangerous times of machine-made assassinations, use of social media to create hysteria against a person/organization, climate change and information expressway, which the Chinese call the 'digital silk road'.

Let me explain it in simple terms. We Indians have our Kumbha Mela, the biggest gathering in the world. It means in simple language a group activity. Group activity leads to the seven Cs – connection, communication, collectivity, contacts, creativity, circulation and consciousness. The Sanskrit word '*kumbh*' actually means Aquarius in English, and the beauty of it is we are now in the Aquarian age. The additional factor is technology and science.

The million-dollar question is whether this technology will overtake us and be finally our master or will we be able to share our life with this new technology. It is said that in Japan, man actually sleep with robots. They are very comfortable with it. I admit that this is only a rumour. It may or may not be true. But it certainly indicates what we are heading for. One thing is certain. We are masters of mass destruction but not of universal happiness despite all our technology, knowledge, understanding, psychology and a powerful grip on the basics of human nature. We are now in a position to discover, analyse and cure neurological disorders. We can also prevent it by early detection of diseases. That is indeed a very major achievement.

Let me put it very simply. We have everything going for us and yet we are so miserable. Terrorists sometimes rule our lives or at least make us absolutely miserable. There are giants in all the above-mentioned fields. I am only an astrologer. Astrology simply means the right persons at the right place and at the right time. The other term of astrology is Jyotish. '*Jyot*' means light and '*Ish*' means God. Therefore, to us Indians, Jyotish is the light of God. I do not pretend to be a superman, a religious leader or a guru. I can only say that I have met three prime ministers of India, helped people in whatever way I can and now, at eighty-eight, this is what I predict in the name of my Master and Lord Guru.

URANUS

In this Aquarian age of technology and humanity, I take three main planets, namely Uranus, Jupiter and Saturn. Uranus signifies technology, revolution and evolution. No Uranus, no Aquarian age. Uranus, therefore, is the main significator of the Aquarian age. It might amaze readers to know that in astronomy, Jupiter is the heavyweight of the zodiac. It has great magnetism. Jupiter attracts planets to itself so that they may not go to the Sun and combust. Therefore, by astronomy, Jupiter is also the protector of the planets. The same is true of Jupiter and astrology. In 2020, Jupiter and Saturn will clasp the hands of each other and therefore Jupiter (protection) and Saturn (stability) will be much more than at other times. But the real pivot, the turning point of our entire existence will be from 20 December 2020 to end of December 2021. I am not a scientist. Instead of 2021 it could extend to 2022. But whatever intuition, imagination, experience of sixty-five years and Ganesha's grace tell me, it is that between 2020 to December 2021, our future will be cast and made.

THE FINAL CUT-OFF YEAR IS 2080

There is another side to the age of Aquarius. It is complete objectivity, experimentation, progress in science and the development of all our capacities of which we are not fully aware, including neurology, which will come to the fore. Therefore, we live in the most exciting century in the history of mankind. In the words of William Faulkner, the Nobel Prize winner, 'We will not only survive but prevail.' Now I am using all my mental faculties, my great compassion for humanity, the grace of my Lord and Master Ganesha, the force and power of Nature and the galaxies, the cosmos, to say that rightly or wrongly, in 2080, latest space travel will be common and we will be able to use gravity, magnetic forces, our own life force and also other forces, which we are not aware of right now, for the union, use and joy of technology and humanity. On Tuesday, the day of Ganesha, I say very humbly that this is my last word.

Achievements

BEJAN DARUWALLA

Bejan was invited to the wedding ceremony of Kapil Sharma, the well-known comedian. Bejan had predicted his success. The CNBC, Zee Business and ANI where invited and Bejan told them categorically that Modi will win the game and scatter the Opposition to the four corners of the world.

Just for the record we state that Bejan was acknowledged as one of the hundred great astrologers in the last thousand years in the great *Millenium Book of Prophecy*, published by HarperCollins, USA.

He was awarded the highest degree of Vedic astrology, 'Jyotishi Mahamahopadhaya', by the Federation of Indian Astrologers.

He was the astrologer in residence at the Manila Hotel, Philippines.

Bejan featured on the BBC, in Hard Talk India, August 1999. Bejan was born on 11 July 1931. He has a family of five, including his wife and three children. He loves them more than his life.

His hobbies are watching cartoons and sports, listening to music, telling jokes, reading books on philosophy and laughing at himself.

Among the supporters and patrons of Bejan he specially mentions Behram Mehta. Behram Mehta is the producer and promoter of the internationally famous Aava mineral water. It might be interesting to know that Aava is the pious and holy river of the Parsees. Behram was mainly responsible for motivating and inspiring Bejan to write this book because the latter felt washed out. Old supporters and patrons – Lakshyaraj Singh Mewar, City Palace, Udaipur, Neeraj Bajaj and Vikram Singh – deserve Bejan's salute. He acknowledges his love and respect for Shri Devendra Fadnavis, chief minister of Maharashtra, Shri Bhupendra Chudasma, education minister of Gujarat, Shri Parshottam Rupala, and Shri Vijay Rupani, chief minister of Gujarat, Dadi Mistry and Jimmy Mistry. He is on very happy and cordial terms with them.

Kishore Kumar Kaya, the owner of the ancient hotel Savoy, hosted his entire family in a royal style at Mussoorie. Bejan tried to guide him to the best of his limited ability. He found Kishore and his wife Madhu very religious and charitable. Hotel owners come no better.

Ekta, the beautiful and brilliant leading lady of Radio Mirchi, came to Bejan's place and he recited two poems on our prime minister Narendra Modi. Both of them approved of the idea and the poems.

NASTUR DARUWALLA

Nastur and his wife, Meetu, went with great pride and honour to pay their respects to the scintillating, peerless Prince Lakshyaraj Singh Mewar of City Palace, Udaipur, and the Royal Princess Nivritti Singh Mewar as the divine royal daughter was born to this royal couple. Prince

Lakshyaraj Singh Mewar is like a son to Nastur's father, Bejan Daruwalla, and Bejan says he will bring glory to all.

Nastur clearly predicted in *Amar Ujala*, Lucknow edition, that Chief Minister Yogi Adityanath will defeat the combination of Mayawati and Akhilesh Yadav. It was not easy, but he did it superbly.

In the same paper, he clearly predicted that Shri Narendra Modi Saheb will come back to power and there was no election at all as Narendra Modi Saheb single-handedly took his party to great victory.

Nastur was invited with great love and respect by Shweta Shah from Bhavnagar, who herself is a very good and efficient Reiki master, to inaugurate a centre for different forms of healing and spiritual togetherness by Samarth Vyas. The event was a huge success.

Nastur once again says 'Big God bless you' to Shri Byram Avari Saheb, Avari Group of Hotels, Karachi, and his entire family because seldom such noble people are born and they have made the Parsee community and the world proud by their humanitarian actions.

Personalities

Ganesha says hats off to Premji for his philanthropy, integrity, ability to create a mighty organization and influencing a generation into wisdom and generosity as well as an exuberance of spirit, adventure and kindness. Both Premji and his counterpart Murthy, of Infosys, are Leos. To me Leo means pure radiance. That says it all.

Under the excuse of 'America First', Donald Trump has proved his negativity, insularity and his combativeness in trade war with China, and Mexico in particular. I admit I could be wrong but he is certainly not the most respected and loved president of America.

Pritish Nandy, a genius, former editor of the *Times of India*, a poet of repute and a man who knows his own mind, and is not afraid to say it, deserves my admiration and praise. I have known him for a thousand years so to say. This Capricorn is both genuine and generous.

I have said a million times that Narendra Modi is the future of our country. I have already said in my 2019 book that BJP will again be in power. There is a poem on him. It says it all.

Anupam Kher, the well-known film actor, producer and director is a Piscean. I have met him thrice and with his brilliance and sheer imaginative sympathy, he does, and will continue to, shine like a star.

Yes, I have met and dined with the Cancerian Gautam Adani along with the famous Virgo spiritualist Sadhguru. I know Gautam Adani is a giant industrialist. But to me it is much more important that he has built a first-class hospital where the poor and needy can find solace and help. Sadhguru is one of the greatest personalities of the world. This is my personal belief.

I have often said that Angela Merkel of Germany – the Cancerian – is perhaps the greatest leader of the world. But I cannot say the same for Libran Vladimir Putin of Russia and Kim Jong-un of North Korea. Shinzo Abe, the Virgo, has my full admiration and praise. Above all, I am convinced that the Dalai Lama, the Cancerian, is sent by God almighty for spreading compassion in the world. I may be right or wrong, but to me compassion and consciousness are twins.

Right now, as I am writing this piece on 7 June 2019, the World Cup is on. Virat Kohli, the Scorpio, is flamboyant and has tucked many runs under his belt. But to me, for whatever it is worth, Taureans Sachin Tendulkar and Brian Lara are slightly superior and I certainly know my cricket. Rohit Sharma is also a Taurean and Bradman, perhaps the greatest cricketer the world has ever produced, is a Virgo. My observation is that the Virgos and Taureans, both earthy signs, make the greatest batsmen. But I admit openly that time could prove me wrong. In other words, a batsman of any sign has the ability to be the greatest ever. In other words, the key to life, cricket and love is to keep an open mind and admit that one could go wrong.

I repeat what I said before, 'In love and in cricket
Even the great Daruwalla can lose his wicket.'

Modi and India

> The Ganges, your mother/the Himalayas, your father/ beckon you for a blessing/they say/'the good and the great/are seldom knit/in the same human/but may you have both/May your feet of clay/alchemize into tensile steel/ not intelligence, not cleverness, not sharpness,/ but wisdom and an open mind/will enable you/to do the right thing at the right time and the right place/ It is your dharma and your karma/to make India shining clean/from sole to soul/you will help to heal the world and make it whole/Narendra, this is your real destiny/Fulfil it.'
>
> – BEJAN DARUWALLA, *Spiritual Sizzlers*, HarperCollins (2015)

Ganesha says my devotee Bejan Daruwalla predicted the mighty success of Narendra Modi as early as 29 March 2012 in Kanoria Centre for Arts, Ahmedabad. Bejan said that Modi will tear the Opposition to shreds and then light a fire with them. Terrible words. How true. Actually, he said Modi will do the TFCD (Todi, Fodi, Chiri, Dhoi Nakhse) which is the Gujarati equivalent to the above. Bejan has met Modi twice. Here is a quote from the *Times of India*, 29 May 2019: 'What the country does in the next five years will determine its destiny. All hesitations and frictions characterising our complex bureaucratic system must be overcome and wheels of the economy freed from the mud and sand that keep it from racing to double-digit growth.'

Astrology is all about timing. The secret of Modi's success is that he has the capacity, the intelligence and the ability to think, observe and deliver the goods. Very surprisingly, the sheer personality of Modi and his oratorical skills have a multifold impact on the masses. Personality is the result of all your experiences and magnetic force, which is difficult to define – either you have it, or you do not have it. Yes, I agree that these are plus points, but Modi is a Virgo. Virgo means purity and cleanliness. Therefore, along with all the other good qualities, it is my prediction that Modi is born to cleanse Mother Ganga. I support this statement as Modi was born on 17 September. The Tarot card shows a lady pouring water to nourish the earth. The title is 'the star'. To me, Mother Ganga is divinity. When I met him, he asked me only question: 'Will our India be great?' Just as human beings have their birthdate, countries also have their birthdate. By Western mundane astrology, India certainly comes under the sign Capricorn. Jupiter, the planet of plenty and prosperity, will be in the sign Capricorn from 2 December 2019 to 18 December 2020. Jupiter will join hands with Saturn (responsibility, religion and duty), which is also in Capricorn. Therefore, this extremely powerful double thrust will push, drive and motivate our country to great success. It is a magnetic turbo for India. I know very well that results take time. India is multicultural, plural and has many tongues, traditions, customs, rituals, ceremonies and all the religions of the world; and we Indians have the freedom to express our own opinion and ideas. It is the way democracy works. Yes, it takes time to deliver the complete results. Therefore, the predictions of this Ganesha devotee is that from 2020 to 2026, India will attain the status of a superpower. More importantly, India will help to make the world united, happy and peaceful.

The astrologer is mainly a visionary. I use Indian astrology, Western astrology, the Tarot card, palm reading, runes and my own invention of the dice. Above all, I pray to Mother Nature and Mother Ganga and say very humbly that I am not a god, but I try my best with my limited ability, and leave the rest to cosmic forces. Though a former professor of English, I have no desire to lecture and preach. I only say may the life force be with all of us.

(Written on 29 May 2019)

AMIT SHAH AND MODI

Ganesha says Amit Shah and Modi make a powerful team together. Why? Amit Shah was born on the twenty-second day of a month. 2 + 2 = 4. Modi was born on the seventeenth. 1 + 7 = 8. Four is half of eight and India's ruling number is 8, example 26 January, our Republic Day, i.e., 2 + 6 = 8. Also, Amit Shah's Jupiter is in the sign Taurus, an earthy sign. Normally, Jupiter in Taurus makes slightly plumb. Modi's sign is Virgo also an earthy sign. Therefore, a beautiful and complete match. Usually, I do not go into the technicalities of astrology and numerology. But here I make a difference.

The million-dollar question is: Can Amit Shah do for India what he has done for the BJP? My answer is yes. The main reason for it is that Amit Shah combines organizing ability, a certain degree of tolerance, the vision to see ahead for the good of all and, above all, the Libra charm of persuasion and the Scorpio instinct for investigation and probing when he gets into the heart of things. This is the master key to his success.

In a telephonic conversation, Amit Shah told me that his favourite colour is pink. Pink is a combination of red and white. Red stands for Mars. Mars means energy, investigation and results. White stands for Sun. Sun means politics, limelight, publicity and prominence. This fits the bill for Amit Shah.

The real time for delivering the goods for our country is the next year itself. The next year decides the fate of India for the whole of the remaining twenty-first century. I know very well that this is a bold statement. But I have eighty-eight years in my pocket. My Lord and Master is Ganesha and, while not a god, I work very hard in my profession and I believe I have the vision, though it might be incomplete, to look into the future. I call upon the cosmic force of the universe and respect all religions. The years 2022 and 2023 will very possibly be the finest ones for our country. India could well be the superpower. I say this very humbly because I am not a god.

In Memorium

I miss my guru, Vashisht Mehta, very much. I remember his key word. Astrology is the art of synthesis. Synthesis means the art of putting everything together in the right place at the right time.

Malay, the son of my mighty good friend the late Gautam Vimal Shah, met his end in May 2019.

It was a double blow to me. Whatever people may say about death, I openly admit that it shakes me up completely and I do not reconcile myself completely to it. That's the way with it.

Astro-analysis of Terrorists and Suicide Bombers

Ganesha says it is time to go digital and explain about the terrorist and suicide bomber in this way: Mars (violence, confidence, powerful determination to accomplish the objective; energy put into action) + Mercury (superb communication and secrecy and deceit and camouflage of real purpose) + Sun (need for prestige, power, position) + Uranus (the actual making of the bomb. Pluto is associated deeply with the atomic bomb itself) + Saturn (attention only on target. Not caring for the results on others and the sufferings it will cause).

Pluto is power plus.

I am not going to give lectures about the suicide bombers and the terrorists. But in the words of Webster, the horror and impact of the heinous actions of the terrorists can be summed up as 'horror piled upon horror'. Devastation of entire families moves me tremendously. But by 2020–21, the terrorists will be completely nabbed, imprisoned and out of action.

But this is my last word. The terrorists and the suicide bombers show us a horrible waste of life which could be used for better purposes as the terrorists and the suicide bombers could have had many good things going for them and for others. This is the tragedy.

ESP and Astrology

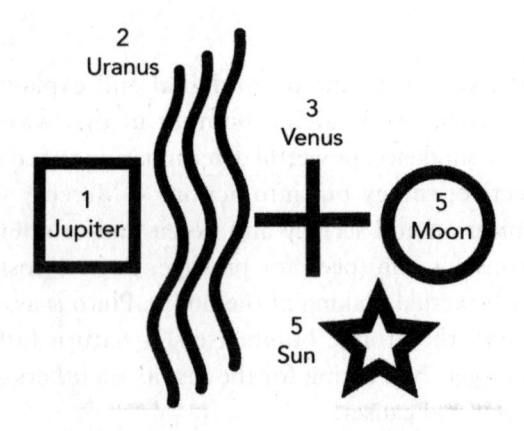

2 Uranus
1 Jupiter
3 Venus
5 Moon
5 Sun

Take a good look at these symbols. We are going to test your ESP (extrasensory perception) by them. Later, we are going to blend it with astrology. The symbols are actually cards designed at the Parapsychology Laboratory (Duke University, USA) to test ESP. ESP is the faculty of seeing mentally what is happening or existing out of sight. You can call it intuition, or the sixth sense.

Yes, I have converted these symbols into planets and astrology with my experience and imagination and research. I do not claim it as final. But I am presenting it to you for what it is worth. There are various other methods of testing: the GEST test, the BT clairvoyance test, the DT clairvoyance test and the matching clairvoyance test. Those of you interested

ESP AND ASTROLOGY

in these and the pack of cards, may get them from Haines House of Cards, Norwood, Ohio 45212. Alternatively, no harm in having, that is, devising your own cards, carrying these five symbols. Twenty-five cards, each symbol of five cards, are enough. Should you feel like probing further into the mysteries of the ESP card, please read *Parapsychology, Frontier Science of the Mind*, by J.B. Rhine and J.G.Pratt (Charles C. Thomas, 1957).

Generally, those who select the Star as the first preference are ambitious and dominating. If you like the Cross best, accept sensuality, as well as sacrifice, as part of your make-up. If the Circle be your first love, it shows spiritual tendencies, a hypersensitive nature, wild imagination and a streak of femininity even in the males (nothing wrong in it, if you ask me, as most poets have feminine souls!). Those who love the Wavy Lines, will do splendidly in the arts as well as the sciences but not commerce. If the Square is your first love, you'll be lucky, find protection and money, and never remain poor.

The third card you choose is the balance wheel of your personality. Often, it shows what helps you from going off your mind. By my findings, the Sun gives results in your first, tenth, nineteenth, twenty-eighth, thirty-seventh, forty-sixth, fifty-fifth, sixty-fourth, seventy-third, eighty-second and ninety-first year. Venus around your sixth, fifteenth, twenty-fourth, thirty-third, forty-second, fifty-first, sixtieth, sixty-ninth, seventy-eighth, eighty-seventh, ninety-sixth. The Moon around your second, eleventh, twentieth, twenty-ninth, thirty-eighth, forty-seventh, fifty-sixth, sixty-fifth, seventy-fourth, eighty-third, ninety-second. Jupiter around your third, twelfth, twenty-first, thirtieth, thiry-ninth, forty-eighth, fifty-seventh, sixty-sixth, seventy-fifth, eighty-fourth, ninety-third. Uranus around your fourth, thirteenth, twenty-second, thirty-first, fortieth, forty-ninth, fifty-eighth, sixty-seventh, seventy-sixth, eighty-fifth, ninty-fourth.

I have always applied Western astrology to Vedic mantras. That has given me excellent results. If you like the Square, the main planet is Jupiter for it and the mantra is '*Om Jhram Jhreem Jhroom Sa Gurave Namah*'.

It would be interesting for the readers to note that by astronomy, Jupiter is the heavyweight of the zodiac and attracts other planets to it, so that the other planets do not go to the Sun and get totally combusted. To me, personally, Jupiter is the saviour of humanity. The other mantra is for the Sun: '*Om Hram Hreem Hrom Sa Suryaya Namah*'.

I do not know why but I do not take the other mantras into consideration for the other planets. I can only say that this is the way I am made. Finally, one can combine it with the horoscope, as I do, or use this method by itself. It is exciting, informative, but not infallible. Nothing ever is!

Cartoons and Comedy (Effect of Mercury)

Ganesha says cartoons and comedy are the finest ways to relax, have fun and laugh away to glory. Why? In cartoons, normally, nobody dies. You can fall from a mountain, fight, love, leap, dance and be larger than life itself. Normally people identify with the cartoons and therefore they can be larger than life and be whatever they want. It is a sort of wish-fulfilment. One does not need astrology to understand this but just for your information, Mercury, the planet of communication, contacts and versatility (ability) is the chief planet for it. Taking an example from sports even, cricket and tennis very specially come under the impact of Mercury. Why tennis? Mercury refers very specially to the arms and in tennis service, volleys, backhand and forehand are most important. Finally, let me say that Mercury juggles the neurological nervous system in the brain. Mercury has much to do with a sharp and brilliant brain.

Ramana Maharshi's Truth

> There is neither creation
> nor destruction,
> neither destiny
> nor free will;
> neither path
> nor achievement.
> This is the final truth.
>
> – RAMANA MAHARSHI

Something in my genes, blood, bones, the subconscious, the mind, the heart and the soul responds instinctively to this saying of Ramana Maharshi. Maybe it is being an Indian and an astrologer that makes me zero in. This I *feel*. If anybody knows what truth is, it is the great seer and sage Ramana Maharshi.

Your Bonus for 2020

KNOW YOUR JUPITER

Whatever defect I have – of eye, of heart, of mind, or whatever excess there is – may Brihaspati (Jupiter) remedy it. Gracious to us be the Lord of the world.
— YAJUR VEDA 36.2

Yes, Jupiter in Indian astrology is best known as the 'Lord of the world'. Ganesha has enlightened me with this unique combination of Jupiter and the Vedic hymn:

Many are the gifts of His Spirit,
His blessings – never exhausted,
For He showers His worshippers
with fullness of knowledge and light.

Jupiter has a big-bellied body with a broad, prominent chest and a voice like a lion. His body, hair and eyes are of a tawny hue that shines like pure gold. Predominantly *kapha* in constitution and fond of sweets, he wears yellow clothes and yellow flowers. The Brahmana Jupiter knows the Vedas and is an expert in all forms of knowledge. He possesses all virtues and is modest, forgiving and happy. His mind and senses are disciplined and his intellect subtle. Attached to ritual, he follows the path of righteousness. His metal is gold and gem topaz.

Lord of the body's fat, of the north-east, of Thursday, and of the constellations Sagittarius and Pisces, Jupiter is known as the Lord of worship and the guru. His titles are teacher of the immortals, the soul, the advisor, the lord of speech, the golden, the creator, the irresistible, he who wears yellow, the young, the worthy of worship throughout the world, the compassionate, creator of polity, remover of oppression, and the peaceable.

Dear readers, I have given you an excellent image of Jupiter as seen in Vedic Indian astrology! Now let me elucidate the uses, benefits and influences of Jupiter in simple and plain language so that you get the most mileage of megabytes:

1. Essentially, it is the planet of good luck, or the greater fortune.

2. Jupiter stands for joviality, earlier called as love.

3. It is the planet of the three Ws, namely, wealth and wisdom and worship, and obviously that's saying a great deal.

4. Jupiter signifies a robust and even rumbustious and boisterous attitude to life. In other words, Jupiter is both cheerful and noisy.

5. This is the planet of expansion – that means weight problems, sincerity, the readiness and ability to learn as well as teach, a truly grand vision of life, easy access to money, popularity, power, position, prosperity, the four Ps that I like to use.

6. Comforts and luxuries fall under the bracket of both Jupiter and Venus. Vehicles and pomp and flair for doing things with savoir faire also come in the ambit of Jupiter and Venus.

7. Jupiter is wise and generous, whereas Mercury is clever and shrewd.

8. Jupiter is friendly and good for practically everything: you can deal with bankers, influential people, get a job, start long journeys, begin religious ceremonies and rites.

9. Jupiter refers to charities, gold, honey, cows, chariots, elder brother, the north-east direction; and among body parts and organs – tantra and mantra, right conduct, yellow topaz; and among body parts and organs – liver, gall bladder, pancreas, spleen, fat, blood arteries, thighs, ear, sense of smell; and among afflictions – anaemia and laziness. Colours will be royal purple, yellow, indigo and red in combination. Jupiter also stands for treasures, wealth and ancient language. His day is Thursday, and his flower, the chrysanthemum.

10. Many astrologers also take tin as the metal of Jupiter and turquoise as the gem. Personally, I take the number 3 and its series, 21=2+1 =3, 12=1+2=3, as the lucky number of Jupiter. Many a time, Jupiter in your horoscope speaks of remarkable organizing ability and managerial excellence.

11. In short, Jupiter is the bestower of goodies; call him Santa Claus if you will.

MIGHTY ASTRONOMICAL FACT ABOUT JUPITER

Jupiter helps you, both by astrology and astronomy. By astronomy Jupiter is the saviour of the planets because it attracts all the planets. If it does not do so, the other planets will go towards the Sun, which will burn them all out of existence. Therefore, by astrology and by astronomy, Jupiter is the saviour of our universe.

JUPITER IN CAPRICORN FROM 2 DECEMBER 2019 TO 18 DECEMBER 2020

Walt Disney, the king of cartoons, Charlie Chaplin, the ultimate cinema comedian, Danny Kaye, another giant of comedy, all had Jupiter in Capricorn in their sun signs. Why? Capricorn is a solid, steady, stable sign. But Jupiter is lively, cheerful, as bouncy as a tennis ball. Jupiter enjoys both love and laughter as I said at the outset. Therefore, the comic aspect of Jupiter in Capricorn is strongly reflected.

At the other and of the scale we have Adolf Hilter, Richard Nixon and Robert F. Kennedy, with Jupiter in Capricorn. All three were in their own way powerful leaders. Hitler was an evil genius. Nixon was charged for impeached. Kennedy had numerous love affairs, ruffled the feathers of many people, and was finally shot dead. In other words, all three, though, totally different in mental make-up and the use of power, came to a very sorry and tragic end. The power and the tragic end were both because of the sign Capricorn. The charm and magnetism were the influence of Jupiter. Ganesha says this is the wide range of Jupiter in Capricorn.

Your best luck comes to you through your industry and ambition. While you will do well in almost any career you choose to follow, you are particularly fortunate in occupations that have to do with politics, cinema, entertainment, business, leadership, empire building, industry, real estate, construction, geology, mining, farming, financing. In other words, you have many options.

You can be generous and tight-fisted at the same time, reach the topmost position of excellence, work hard and be the perfect taskmaster. You will always have strong likes and dislikes.

In personal relationships, goals, status, sense of purpose and social climbing, integrity and honesty will be very important, as important as love itself. In other words, in a relationship you will work hard and long for both material success and real joy which comes from sincere efforts. I do not have Jupiter in Capricorn. But I do endorse the tremendous effort and sacrifice those with Jupiter in Capricorn make. Hats off to them!

JUPITER IN AQUARIUS FROM 19 DECEMBER 2020 TO 28 DECEMBER 2021 (ROUGHLY)

Ganesha says with Jupiter in Aquarius the modern age of science and technology will be at full speed for the remaining year. Albert Einstein, the man of the millennium, the father of modern science, had Jupiter in Aquarius. Why? Aquarius is the sign of the New Age, the millennium, the modern times, the twenty-first century, and Jupiter is the planet of both knowledge and wisdom. Therefore, Jupiter in Aquarius leads to inventions, research, new methods and modes which improve the quality of life. It speaks of television, computers, electronics, aviation and the space industry. So powerful is this New Age influence that I am making an exception and quoting at length.

> You have strong intuitions and original ideas, and you like to cultivate your mind. You do not value money for its own sake, but for what it can do to satisfy the material needs of others. You are a humanitarian first and foremost. Purely commercial ventures bore you. You make excellent scientists, doctors, lawyers, architects, investors, bankers, ambassadors and statesmen. You would do well as teachers, speakers, scientists, labour leaders and psychologists. You may also be fortunate in the many fields of entertainment, and particularly in music. You are likely to be active in charitable or social work, and you can excel in jobs connected with transportation by air. Often, also, your best opportunities lie in government or other big organizations, or where it is an advantage to be popular with the masses.
>
> – JOAN QUIGLEY

The numbers 3, 4, 8 often play an important part in your life. The colours blue and aquamarine (and the stone) will be lucky for you.

In relationship you will realize your ideals and hopes and they will come from sharing. Yes, you will make lasting friendships and marriage should be good for you. It will also be an enduring relationship. Ganesha says you will think positively and that will lead to happiness. The best part is you will stimulate your friend, mate, partner, associate, and all those who come in direct contact with you. You will be an evolved human being. That's saying everything.

FOR READERS

It is quite possible that you may find my view of your own placing of Jupiter not perfect and sometimes not totally applicable to you. The reason is that Jupiter in any sign is not the only placing. We also have Saturn, Mercury, Venus, Sun, Moon, Pluto, Neptune and Uranus in any of the twelve signs. All of these have an influence and therefore an impact on your horoscope. Therefore, no one planet in one sign can be truly enough, or representative of your total personality and complete character. This is what makes the horoscope so fascinating and difficult to read and interpret.

Bejan Opens Out

Ganesha devotee Bejan Daruwalla is writing this piece on 8 June 2019 as the World Cup is on. Just as in the World Cup there are opening batsmen, Bejan also open the innings of his life and his heart. Bejan says one never asks a painter what he paints. The simple reason is that the whole world is the canvas of the painter. In the same way, not only the world but the cosmos is the area of the astrologer. We are a box of assorted chocolates. Twelve signs, therefore, at least twelve different people. The one problem which has beaten me is that we have everything going for us and yet we continue to fight, squabble and make ourselves miserable and unhappy. This has been going on since time immemorial. I agree there have been prophets, leaders, peacemakers and visionaries who have stepped in from time to time to ease our pain and often make us happy. But it is for a short time.

Now, to me the twenty-first century is the biggest, best and brightest in the history of mankind. Mankind is getting into artificial intelligence, genes, microbiology, the sheer abundance and variety of Mother Nature, modern amenities, the neurological power and possibility of our brain which we are now learning to use completely, a chance to do away with sickness and disease and improve our own way of life and thinking, adjustment and even mitigation climate change and, above all, creation of a new efficiency for ourselves and the world. We human beings are of the Earth, but we can not only reach out to the stars but actually go there and create a brand-new world. To put it simply we have a chance to be happy in every possible way. We just need to be tolerant and scientifically minded, to accept the changes of the world and yet be our own natural selves. I know it is very easy to say this and mighty difficult to put it into practice. But we human beings can adapt and adopt to each given situation. We are truly masters of resilience. Therefore, taking all of this into consideration, I say with conviction and courage that happiness and well-being is our rightful inheritance and legacy. Three cheers! Many scientists believe God will not be necessary after 100 years. They are welcome to their opinion. I can only say that according to the Upanishads, the nature of consciousness could very well lead us to the final truth of the entire cosmos. That is my final word.

Mantras

Ganesha says we Indians believe in the power, myth, light and vibrations of mantras. Therefore, I am giving a few mantras.

The mantra for Sun is: '*Om Hram Hreem Hrom Sa Suryaya Namah*'.

The mantra for Mars is: '*Om Kraam Kreem Krom Sa Bhowmaya Namah*'.

The mantra for Mercury is: '*Om Bram Breem Browm Sa Budhaya Namah*'.

The mantra for Jupiter is: '*Om Jhram Jhreem Jhroom Sa Gurave Namah*'.

The mantra for Saturn is: '*Om Praam Preem Proum Sa Sanaye Namah*'.

The mantra for Rahu is: '*Om Bhram Bhreem Bhroum Sa Rahave Namah*'.

The mantra for Ketu is: '*Om Praam Preem Proum Sa Kethave Namah*'.

About the Authors

Bejan Daruwalla

Ganesha says that though it may be true that Bejan Daruwalla is one of the 100 great astrologers in the last 1,000 years, he is perhaps the only one who has read the fortune of three prime ministers of India, namely, Morarji Desai, Atal Bihari Vajpayee and Narendra Modi. This Ganesha devotee at eighty-eight believes that goodness and compassion are much more important and certainly universal. He now believes in keeping a very low profile and tries to bless all people sincerely and with all the limited power that he has. In other words, in the wide, wide world, there is no substitute for sheer goodness. Goodness (including integrity) matters a million times more than greatness is Ganesha devotee Bejan's final word.

Nastur Daruwalla

How can I ever forget the scintillating prince, Lakshyaraj Singh of Mewar City Palace, Udaipur, who is like a son to me, as he has the divine blessings of Lord Ekling-ji of Shakti Peeth as the temple belongs to his great royal ancestors. If you have Lord Shiva with you what is more to say. My son Nastur stays in the heart of Prince Lakshyaraj Singh who is always ready to help the needy and downtrodden in life.

My son got blessings from the top industrialist of India, Shri Neeraj R. Bajaj, son of my patron Ramkrishna Bajaj for progress in life. I call Neeraj Bajaj my divine son as our relationship is at least fifty years old.

The coming back to power of the chief minister of Gujarat, Shri Vijay Rupani, was the bold and correct prediction of my son when all others were thinking that the chief minister will be changed. My son again got encouragement and blessings for progress in life and for writing this book from the education minister of Gujarat, Shri Bhupendrasinh Chudasma.

My another beloved son and top industrialist of Mumbai, Shri Jimmey Mistry, gave his good wishes so that my legacy can continue in the form of my son Nastur.

Contact Information

WhatsApp/Call

+91 8141234275

Email

info@bejandaruwalla.com

Website

www.bejandaruwalla.com